Educational Change and the Political Process

Educational Change and the Political Process brings together key ideas on both the system of educational policy and the policy process in the United States. It provides students with a broad, methodical understanding of educational policy. No other textbook offers as comprehensive a view of the U.S. educational policy procedure and political systems.

Section I discusses the actors and systems that create and implement policy on both the federal and the local level; Section II walks students through the policy process from idea to implementation to evaluation; and Section III delves into three major forces driving the creation of educational policies in the current era—accountability, equity, and market-driven reforms.

Each chapter provides case studies, discussion questions, and classroom activities to scaffold learning, as well as a bibliography for further reading to deepen exploration of these topics.

Dana L. Mitra is Professor of Education (Educational Theory & Policy) at The Pennsylvania State University.

Educational Change and the Political Process

Dana L. Mitra

Routledge
Taylor & Francis Group

NEW YORK AND LONDON

First published 2018
by Routledge
711 Third Avenue, New York, NY 10017

and by Routledge
2 Park Square, Milton Park, Abingdon, Oxon, OX14 4RN

Routledge is an imprint of the Taylor & Francis Group, an informa business

Library of Congress Cataloging in Publication Data
A catalog record for this book has been requested

ISBN: 978-1-138-69273-2 (hbk)
ISBN: 978-1-138-69274-9 (pbk)
ISBN: 978-1-315-53177-9 (ebk)

Typeset in Utopia
by Wearset Ltd, Boldon, Tyne and Wear

Brief Contents ●●●●●

Contents ● ● ● ● ●

Preface ● ● ● ● ●

In a shifting political climate, the policy process can be confusing and alienating for educational leaders. The textbook is designed to help educational leaders—teachers, principals, superintendents—make sense of the policy landscape and learn to be strong change agents within that context. It is also designed to teach future researchers, policy makers, lobbyists, and funders how to analyze and interact within the process. Readers will take away an understanding of what lies beneath the formal structures of governance, how politics shape policy, and how actors can influence the system.

This core textbook on educational policy and politics provides a comprehensive overview of the major topics offered in graduate and advanced undergraduate courses on policy and politics of the U.S. educational system. In a time of increasing dissonance and polarization of perspectives, it is increasingly important how the structures, process, and ideals of the policy system work together to enact and to prohibit change.

● ● ● ● ●
Why This Book?

The book is a synthetic text designed with a particular focus on the political landscape in the past 10 years. No other textbook offers as comprehensive a view of the U.S. educational policy process and political systems. It offers a comprehensive resource on the U.S education policy system that can stand alone as the required reading for a course.

The text brings together the best of previous educational policy textbooks and updates them to include the most current research and commonly used theory and frameworks. The book is grounded theoretically in a political approach to policy analysis that draws heavily on organizational theory and institutional change, with a focus on the latest research on topics such as foundations, intermediary organizations, social networks, improvement science, and student voice research.

● ● ● ● ●
The Structure of the Book

The book is organized into three conceptual sections. The first section defines the formal and informal structures of the U.S. policy system. The second section explores the policy process that occurs within these structures. The third section explores the ideas that shape policy, including equity and market-driven reforms. Together, these three sections provide a comprehensive and detailed examination of U.S. education policy and politics.

Each chapter provides a clear description of content, explaining theory in easy-to-understand language and providing extended examples and case studies. To facilitate learning, the chapters include discussion questions and case studies to scaffold learning, and a bibliography for further reading to deepen learning for advanced students.

Section I: The Structure of the U.S. Educational System

This section considers the layers of educational structures that form the U.S. system. Unlike most nations that have national ministries of education, the U.S. system consists of a complex system of layers. It discusses the layers of educational policy: federal, state, and local systems. It also explores policy actors with an emphasis on new influential actors: foundations, intermediary organizations, think tanks, and other interest groups.

Chapter 1—Federal Education Policy

This chapter provides an overview of the federal legislative and executive systems in relation to educational policy. It provides a review of foundational U.S. government themes in the context of educational issues, including key committees at the federal level for educational reform. It also provides a brief overview of education policy history from *A National at Risk* to the *Every Student Succeeds Act* to understand the key issues of the most recent wave of educational reforms.

Chapter 2—State Systems of Education

Shifting the focus to the state level, this chapter examines the state policy system. States within the U.S. educational policy context encompass significant variability. The chapter begins with the history of state control and an overview of different state educational structures. It includes an exploration of Common Core State Standards as a case study of educational change on the state level.

Chapter 3—Local School Districts, Citywide Change, and Rural Dilemmas

Examining the local level of policy and politics in the U.S., this chapter begins with an overview of local educational structures, including districts, school boards, and community control. The chapter also explores mayoral control of cities and the concepts of civic capacity and urban regimes.

Chapter 4—Influential Policy Actors

This chapter introduces the interest groups who have the greatest influence in the education policy system. It provides an overview of teacher unions, educational foundation, education management organizations, think tanks, and the American Legislative Exchange Council. The chapter also examines the means by which policy actors can engage with different levels of education policy.

Section II: The Policy Process

The section details the policy process. While problematizing a linear model of policy, this section addresses issues of problem formation, agenda setting, policy formation, implementation, sustainability, and scale.

Chapter 5—Public Policy and Power

This chapter defines the concept of policy and introduces the policy process. It provides a theoretical focus on the strong distinction between a rational approach to policy as decision making and a political model focusing on evidence, argument, and persuasion. It also provides an understanding of the policy process based on steps of the policy system while also problematizing their linearity. Ideas of problem formation/agenda setting, policy formation/adoption, implementation, and scale are addressed. Additionally, specific examples of educational policy from the last three decades are interwoven to provide case studies and to illustrate the conceptual ideas presented.

Chapter 6—Problem Formation, Agenda Setting, and Framing

Building from a political model of education policy, this chapter spirals deeper into consideration of what type of education policy ideas get on the agenda and why. The chapter considers who has a voice in the policy system and who does not. It also considers the importance of crafting argument and negotiating with constituencies and interest groups to understand how education policy is created.

Chapter 7—Policy Formation

This chapter considers what happens during the drafting and passing of legislation. A major focus is the intersection between policy instruments (mandates, incentives, systems changing, and hortatory) and the role of target populations. The chapter examines how perception of power and the likeability of educational actors influence what types of policies are created.

Chapter 8—Policy Implementation

In educational policy research, implementation has become one of the main topics of education policy research in the past three decades. This chapter focuses on the framework of the relationships policy and practice, including the difference between a top-down approach to policy making and a bottom-up view that includes grassroots and teachers' perspectives. It considers the research on sensemaking, garbage can theory, co-adaptation, will and capacity, metapolicy, and street-level bureaucrats in the new era of accountability.

Chapter 9—Sustainability and Scale

This conceptual chapter explains why change is so hard, using neo-institutional theories and loose coupling as counterpoints. The chapter provides a framework for understanding power and influence via organizational theory and institutional theory to help to understand how power influences which voices are heard. It also considers when and why sustaining change, spreading ideas, or going to scale works. The chapter explores the latest work in innovation science and research/practice partnerships as contemporary means to conceptualize educational change as an ongoing change process.

Section III: Ideals of the U.S. Educational System

Since the first chapter of this book, we have defined policy as a struggle over ideals. This section involves how deeply held beliefs transform into creative solutions to address longstanding concerns. This section explores what ideals are central within the U.S. political structure and the beliefs of the major U.S. political parties.

Chapter 10—Understanding U.S. Ideals

This chapter provides a review of U.S ideologies that influence educational politics and also policy research—equity, efficiency, and social order. It also considers the range of political parties in the United States, including the range of perspectives within the Republican and Democratic parties today.

Chapter 11—Market-Driven Reform

This chapter focuses on market-driven theories of competition and rational choice theory, which have emerged as a strong influence on educational reforms. The chapter includes an examination of vouchers and charter schools as market-driven strategies for reform.

Chapter 12—Equity

A balance between excellence and equity has always been a tension in education policy. Often these tensions are explored through critical theory and critical race theory. After discussing these frameworks, this chapter considers the role of the courts in equity-based reform. It also examines equity-oriented policies, including Opportunity to Learn standards, desegregation, early childcare education, and wraparound services. The chapter concludes with a review of student voice reform.

●●●●●

Putting It All Together

The book is designed to ensure students will be prepared for their work as practitioners and educational leaders, scholars, policy makers, and/or informed citizens by providing a deep understanding of U.S. politics and policy. It offers the breadth of coverage needed for a course in politics and policy by providing a systematic, comprehensive examination of the policy process, the actors and systems behind the creation and implementation of policy, and the main ideas shaping contemporary education policy. The book also offers the depth of explaining concepts coherently, incorporating foundational theories with new research. Case studies make the concepts come to life, and provide opportunities for students to make direct connections to their own work. With additional suggested reading and resources, the textbook provides a reference tool for understanding policy processes and a springboard for further work on educational issues.

Acknowledgments ● ● ● ● ●

Deepest gratitude to Eric McGinnis, who served as the primary editorial assistant on this project. He took an ambiguous, ever-expanding project and tackled each detail with precise attention and patience. He is the consummate professional.

Daniella Hall, Assistant Professor at Clemson University, co-wrote two chapters of the book and read each word of the chapter with a keen eye. She possesses an encyclopedic understanding of educational policy. She elevated my understanding of the most recent research and taught me things I knew nothing about.

Thank you also to Stacey Rutledge for her wide lens of what was missing and the need to tie the project together at the macro level.

Samantha Holquist graciously offered to read the draft for glaring holes and mistakes, and caught quite a few.

Mariel DiMidio provided the first round of editorial assistance and got me off to a great start.

Brian Huff provided assistance with tables and figures.

Thank you to Mike Kirst and Milbrey McLaughlin for their encouragement of the project.

My courses in Education Politics and Policy and Politics at Penn State served as guinea pigs on my early drafts, and especially helped me to brainstorm the U.S. ideals chapter. Thank you for your feedback and support.

To my family—Todd, Kaden, and Carson—for enduring my endless writing, researching, and rewriting. To Tenzi the dog for sticking next to me for most of the work.

I

● ● ● ● ●

The Structure of the U.S. Educational System

Unlike most nations that have national ministries of education, the U.S. system consists of a complex system of layers. This section discusses the federal, state, and local systems. It also explores the informal but highly influential policy systems created by foundations, intermediary organizations, think tanks, and other interest groups. By focusing on the structures of the policy system, it sets the stage for exploring the policy process in Section II.

1

● ● ● ● ●

Federal Education Policy

This chapter provides an overview of the federal legislative, executive, and judicial systems in relation to educational policy. It reviews basic U.S. government themes in the context of educational issues. It also provides a brief overview of education policy history from post-World War II to the present day, and the key issues in educational reform.

Policy formation in some aspects is what we may have once thought is all that matters—how a bill becomes a law. Section II in this book will show how the policy process has many steps before a public idea rises to the point that it gets placed into the formal policy process.

The passage of a bill to a law contains many steps in the U.S. legislative process. The basic steps of the process are:

■ Bills and joint resolutions can be introduced in the House or the Senate by a member of Congress. They have similar processes. Bills are the most common; joint resolutions tend to be reserved for continuing or emergency appropriations. Joint resolutions can also amend the constitution by gaining support of two-thirds of both chambers and three-quarters of the states. *Simple resolutions* can be passed within one house alone and do not have the force of law. They are also used for the recognition of people and events (such as National Ice Cream Day or the offering of condolences due to the death of someone of significance).

■ The Speaker of the House or the President of the Senate assigns the bills to a committee.

■ The committee (and subcommittees) can amend or change the bill and choose to pass it or not. Hearings are held to collect information.

■ The Hearings Committee markup can amend bills or let them die and go no further. In the House, the Speaker also can amend the bill at this point. A final reading of the bill and vote by the committee occurs. A report is created that provides justification for the bill, including how it changes existing law and the potential cost of implementation.

■ The Rules Committee in the House and the majority leader of the Senate can amend the bill again.

■ The bill is put on the calendar to move to the full body (Senate or House) for discussion, debate, and a vote. It can be amended or die at this process.

- If the bill passes the House or Senate, the Congressional Budget Office must confirm that the bill adheres to spending constraints.
- The bill then moves to the other body for amendment and a vote on the House/Senate floor.
- A Conference Committee comprised of members of both chambers meets to take both the House and the Senate versions of the bill to come to consensus and to create a conference report.
- Both houses must vote on the new version of the bill.
- The president then signs the bill, vetoes the bill, or if the president does neither, the bill automatically becomes law after 10 days.

The federal role of education has always been tenuous in the United States. Most other nations have a strong federal role in shaping education through a ministry of education and strong top-down direction on curriculum, training, and related issues. In the United States, local and state governments have been responsible for education. The nation's large geographic size and the design of the constitution contributed to the staying power of local control.

The U.S. constitution does not mention education. The Tenth Amendment of the constitution reserves to the states powers not delegated by the constitution. The federal government historically has taken a permissive role in education, consistent with the metaphor of *layer-cake federalism* (Grodzins, 1966). Also called *divided sovereignty* or *dual federalism*, this concept explains the division of power between the federal and state governments, whereby state governments exercise the powers not assigned to the federal government. Therefore, the states assume primary responsibility to be in charge of education policy. Ninety percent of funds for schools come from state and local governments (Jennings, 2015, p. 16). For education, the federal government's layer of the cake would just be a thin layer compared to the bulk that is state and federal.

Federal involvement increased in schools dramatically after World War II. The U.S. Office of Education was transferred from the Interior Department to the Department of Health, Education and Welfare, including increasing its staff to 300 people and taking on a budget of $40 million. During this era, Congress created a national vocational education program and provided tuition assistance for veterans to attend college. Fearing that the Russians were outperforming U.S. students as the Soviet Union spacecraft Sputnik launched into outer space in 1957, federal funding increased to help to improve educational outcomes, including the National Defense Education Act of 1958 signed by President Dwight Eisenhower with the intent of increasing U.S. global competency in math and science. The bill was passed due to the perception that the Soviet Union was surpassing the United States in education—and especially in subjects that could translate into technical and military expertise. The bill had two main purposes. The first purpose was to increase shortages in personnel in defense-related industries, including mathematics, engineering, technology, and foreign languages. The second purpose was to provide financial assistance

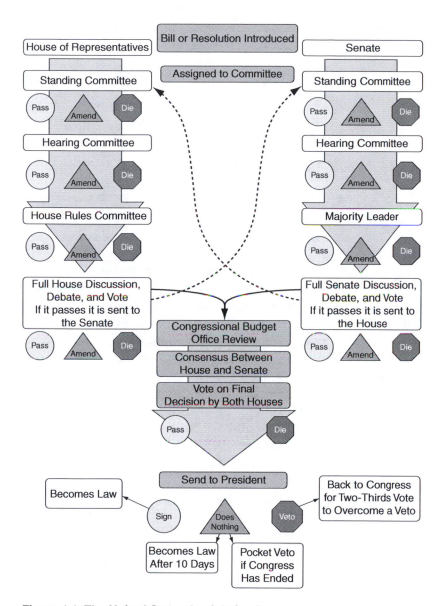

Figure 1.1 The United States Legislative Process.

to students in these fields to encourage enrollment into colleges and universities, called the National Defense Student Loan program.

While education was not to be a direct target of federal policy, education has long been viewed as a policy space in which governments attempt to address social issues. *Brown v. Board of Education of Topeka*, Kansas, ordered the desegregation of schools. In the 1960s, civil rights legislation included a focus on schools being a space in which the government could target the needs of the poor.

The Great Society reforms of the Johnson administration of the 1960s included the passage of the Elementary and Secondary Education Act (ESEA) of 1965.

Initially a poverty policy, the intent behind the legislation was targeted money to needy students with the idea that increased tutoring and one-on-one assistance for poor kids could lead to improved educational outcomes, which would lead to getting these children out of poverty. The problem of low-performing needy children was believed to be solvable through an increase in money into schools. The ESEA was a mechanism to increase funds to poor children.

The passage of this act dramatically increased the federal role in schooling. Federal involvement in education prior to ESEA was prevented due to several controversies (Jennings, 2015). The Kennedy administration in the 1960s opposed federal involvement because it did not include aid for Catholic schools. Private-school supporters also blocked federal aid. Nixon opposed increased aid due to concern over federal intrusion in schools. Southern members of Congress feared a federal role in education due to increased pressures to desegregate schools.

The first ESEA law provided a massive allocation to education—$1.1 billion. This size of investment was viewed as historically large at the time (Jennings, 2015). Congress is expected to reauthorize the ESEA every four years (although the last reauthorization was 12 years overdue). For most of these revisions, the changes resulted in an expansion of federal aid through creating new programs and expanding the budgets of current programs. Interventions included funding for neglected children, migrant farm workers, at-risk students, homeless children, English language learners, students with disabilities, and racially segregated students. ESEA also served as a model for the development of other legislation that bolstered funding and programs through the educational system, including the Individuals with Disabilities Education Act of 1975.

In the 1970s, a focus of the program included training of parents as well as students. One revision encouraged the use of parents as *paraprofessionals*—minimum-wage positions within classrooms as teacher assistants. The initial idea was that mothers from local communities could work in the school, thus providing additional wages for the family while also helping to educate these mothers on the expectations of schooling to help align family life with school habits. Since the 2002 reauthorization, paraprofessional requirements were radically increased, including the requirement that all have an associate's degree rather than solely a high school diploma.

The first 20 years of ESEA focused on efforts to protect the funds from graft, such as funding building projects and even swimming pools. Keeping budget lines separate meant separating and isolating children from their peers, however. While it is cleaner to have pullout programs for struggling children, research shows that integrating children within classrooms could lead to more effective learning outcomes for at-risk children (Baker, 1995). As knowledge on learning outcomes grew, the ESEA legislation funding streams shifted from supporting the tutoring of individual children to incentivizing schoolwide reforms.

In the late 1970s, the Carter administration helped to fortify the federal role in education by creating the cabinet-level U.S. Department of Education. The Carter administration also oversaw the largest authorization of categorical aid in ESEA through the creation of new targeted assistance programs, including the creation of a federally funded school lunch program and several federal post-secondary loan programs (Jennings, 2015).

Jack Jennings (2001), former staff director and general counsel for the U.S. House of Representatives' Committee on Education and Labor from 1967 to 1994, reflected on how departmental charges reflected the values embedded in the role of education in the United States. He saw this period in history as reflecting the values of: civic education to instruct citizens on how to participate in democracy; workforce preparation to ensure economic productivity; increasing equality of opportunity to succeed; and protecting the nation by strengthening national defense.

Since its creation by Carter, the Department of Education has served several purposes (Wirt & Kirst, 1997, p. 249):

- Provide financial assistance to schools without any restrictions or expectations in return, called *general aid.*

- Provide funding to schools in exchange for specific purposes, often aimed at changes in school behaviors—called *categorical aid* or *differential aid.* Such assistance requires extra costs of monitoring to determine compliance.

- Regulate behavior, including licensure, certification, and standards requirements established by federal law.

- Encourage knowledge creation and innovation through federal granting agencies, including the National Science Foundation (NSF) and Institute for Education Sciences (IES), which includes the National Center for Education Statistics (NCES).

- Provide consultation and technical assistance to implement other federal laws, such as desegregation orders.

- Influence opinion, steer vision, and create moral values of education through the bully pulpit of hortatory persuasion.

The department also must take the laws passed by Congress and add greater specificity—a process called *rulemaking.* The department (or other agency) publishes proposed elaborations and changes in rules in the Federal Register to seek public comments. The Federal Register houses the final versions of rules as well, along with the comments received and responses to comments.

●●●●●

A Nation at Risk Catalyzing Education Reform

An effort to eliminate the Department of Education continued to be a focus until the Reagan administration. (It was thought to have been a dead issue since the late 1980s, but it has been raised again by the Trump administration.) Reagan also sought to reduce categorical aid in favor of general aid through the consolidation of programs into block grants. The department survived the Reagan years due to a coalition of moderate Republicans and Democrats in Congress. The cause of education also was bolstered by the secretary of the department disregarding Reagan's intentions of shrinking the department. Instead, he spearheaded the development of *A Nation at Risk* report (Gardner, 1983).

Ronald Reagan commissioned a report by his secretary of education, Terrence Bell, with the purpose of reducing the role of education at the federal level. Instead, Bell oversaw the writing of the report for the opposite purpose. Bell was supportive of a federal role for education based on his experiences in the Nixon administration as the commission of education in the 1970s. Bell established an independent panel to study the state of education with the hope that a positive image of education would emerge (Vinoviskis, 2009). The 18-member National Commission on Excellence in Education was established on August 26, 1981 under David Gardner, president of the University of Utah.

Written to be an inflammatory policy document that takes advantage of the bully pulpit of the federal government, the short pamphlet was targeted toward media outlets and intended to increase national concern about the role of education. Citing a lack of international competitiveness, the report used the following language:

> Our nation is at risk. Our once unchallenged preeminence in commerce, industry, science, and technological innovation is being overtaken by competitors throughout the world. ... If an unfriendly foreign power had attempted to impose on America the mediocre educational performance that exists today, we might as well have viewed it as an act of war. We have even squandered the gains in student achievement made in the wake of the Sputnik challenge. Moreover, we have dismantled essential support systems that helped make those gains possible. We have, in effect, been committing an act of unthinking, unilateral educational disarmament.
>
> (Gardner, 1983, p. 5)

A Nation at Risk increased national focus on education and dramatically swayed public opinion from thinking favorably about schools to perceiving schools as problems that needed to be solved.

● ● ● ● ●

The Governors Catalyze Stronger Federal Involvement

The election of George H. W. Bush represented a sea change in the view of Republican presidents toward education. Bush sought to strengthen the federal role in education policy. In his 1990 State of the Union Address, President George H. W. Bush proclaimed educational goals, including:

■ Children would start school ready to learn.

■ The high school graduate rate would increase to 90 percent.

■ Students would demonstrate competency in grades 4, 8 and 12, and students would be first in the world in math and science achievement.

■ Every adult American would be literate and possess skills to compete in a global economy and exercise the rights of citizenship.

The creation of voluntary education goals through the America 2000 Act signaled a change in direction toward an increasing federal role in educational policy. Although the legislation did not pass, the National Governors' Association strongly endorsed these goals (Vinoviskis, 2009).

The role of the nation's governors was most evident in the Charlottesville Summit in 1989. The issue of standards-based education accountability was placed at the center of a coordinated state education policy agenda. The governors proclaimed that the country needed to set educational goals. President H. W. Bush attended parts of the meeting, but at the time the concern of the federal government was not to be involved in such discussions directly, causing Bush not to stand with the governors during the final press conference. This event also saw the rise of the "education governors," all elected at the end of the 1970s, including Republican Lamar Alexander of Tennessee, Democrat Bill Clinton of Arkansas, Republican Bob Graham of Florida, Democrat James Hunt of North Carolina, Republican Tom Kean of New Jersey, Democrat Dick Riley of South Carolina, and Democrat William Winter of Mississippi.

When Bill Clinton assumed the presidency, his focus on education was influenced by his time as a governor of Arkansas and a member of the leadership of the National Governors' Association, which worked on the creation of academic standards and accountability. When Clinton took office, he continued the effort toward national goals with Goals 2000, which built upon the Bush plan. He also adjusted the focus of ESEA in the 1994 authorization to switch from classroom to whole-school as the leverage point of change. Based on research at the time of the value of whole-school reform as the best strategy for improving student outcomes, the Improving America's Schools Act of the Clinton administration provided funding for high-poverty schools to choose a whole-school reform model for implementation. This reauthorization was also the first to begin to focus on accountability for children through the introduction of expectations for voluntary system-wide standards.

While Congress scaled back the focus on standards during the first Clinton administration, the governors and the White House created the National Education Goals Panel, initially consisting of six governors, four members of the administration, and several members of Congress. The organization issued its first report in 1991.

Congressional Republicans gained strength during the first midterm election in the Clinton presidency. With the Gingrich Revolution in Congress, a name for the 1994 midterm elections that led to a net gain of 54 seats in the House of Representatives and 8 in the Senate, the Republicans scaled back much of the educational legislation of the Clinton administration. This reduction included gutting the funding for many of the initiatives—a dramatic retrenchment set the stage for a presidential election battle focused on education. Robert Dole's presidential platform continued to be removing the Department of Education and reducing the federal role in education during this election. Dole's sound defeat signified a solidification among the American electorate of the role of the federal government in education policy. The second term of Clinton included much more Republican Congressional support of education issues and the abolishment of the federal role of education no longer had a strong backing from most Republicans.

Clinton's number two person in the Department of Education, Marshall Smith, was one of the architects of a *systemic* vision of education. Publishing with his former graduate student Jennifer O'Day, prior to his service in the U.S. Department of Education, Smith published a vision of a systemic view of education that created *coherence* at the state level. The framework suggested that the problems with educational reform were due to a wide range of goals and visions sending multiple messages to districts. Successful change according to this theory involved the alignment of pieces of the education process with a united vision. Alignment included sending reinforcing vision and focus in the curriculum, textbooks, teacher training, professional development, and assessment at the state level. A unified vision also could lead to a streamlining of the educational process and an increase in excellence and accountability.

The work of the Clinton administration helped to build capacity for this alignment, but a strong role of accountability in federal reform was not evident until George W. Bush's 2001 reauthorization of ESEA, the passage of the No Child Left Behind (NCLB) Act. Following in his father's footsteps, George W. Bush viewed strengthening education as a national imperative. He considered education "the civil right issue of our time" (Jennings, 2015, p. 10).

Taking the ideas of Marshall Smith and adding a layer of distrust for education professionals, the NCLB Act marked a dramatic increase in the federal role in educational policy. Considered by most to be an *unfunded mandate* (defined and discussed in Chapter 7), it tied federal funds to the creation of a yearly accountability process. States had to begin testing students within a year of the passage of the act, or the large amounts of federal funding for education that had become a central part of state budgets would disappear.

The focus of assessment was at the school level, with states having to publish the test results each year. Testing was to occur each year in grades 3–8 in reading and math, and once in high school. Science testing was also phased in. Incremental improvements on the tests had to happen each year or schools would be deemed as failing to make 'Adequate Yearly Progress.' Schools not making progress were placed in a 'Needs Improvement Path' with very narrow options for how to improve. Failing students could be tutored in pullout programs that seemed more similar to ESEA legislation from the 1970s than evidence from recent research on how to improve outcomes for children. Students also were supposedly allowed to switch to other schools if their school continued to have problems. After five years of struggle, schools could be reconstituted or taken over by state officials.

The most stringent part of the legislation was the expectation that improvements would continue so that 100 percent of students would be "proficient" in reading and math by the year 2015. A feat considered statistically impossible, some pundits speculated whether this legislation was designed to fail, to prove that the public-school system was insufficient at meeting the needs of children and perhaps private systems should be considered instead.

Equity advocates lauded the disaggregation requirements of NCLB—not only did scores need to be reported by each school, but they also needed to be reported for subgroups, including race, socioeconomic status, gender, immigrant status, disability and English language learners. All subgroup reports also had to make Adequate Yearly Progress. Proponents of this piece of the legislation noted that it was the first time in U.S. educational policy history that a systemic and ongoing documentation of equity in schools had been implemented with strong accountability to address the inequities.

●●●●●

The Obama and Trump Administrations

The ESEA legislation was expected to be reauthorized early in the Obama administration as it was due to expire in 2007. Due to a Great Recession of the 2000s, Obama's team focused on pushing forward a national economy recovery plan instead of new educational legislation. Included in this massive spending package was the American Recovery and Reinvestment Act of 2009 (ARRA)—the greatest federal expenditure for education in the history of the United States. Most of the money went toward a temporary funding of teachers' salaries to avoid massive teacher layoffs and toward building construction to help state governments regain their footing during the recession.

Part of this funding allocation included the creation of *Race to the Top* (RttT)—a nationwide competition aimed at four goals—adopting state standards, improving data systems, evaluating teachers, and targeting the improvement of the lowest performing schools. In the first round of competitive funding in June 2014, only Delaware and Tennessee received funding. Ten states (including DC) received funding in the second round and seven received funding in the third. The rounds took place from 2010 to 2011. After a third round, eventually 18 states and DC received grants ranging from $25 to $700 million. States also had to agree to no longer limiting the number of charter schools and to use test scores as a significant factor in evaluating teachers (Jennings, 2015) and to consider the implementation of one of the plans for Common Core Standards (discussed in Chapter 2).

Many of the winning states spent large sums of money to work with three consulting firms to design their proposals. Education First Consulting, McKinsey & Company, and Wireless Generation provided advice to states on Race to the Top Applications. The Race to the Top Technical Assistance Network, run by ICF

International, was funded by a $4.9 million federal grant to help the chosen districts to implement the plans (Brownstein, 2011).

Although only a fraction of the states received these RttT grants, the size of the awards was so great that this incentive-based grant program dramatically reformed most state governments as they scrambled to make themselves eligible for RttT monies. While not all chose to apply, many more states than those receiving funding did develop statewide data systems and tighten accountability across their systems. Thus, the competition leveraged greater change than it might have accomplished if all states were funded. Such a system cannot be used often, since undoubtedly the fact that most states did not receive the money after all might create a disincentive to work as hard in the future for such programs. In the immediate sense, however, the federal incentivization structure created unprecedented statewide educational changes.

In addition to the RttT legislation, the Obama administration created a waiver system for the expired NCLB Act rather than working to pass new legislation. Most states applied for waivers since they were not going to make the 100 percent proficiency goal by 2015. Yet, they felt that the waivers were "NCLB plus"—rather than exempting states from NCLB demands, the waivers added new demands on top of the educational testing expectations. The waivers required states to accept standards and for teachers to undergo evaluations that incorporated student performance (Klein, 2015). Notable also are states that failed to comply with NCLB standards, such as the state of Vermont. All schools in the state did not meet the proficiency standards set by the federal government due to state refusal to comply with the law. Yet, Vermont never incurred federal intervention despite the resistance.

In addition to RttT, ARRA transformed the size and the scope of the federal School Improvement Grant (SIG) program. The Obama administration announced a plan to support the improvement of the most failing schools in the nation by using the SIG program to provide support to the nation's 5000 lowest-performing schools. The federal government provided temporary funding requiring dramatic reforms at the school level. Fitting with market-driven reforms of the business world (see Chapter 11), this vision involved massive layoffs of teachers and administrators with the assumption that a school could be shut down and reopened as a new organization with a new outcome in the same geographical space. The Obama administration called the concept "turnaround schools." With the SIG re-visioning, the Obama administration specifically required one of four processes of reconstitution for turnaround schools (Trujillo & Renee, 2015):

- *Turnaround*: All personnel are fired (teachers and students) and only half of the teachers can be rehired.
- *Transformation*: Principal is fired and a teacher evaluation system that includes evaluation based on student test scores is implemented, as well as new systems for teacher recruitment, retention, and training, and a reward and sanction system for teachers and administrators.

■ *Restart*: All personnel are fired and school reopens as a charter school.

■ *School closure*: The school is closed and all students are sent elsewhere.

In an extensive review of the literature on reconstitution and turnaround policies, Trujillo and Renee (2015) found that this style of reform has not been found to improve outcomes for kids or improve organizational performance. The paper suggests that changes in future turnaround reform strategies should include: increasing funding for reform focusing on teaching and learning quality rather than organizational structures, involving community stakeholders in turnaround plans, and broadening indicators of effectiveness beyond test scores.

In the final year of the second term of the Obama administration, ESEA was finally reauthorized by Congress, eight years late. The Every Student Succeeds Act (ESSA) kept most of the standardized testing system intact. Students still had to take exams every year for grades 3–8. However, the law greatly restricted the federal role of education, including explicitly stating the ways in which the secretary of education could no longer make demands on state governments. Power to implement accountability was squarely placed back in the hands of state governments. Additionally, standardized testing only had to comprise 51 percent of how states evaluated school quality. Other measures focusing on opportunities to learn could also be included in the state policy for assessing school quality. Such measures could include the assessment of portfolios, projects, or extended performance tasks (ESSA, 2015).

During the presidential campaign, Trump pledged to eliminate the Department of Education and to create policies that would discourage the adoption of the Common Core by state governments. Once in office, he appointed the polarizing figure of Betsy DeVos as Secretary of Education. DeVos came to the government from being the head of a school choice advocacy organization, the American Federation of Children, which promotes parental school choice options including private schools. Her controversial appointment hearing attracted unprecedented attention to the nomination of a secretary of education, and tension and protest at public events of the Secretary symbolize the divisive nature of politics during the Trump presidency.

Efforts to shift policy in the Trump administration have focused on ways to decrease the federal role in education, including major budget cuts overall but an increase in funds for school choice policies. Trump also issued an executive order that calls for a review of federal outreach in education and the supported congressional resolutions to repeal the requirement that states submit accountability plans and the guidelines for teacher preparation programs under ESSA. The Trump administration through the Justice and Education department are also rolling back the protection of civil rights, including bathroom access for transgender students, sexual assault enforcement under Title IX, and exclusionary discipline policies for minorities.

● ● ● ● ●

Comprehension Questions

■ How did the Elementary and Secondary Education Act begin and how has it evolved over time?

■ What was the role of governors in defining the federal education agenda?

■ What was the significance of *A Nation at Risk* in educational policy history?

■ How did the actions of the Obama administration influence the way in which Congress designed the latest authorization of the ESEA?

● ● ● ● ●

Discussion Questions

■ What was the purpose for designing the legislative process with so many steps and actors? Does the system still work the way it was intended? What evidence do you have?

■ Educational policy has been remarkably bipartisan in the past 20 years— why might that be the case? In the current administration, will this trend change?

● ● ● ● ●

Activities

■ The famous television video *I'm Just a Bill* (Frishberg, 1975) provides an entertaining way to review the process as the cartoon character of a policy bill sits on the steps of Congress, worrying that he might never become a law. View the cartoon and discuss its accuracy in depicting the legislative process.

■ Make a drawing/infographic of how a bill becomes a law. Compare to the infographic presented in Figure 1.1.

■ Many websites provide interactive ways to practice how a bill becomes a law, including the game "Lawcraft" available on the website "Gamepop."

■ Have the class make its own timeline of key education policy instances— compare it to the 25-year interactive timeline of standards developed by *Education Week* (Klein, 2015).

■ Listen/read the report *Obama's Impact on America's Schools* (January 13, 2017, 6:38 AM ET).
Find on the web using the following search terms:

NPR; January 13, 2017; Obamas impact American schools

■ Listen/read the report *A Former Education Secretary's Advice for Betsy DeVos* (January 16, 2017, 12:01 PM ET).
  Find on the web using the following search terms:

  NPR; January 16, 2017; former education secretary advice; Devos

●●●●●

Further Reading

Hess, F. M. & Eden, M. (2017). *The Every Student Succeeds Act: What It Means for Schools, Systems, and States.* Cambridge, MA: Harvard Education Press.

Jennings, J. (2015). *Presidents, Congress, and the Public Schools: The Politics of Education Reform.* Cambridge, MA: Harvard Education Press.

Mehta, J. (2013). How paradigms create politics: The transformation of American educational policy, 1980–2001. *American Educational Research Journal, 50*(2), 285–324.

Trujillo, T. & Renee, M. (2015). Irrational exuberance for market-based reform: How federal turnaround policies thwart democratic schooling. *Teachers College Record, 117*(6), 1–34.

Vinoviskis, M. (2009). *From A Nation at Risk to No Child Left Behind: National Education Goals and the Creation of Federal Education Policy.* New York: Teacher's College Press.

●●●●●

Reference List

Baker, E. T. (1995). The effects of inclusion on learning. *Educational Leadership, 52*(4), 33–5.

Brownstein, A. (2011). Consultant in high demand as ARRA's clock ticks. *Education Week, 30*(20), 16.

Every Student Succeeds Act (ESSA) of 2015, P.L. 114–95, 20 U.S.C. § 6301 (2015).

Frishberg, D. (Writer). (1975). *I'm Just a Bill* [Television series episode]. Wharburton, T. (Director), Rushnell, S. (Creative Producer), *Schoolhouse Rock!* New York, NY: American Broadcasting Company.

Gardner, D. P. (1983). *A Nation at Risk: The Imperative for Educational Reform. An Open Letter to the American People. A Report to the Nation and the Secretary of Education.* Washington, DC: U.S. Department of Education.

Grodzins, M. (1966). *The American System: A New View of Government in the United States.* New Brunswick, NJ: Transaction Publishers.

Individuals with Disabilities Education Act of 1975, 20 USC § 1400 et seq. (1975).

Jennings, J. (2001). *A Brief History of the Federal Role in Education: Why It Began and Why It's Still Needed.* Washington, DC: Center on Education Policy.

Jennings, J. (2015). *Presidents, Congress, and the Public Schools: The Politics of Education Reform.* Cambridge, MA: Harvard Education Press.

Klein, A. (2015). The nation's main K-12 law: A timeline of the ESEA. *Education Week Magazine, 34*(26), March 31. Retrieved from: www.edweek.org/ew/section/multimedia/the-nations-main-k-12-law-a-timeline.html.

National Defense Education Act of 1958, P.L. 85–864, 20 U.S.C § 401 (1958).

No Child Left Behind Act of 2001, 20 U.S.C.A. § 6301 (2001).

Trujillo, T. & Renee, M. (2015). Irrational exuberance for market-based reform: How federal turnaround policies thwart democratic schooling. *Teachers College Record, 117*(6), 1–34.

Vinoviskis, M. (2009). *From A Nation at Risk to No Child Left Behind: National Education Goals and the Creation of Federal Education Policy.* New York: Teachers College Press.

Wirt, F. M. & Kirst, M. W. (1997). *The Political Dynamics of American Education.* Berkeley, CA: McCutchan Publishing Corporation.

2

• • • • •

State Systems of Education

With the federal constitution lacking mention of education, the responsibility of creating education policy primarily falls to the states. State government is responsible for overseeing most components of the education system. The state often chooses to delegate many of these responsibilities to districts, often called local education agencies (LEAs). Ultimately it is the state's discretion when it wants to reclaim that authority. While states choose different patterns of control over education, they tend to act similarly in developing and governing the following functions (Marshall, Mitchell, & Wirt, 1989; Wirt & Kirst, 1997):

- *Funding.* States fund schools through a formula that consists of a mix of levying local property taxes and providing funding directly to districts. Most states require local districts to levy a minimum property tax and to guarantee a base level of expenditures toward education. The state responsibility for funding education increased dramatically in the second half of the twentieth century. State funding increased from 30 percent in the 1940s to 50 percent in the 1980s—the first time that states had a greater financial responsibility for schools than local districts (Fuhrman, Goertz, & Weinbaum, 2007; Wirt & Kirst, 1997; Verstegen & Knoeppel, 2012). Court cases questioning the equity of the educational system helped to shift funding from local districts to states. In California, *Serrano v. Priest* (1971) argued that the funding system relied too heavily on local property taxes and that the system violated the Equal Protection Clause. The ruling dramatically shifted the funding of schools to state revenue. *Abbott v. Burke* (1975) in New Jersey considered whether the public-school system of the state was unconstitutional because the funding structure did not provide a "thorough and efficient" education to students. Universal preschool and school renovation efforts occurred as a result of this ruling.

- *Licensure of personnel.* States create accreditation programs and processes to license teachers, principals, and other educators. They increasingly are also creating non-traditional programs for licensure.

- *Curriculum and testing.* States outline minimum curricular and graduate standards and, since the 2000 No Child Left Behind legislation, they determine statewide testing and assessment. Some states also mandate textbooks. The

2015 ESSA legislation also reaffirms that the federal government should not interfere with state choice of standards or provide incentives regarding testing and standards choices.

■ *Governance.* States determine the size and organization of local school districts.

■ *Standards and guidelines.* States also set minimum standards for school attendance, safety guidelines, and building and facility/issues, and regulate and enforce these minimum standards.

■ *Program definition.* Most states design the scope for an array of student services and programs, such as gifted and talented education, special needs education, and education for English language learners.

Some states have a meso-layer of structures in between districts and states. Some states call them Intermediate Units (IUs), such as Pennsylvania. Others call them Boards of Cooperative Educational Services (BOCES), such as New York State. These systems provide concentrated support mechanisms for districts. With intentions of creative cost-effective and efficient services, these structures offer services that districts struggle to provide alone. They are particularly used in states with large rural populations. They can offer a range of programming, including special needs services, professional development, career and technical education, early intervention programs, literacy training, adult education programs, and assistance with implementation of state initiatives.

● ● ● ● ●

History of State Control

For most of American history, states delegated most of their educational responsibilities to LEAs. State infrastructures tended to be small and followed a policy of local control with minimal interference (Cohen, 1982). State reform in the first half of the century focused on increased professionalism in education, standardization of time in school, and the duration of classes. Districts also consolidated dramatically around World War I. By 1925, one-third of states established minimum facility standards for types of classes, building code, and professional qualifications of teachers. In 1900, no state required a university degree as a minimum standard to teach; by 1965 all 50 states required a university degree (Wirt & Kirst, 1997, p. 203).

State reach increased dramatically in the second half of the twentieth century, in large part due to expectations created by federal programs (Fuhrman et al., 2007). The original 13 state constitutions made no mention of education. Now all states discuss education. Connecticut's constitution has four brief statements that address education. The California constitution's education article is more than 2500 words (Wirt & Kirst, 1997, p. 202).

As states increased their influence in educational matters, state staff and capacity to design, implement, and enforce policy greatly increased. The passing of the federal Elementary and Secondary Education Act of 1965 created mounting expectations for states to be involved in education to receive the federal funds. Legislative staff increased 130 percent between 1968 and 1974 (Wirt & Kirst, 1997, p. 203). In 1972, over three-quarters of state education staffers had not held their positions for three or more years (Wirt & Kirst, 1997). Title V of the act helped with this expansion by providing support for state administrative services. With this growing staff, state influence showed dramatic increases in areas of finance, accountability and standards, and attention to special needs and English language learners (Fuhrman et al., 2007; Wirt & Kirst, 1997).

Categorical programs were developed to respond to state needs but were underfunded and underdeveloped (Fuhrman et al., 2007). The structure of these emerging state agencies tended to mirror the structure of federal government. Programs occurred in *silos*, meaning that they did not talk to one another regularly. Consideration of the holistic needs of students or the holistic needs of states and districts was not a priority. For example, pre-school programs tend to be housed in Health and Human Services departments, separate from Education departments. Students with health issues identified at schools must be coordinated with Health and Human Services as well. The school lunch program is coordinated through the Agriculture department.

The work of the "education governors" in the 1980s (discussed in the previous chapter) helped to redefine education policy's relationship between the federal and state level (Schwartz, 2003). They defined improving education quality as the central policy strategy for building a strong economy.

Coherence at the state level was a central focus of Bill Clinton's presidential administration (1993–2001)—an outgrowth of Clinton's participation as an education governor. The coherence strategy was meant to solve the problem that most state systems lacked alignment between the components of an educational system, including teacher training, curriculum, textbooks, assessments, and more. Jennifer O'Day and Marshall Smith (who became the undersecretary in the U.S. Department of Education during the Clinton administration) drafted a series of papers (O'Day & Smith, 1993) on the value of alignment and particularly on the value of making progress toward state-level standards that could serve as the anchor point for the state educational system. During the following decades, every state and national organization created and supported state standards (Fuhrman et al., 2007).

An understanding of state role was especially strengthened by the creation of the Consortium for Policy Research in Education (CPRE), which was formed among Harvard, Stanford, University of Pennsylvania, and Michigan to explore state education policy (McDermott, 2009).[1] Much of the CPRE research developed case studies of state policy, which eventually allowed for a policy brief on state education drawing on 19 states (Fuhrman, 1994). A focus of the initial work of CPRE considered the extent of state intervention into local districts, from deregulation to state takeover (Fuhrman & Elmore, 1992, 1995). More recent research has tracked state assessment and accountability systems and Common Core Standards adoption and implementation.

The reauthorization of the Elementary and Secondary Education Act of 2000 (No Child Left Behind) also further increased expectations of state role in education. Through federal pressure, the state was established as the policy level that administers assessments and enforces sanctions for schools not meeting the standards that the states also set.

The increased focus on testing came at a time when state budgets were in freefall due to the recession that accompanied the end of the George W. Bush administration. Over the course of the first decade of the twenty-first century, state departments of education and state legislatures cut staff dramatically, sharply reducing the capacity for educational policy. In 1995, 30 states considered reorganization of state education agencies. Texas, for example, repealed a third of its education code. Cuts in state education agencies limit the ability of states to enforce current law and tend to lead to a shrinking of programs (Wirt & Kirst, 1997). Much recent fiscal research has looked at the harsh impact of the Great Recession on schooling, including shifting the costs of higher education from public subsidies to individuals (Barr & Turner, 2013).

One of the greatest shifts in state governments was instigated by Obama's Race to the Top Initiative (discussed in the previous chapter). The forcing of states to reform prior to receiving a large grant led to far more states reforming than receiving funding. States' changes included developing college and career readiness standards (often aligned with Common Core), developing data systems, and redesigning how to address the most failing schools—all at a time of shrinking state capacity. The latest reauthorization, the Every Student Succeeds Act of 2015, placed even greater expectations on the state as the primary authority for evaluating equity and excellence through standardized testing and other related measures.

● ● ● ● ●

State Education Structures

States vary in terms of how educational decision making is structured. This section examines the roles of the major state actors and the varying relationships between them. The predominant framework for examining state political cultures dates back to 1984 by Daniel Elazar (see Figure 2.1):

Traditionalistic: focus on maintaining the status quo and to ward off change. Participation in politics is considered a privilege restricted to the elite; power kinship and social connections are important. Many southern states have a history of this type of power due to a history of plantation and county-based educational systems. This system also tends to have districts at the county level rather than smaller districts that favor local control (see Figure 2.2).

Individualistic: focus is on sustaining a capitalistic, market-based system that responds to favors and exchanges of information and negotiation. Political parties are often a vehicle for negotiations. Common in Middle Atlantic states and Southern New England, this culture focuses on politics as a marketplace, with government maintaining minimum intervention into local affairs.

Moralistic: focus on achieving the community good through positive government action, and parties are not emphasized. With a history of common schools in Northern New England, the focus is on activist government that develops programs when necessary to create a safety net and to support the entire community. Ideas and issues matter and government is viewed positively; efforts to avoid corruption of government are highly prized.

While this framework still has great merit, the introduction of immigrants, shifting populations, and new generations of political leadership beg for more research on this topic (McDermott, 2009).

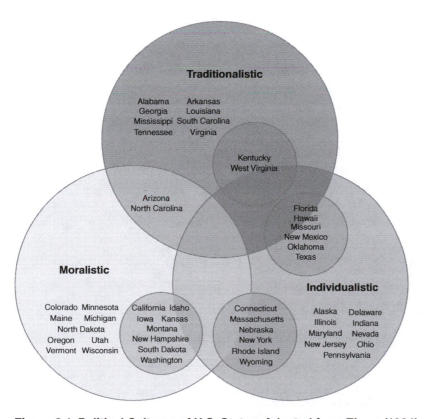

Figure 2.1 Political Cultures of U.S. States. Adapted from Elazar (1984).

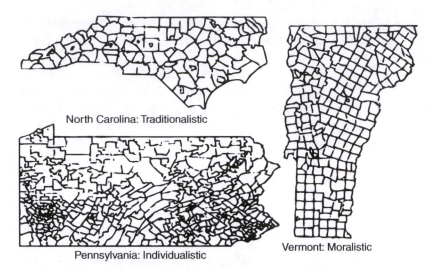

North Carolina: Traditionalistic

Pennsylvania: Individualistic

Vermont: Moralistic

Figure 2.2 District Boundaries in North Carolina, Pennsylvania, and Vermont. Data from U.S. Department of Education (school year: 2013–14).

Within-state dynamics in educational policy focus on interactions between four main bodies in state systems.

Legislatures. State legislatures are increasingly subject to greater demands but without greater infrastructure. They range from highly professional, year-round structures such as in Pennsylvania, where legislators are provided a full-time salary and benefits and robust staffing and resources (see Figure 2.3). In other states, such as Texas, legislatures only meet once every two years and receive limited compensation, staffing, and resources, so that

Largely Unprofessional	Partially Professionalized		Highly Professionalized
Arkansas	Alabama	Minnesota	California
Georgia	Alaska	Mississippi	Illinois
Idaho	Arizona	Missouri	Massachusetts
Indiana	Colorado	Nebraska	Michigan
Maine	Connecticut	North Carolina	New Jersey
Montana	Delaware	Oklahoma	New York
Nevada	Florida	Oregon	Ohio
New Hampshire	Hawaii	South Carolina	Pennsylvania
New Mexico	Iowa	Tennessee	Wisconsin
North Dakota	Kansas	Texas	
Utah	Kentucky	Virginia	
Vermont	Louisiana	Washington	
West Virginia	Maryland		
Wyoming			

Figure 2.3 Professionalization of State Legislatures. Adapted from Patterson (1996).

the elected officials are not professional in nature and must generate an income from elsewhere. State legislatures who support professional elected officials with full-time salaries and benefits and robust staffing and corresponding resources tend to have increased policy-making influence relative to gubernatorial power (Squire, 2007; Mooney, 1995). The relationship between the governor, the State Board of Education, and the Chief State vary greatly, as do the roles of each body. Figure 2.4 maps out the three most common relationships between these key executive offices.

Governor: The executive head of the state and the party of a state is the governor. Overall, researchers indicate that state governors are stronger than ever before in terms of term lengths, budgetary power, veto power, and power to appoint to agencies (Barrilleaux & Berkman, 2003; Henig, 2013). Some states give governors broad power (including West Virginia, New York, Maryland, Massachusetts, Vermont, and Washington), others have governorships with little power; and the legislatures are given most decision-making authority (including New Hampshire, Vermont, Indiana, Rhode Island, and North Carolina). Most recently, Jeff Henig (2013) has documented some noted increases in governor authority, including the governor of Massachusetts restructuring the state education system by creating a new secretary of education appointed by the governor in 2008. In Oregon, a governor created an education investment board that transferred much of the power from the state board in 2011. Governors with strong control can lead to dramatic cuts in the education system. For example, the New Jersey governor cut the pay of two-thirds of all local superintendents in 2010 (Henig, 2013).

State Board of Education or State Education Agency: This organization creates the education code. It is either appointed or elected. It takes the laws passed by the legislature and signed into law by the governor and creates the details needed to create a pathway for schools to follow the guidelines. It develops compliance techniques, such as reports and sanctions, and they help the LEAs with interpreting federal statues (Wirt & Kirst, 1997). Usually the governor appoints the state board of education, but sometimes it is the state legislature or elected directly by the public in partisan and nonpartisan elections.

Chief State School Officer (CSSO): This person is responsible for enacting the education policy created by the state board, the governor, and the legislature. The CSSO has little power unless this person has sufficient staff to enact and enforce education policy. The CSSO is elected in 15 states; it was formally elected directly in many more states until a decline after the 1940s (Henig, 2013). Other formats include the state board appointing the CSSO (a shift from 8 to 24 states) or the governor appointing the CSSO (from zero governors at the turn of the century to 14 in the present day) (Henig, 2013, p. 41).

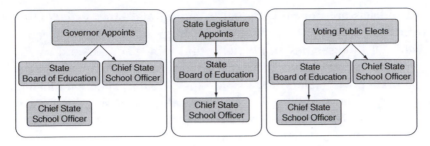

Figure 2.4 Selection Patterns for State Education Leadership. Guthrie and Reed (1986).

●●●●●

Referenda

One way that citizens can appear to have increased their voice in policy is through *referenda*. In states with referenda laws, such as California, citizens vote directly on school matters, such as bonds, levies, and budgets (Rivera, 2016; Wirt & Kirst, 1997). Referenda can be a way to voice concern and dissent for policies.

Referenda laws were created mainly by conservative groups seeking to reduce spending on schools through prevention of bond and property tax measures. Such laws required extraordinary majorities to be passed and increased the ability of property owners to prevent tax increases. As a result, states could not pay their education bills. While not all states have direct referenda, all states except Alabama, Hawaii, and Indiana have laws that require local public votes on school financing (Wirt & Kirst, 1997). Some states have statewide referenda laws. In the case of California's 1978 Proposition 13 referendum, school funding was reduced by one-third overnight, accounting for nearly $3 billion. This referendum marked the beginning of a downward trend in the quality of schools in California based on comparisons of performance measures (Burke, Penner, & Walsh, 2010; Carroll, Krop, Arkes, Morrison, & Flanagan, 2005).

In many cases, referenda are a tool that can be accessed by only the very wealthy. In these states, referenda also have led to policies that dramatically change teachers' rights and classroom instruction. While referenda seem like they are a highly democratic process, garnering enough signatures to get an agenda on a ballot in a large state such as California is a multi-million-dollar process. While some grassroots organizations have developed extensive campaigns to create referenda, millionaires can write a check to fund such campaigns. Proposition 227, *English for the Children,* was developed by millionaire Ron Unz. While the title of the proposition sounds appealing, the law actually prevents teachers from using bilingual methods of instruction for English language learners—teachers can only teach using English, despite research that shows that Limited English Proficient (LEP) students learn English more effectively in a bilingual setting when teachers are well-trained and the program is funded properly (Rossell & Baker, 1996; Krashen, 1999a, 1999b; McQuillan, 1998). The law was especially strong because teachers could be sued and fired for using bilingual strategies in their classrooms. This law was repealed by Proposition 58, in 2014.

●●●●●

Policy Development Across States: The Story of the Common Core

The Common Core State Standards (CCSS) were a state-initiated effort to create simplified, higher quality standards for K-12 Language Arts and Mathematics. Formed between 2006 and 2010, the stalling of the reauthorization of the Elementary and Secondary Education Act created policy space for the development of the standards. The belief behind the creation of common standards was that a lack of coherence across states was an impediment to improving educational achievement and increasing international competitiveness (Kornhaber, Griffith, & Tyler, 2014). All students should be college and career ready if they attended a school designing teaching and learning on the concepts within the CCSS. Proponents of the standards touted their rigor, the incorporation of brain and learning research, aligned assignments, international benchmarking, and the improvement of curricular access for students who change districts (Supovitz, Daly, & del Fresno, 2015).

The development of CCSS occurred in a short period of time with a small number of national actors. The Chief Council of State School Officers (CCSSO) and the National Governors' Association (NGA) championed the bi-partisan effort to create the standards. The federal government created a competitive grant program to fund development of CCSS-aligned assessments. Because the funding was provided to states, applicants had to demonstrate support from multiple states, as well as commit to innovative elements such as computer adaptive assessments. The two primary grant winners were Smarter Balanced, a consortium backed by 31 states in 2010, and Partnership for Assessment of Readiness for College and Careers (PARCC), which was supported by 26 states (U.S. Department of Education, 2010). These consortia then outsourced much of their grant funding to for-profit test developers and data managers, such as McGraw Hill.

Financial incentives from the federal Race to the Top (RttT) grant program developed by the Obama administration provided strong financial support and heavy-handed political leverage to encourage states to adopt the standards. The Gates Foundation and others provided financial support to states to help write their RttT plan (Kornhaber, Barkauskas, & Griffith, 2016, p. 16). However, the stigma of federal involvement also fanned the flames of opposition to the legislation. With a growing trend of presidents who are polarizing figures (McGuinn & Supovitz, 2016; Smith & Seltzer, 2015), CCSS implementation may have been damaged by presidential endorsement (Hess, 2014).

At its peak, 45 states and the District of Columbia adopted the CCSS. Alaska, Texas, Virginia, and Nebraska chose to keep their own state standards (reflecting local opposition to state education politics, Anchorage, AK adopted the CCSS) and Minnesota only adopted English Language Arts (ELA) standards (Supovitz et al., 2015). At the time of the printing of this textbook, four states have withdrawn from CCSS adoption: Indiana, Minnesota (ELA adoption only), Oklahoma, and South Carolina (Kornhaber et al., 2016). Other states have faced significant resistance to CCSS implementation and introduced legislation to repeal. This has generated some state legislatures to rename the standards in an attempt to deflect the stigma attached to CCSS through basic rebranding (Layton, 2014). For example, Florida renamed the CCSS as "Next Generation Sunshine State Standards."

Pushback to the Common Core

Early implementation of CCSS proceeded with little controversy. Knowledge of what common standards were remained low and as a result the developers and advocates of the Common Core did not develop strong idea campaigns for educating the public. As implementation was expected to begin in these states, support for the policy faded (McDonnell & Weatherford, 2016). The lack of intentional messaging by the advocates of the Common Core made the policy vulnerable to opposition (McGuinn & Supovitz, 2016).

As opposition increased against the CCSS, the proponents remained behind the curve in reacting to attacks rather than developing a cohesive communication strategy. Also, the very nature of the receptivity of the creation of the Common Core among states—a widespread coalition of state actors without a centralized ownership of the reform—prevented a cohesive response strategy to reacting to problems with it.

The four years between initial adoption by states and the administration of standards-aligned assessments included political changes in state and local elected offices in half of the states. The opposition to the CCSS came from both edges of the right and the left, a concept called *transpartisan* politics (Supovitz et al., 2015). These groups share their opposition to an issue but would be very unlikely to agree to a policy alternative because their objectives stem from fundamentally different values.

The case of the Common Core opposition efforts also raise the use of symbols and public ideas (discussed in Chapter 6) being used to sway public opinion at the adoption and implementation phases of policy. Opposition groups selectively chose particular aspects of the Common Core to appeal to the values and beliefs of constitutions (Majone, 1989; Moore 1988; Supovitz et al., 2015).

Metaphors used by CCSS opposition included threats of oppressive government intrusion, brainwashed children, threats to freedom, and attacks on American and religious values on the right. On the left, threats of for-profit intrusion into public education, student data collection, excessive testing, and concerns regarding the use of children as guinea pigs for social experiments appealed to liberal opposition (Supovitz et al., 2015). The Common Core became a "proxy war" that represented the broader cultural rifts occurring in the United States at the time (Supovitz et al., 2015).

Progressives, such as the "Bad Ass Teachers Association," raised concerns about teacher evaluations being tied to assessments, about corporatization of the educational system, the dominance of standardized testing in determining student learning and success, and a lack of focus on equity (Supovitz et al., 2015).

The Tea Party and right wing protested the alignment of the effort with Obama administration policies. The federal role was viewed as too prominent. Longstanding concerns about curricula that could run counter to conservative religious beliefs and that supported multi-culturalism were also raised. The reauthorization of ESEA, passed by a Republican-dominated Congress in 2015, explicitly banned the federal government from future efforts to promote standards-based reform, including preventing financial incentivizing of the Common Core.

The Common Core also was one of the first major education policy issues that faced the fate of the shifting use and consumption of media, called "the new landscape of social and alternative media" by McGuinn and Supovitz (2016, p. 16). Often the arguments led to less informed citizenry rather than clearer information. For example, only half of Americans who had heard of the Common Core understood that states and local districts still held the authority to choose standards (Downey, 2014). Donald Trump campaigned to end the CCSS, even though the president cannot change state policies.

Research indicates a self-selection of news that affirms one's beliefs instead of providing a broad spectrum (Epstein & Graham, 2007; Mutz, 2006), called an echo chamber, rather than a source of news (McGuinn & Supovitz, 2015). With the advent of Facebook and Twitter, grassroots movements can spread public ideas much quicker than the previous era of television and radio.

Moving Forward With the Common Core

David Cohen and Jal Mehta (2017) have offered recommendations on the future of the Common Core based upon an analysis of what reforms tend to be successful. They suggest that states and districts and other key players need to create stronger alliances to align support systems for implementation of the standards. They also encourage these actors to look to what is working in their communities and build the Common Core Standards into these successful practices, such as the International Baccalaureate programs in some states. They further suggest enhancement of the work of intermediary organizations to help with capacity building, concluding support for tools and content, assessments, and professional development.

●●●●●

Comprehension Questions

■ What does the U.S. Constitution say is the role of the state government in educational matters?

- How has the state role in education evolved over recent history? How have ESEA law and reauthorizations changed the state role in educational policy?

- What lessons does the experience of Common Core teach about the relationship between state and federal policy? About agenda setting and messaging? About the role of interest groups in influencing implementation?

● ● ● ● ●

Discussion Questions

- What are the range of relationships between governors, departments of education, and chief executive school officers? What are the advantages and disadvantages of each configuration? Which one is the relationship for your state?

- Discuss Elazar's framework of state political cultures. Does this framework still fit with state political cultures? Does your state fall into the mode of traditionalistic, individualistic, moralistic, or something else?

- Who are the key players in state educational politics? Identify these individuals for your state and learn about their positions on key issues.

● ● ● ● ●

Activities

- Identify referenda passed in states such as Arizona and California, including on issues such as taxation and bilingual education. Become familiar with some of the particular initiatives and then discuss the pros and cons of a referenda system.

- View the movie "Building the Machine"—a movie designed to build support to oppose the Common Core. What political symbols are used to elicit an emotional reaction? What evidence and appeals are used for claims?
  Find on the web using the following search terms:

  Common Core Movie; building machine

- Review the state ESSA proposals. What are patterns of how states have chosen to respond to increased agency to define accountability measures?
  Find on the web using the following search terms:

  state ESSA plans; check state plans

- Listen/read "The Return of Bilingual Education in California?" reported by Claudio Sanchez (October 26, 2016).
  Find on the web using the following search terms:

  NPR; Return Bilingual Education California; October 26, 2016; Sanchez

■ Review the ESSA state proposals and develop categories for considering how the states have approached the opportunity for greater agency in defining accountability policy.

Find on the web using the following search terms:

ESSA State proposals 2017

● ● ● ● ●

Note

1 Current CPRE institutions are University of Pennsylvania, Teachers College, Columbia University, Harvard University, Stanford University, University of Michigan, University of Wisconsin-Madison, and Northwestern University.

● ● ● ● ●

Further Reading

Henig, J. (2013). *The End of Exceptionalism in American Education: The Changing Politics of School Reform.* Cambridge, MA: Harvard Education Press.

Marshall, C., Mitchell, D., & Wirt, F. (1989). *Culture and Education Policy in the American States.* Bristol, PA: Falmer Press.

O'Day, J. A. & Smith, M. S. (1993). Systemic reform and educational opportunity. In Fuhrman, S. (ed.) *Designing Coherent Education Policy: Improving the System* (pp. 250–312). San Francisco, CA: Jossey-Bass.

Squire, P. (2007). Measuring state legislative professionalism: The Squire index revisited. *State Politics & Policy Quarterly, 7*(2), 211–27.

● ● ● ● ●

Reference List

Barr, A. & Turner, S. E. (2013). Expanding enrollments and contracting state budgets: The effect of the Great Recession on higher education. *The ANNALS of the American Academy of Political and Social Science, 650*(1), 168–93.

Barrilleaux, C. & Berkman, M. (2003). Do governors matter? Budgeting rules and the politics of state policymaking. *Political Research Quarterly, 56*(4), 409–17.

Burke, M., Penner, G., & Walsh, N. (2010). Prop 13's impact on schools, *KPBS*, San Diego State University, March 26. Retrieved from: www.kpbs.org/news/2010/mar/26/prop-13s-impact-schools/.

Carroll, S. J., Krop, C., Arkes, J., Morrison, P. A., & Flanagan, A. (2005). *California's K-12 Public Schools: How Are They Doing?* Santa Monica, CA: RAND Education.

Cohen, D. (1982). Policy and organization: The impact of state and federal educational policy on school governance. *Harvard Educational Review, 52*(4), 474–99.

Cohen, D. & Mehta, J. (2017). Why reforms sometimes succeed: Understanding the conditions that produce reforms that last. *American Educational Research Journal, 54*(4), 644–90.

Downey, Maureen. (2014). Most Americans support national standards unless they're called Common Core. Time for rebranding? *Atlanta Journal Constitution*, August 19.

Elazar, D. (1984). *American Federalism: A View From the States*. (3rd ed.). New York: Harper and Row.

Epstein, D. & Graham, J. D. (2007). *Polarized Politics and Policy Consequences*. Santa Monica, CA: The RAND Corporation.

Fuhrman, S. H. (1994). *Challenges in Systemic Education Reform*. New Brunswick, NJ: Center for Policy Research in Education (ERIC Document Reproduction Service No. ED315903).

Fuhrman, S. H. & Elmore, R. F. (1992). *Takeover and Deregulation: Working Models of New State and Local Regulatory Relationships*. New Brunswick, NJ: CPRE, Rutgers University.

Fuhrman, S. H. & Elmore, R. F. (1995). *Ruling Out Rules: The Evolution of Deregulation in State Education Policy*. New Brunswick, NJ: CPRE, Rutgers University.

Fuhrman, S. H., Goertz, M., & Weinbaum, E. (2007). Educational governance in the United States: Where are we? How did we get here? Why should we care? In, Fuhrman, S. H., Cohen, D., & Mosher, F. (eds.) *The State of Education Policy Research* (pp. 41–61). Mahwah, NJ: Lawrence Erlbaum Associates.

Guthrie, J. & Reed, R. (1986). *Educational Administration and Policy*. Englewood Cliffs, NJ: Prentice-Hall.

Henig, J. (2013). *The End of Exceptionalism in American Education: The Changing Politics of School Reform*. Cambridge, MA: Harvard Education Press.

Hess, F. (2014). How the Common Core went wrong. *National Affairs, 21*, Fall. Retrieved from: www.nationalaffairs.com/publications/detail/how-the-common-core-went-wrong.

Kornhaber, M. L., Barkauskas, N. J., & Griffith, K. M. (2016). Smart money? Philanthropic and federal funding for the Common Core. *Education Policy Analysis Archives, 24*(93).

Kornhaber, M. L., Griffith, K., & Tyler, A. (2014). It's not education by zip code anymore—but what is it? Conceptions of equity under the Common Core. *Education Policy Analysis Archives, 22*(4).

Krashen, S. (1999a). *Condemned Without a Trial: Bogus Arguments Against Bilingual Education*. Portsmouth, NH: Heinemann.

Krashen, S. (1999b). Bilingual education: Arguments for and (bogus) arguments against. Paper presented at the Georgetown Round Table on Languages and Linguistics, Georgetown University, Washington, DC, May.

Layton, L. (2014). Some states rebrand controversial Common Core education standards. *Washington Post*, 30 January.

Majone, G. (1989). *Evidence, Argument, and Persuasion in the Policy Process*. New Haven, CT: Yale University Press.

Marshall, C., Mitchell, D., & Wirt, F. (1989). *Culture and Education Policy in the American States*. Bristol, PA: Falmer Press.

McDermott, K. (2009). The expansion of state policy research. In Sykes, G., Schneider, B., & Plank, D. (eds.) *Handbook of Education Policy Research* (pp. 749–66). New York: Routledge.

McDonnell, L. M. & Weatherford, M. S. (2016). Recognizing the political in implementation research. *Educational Researcher, 45*(4), 233–42.

McGuinn, P. & Supovitz, J. (2016). *Parallel Play in the Education Sandbox: The Common Core and the Politics of Transpartisan Coalitions*. CPRE Research Reports. Retrieved from: http://repository.upenn.edu/cpre_researchreports/8.

McQuillan, J. (1998). Is 99% failure a "success?" Orange Unified's English immersion program. *The Multilingual Educator, 21*(7), 11.

Mooney, C. Z. (1995). Citizens, structures, and sister states: Influences on state legislative professionalism. *Legislative Studies Quarterly, 20,* 47–67.

Moore, M. (1988). What sort of ideas become public ideas? In Reich, R. (ed.) *The Power of Public Ideas* (pp. 55–84). Cambridge, MA: Ballinger Publishing Company.

Mutz, D. C. (2006). *Hearing the Other Side: Deliberative Versus Participatory Democracy.* Cambridge, UK: Cambridge University Press.

O'Day, J. A. & Smith, M. S. (1993). Systemic reform and educational opportunity. In Fuhrman, S. (ed.) *Designing Coherent Education Policy: Improving the System* (pp. 250–312). San Francisco, CA: Jossey-Bass.

Patterson, S. C. (1996). Legislative politics in the states. In Gray, V., Hanson, R., & Kousser, T. (eds.) *Politics in the American States: A Comparative Analysis* (pp. 159–206). Washington, DC: SAGE/CQ Press.

Rivera, M. (2016). *Inequity and Privatization in School District Facilities Financing: A Mixed Methods Study.* Unpublished dissertation. University of California, Berkeley.

Rossell, C. H. & Baker, K. (1996). The educational effectiveness of bilingual education. *Research in the Teaching of English, 30*(1), 7–74.

Schwartz, R. (2003). The emerging state leadership role in education reform: Notes of a participant-observer in *A Nation Engaged?* In Gordon, D. T. (ed.) *American Education 20 Years after "A Nation At Risk"* (pp. 121–51). Cambridge, MA: Harvard University Press.

Smith, R. & Seltzer, R. (2015). *Polarization and the Presidency: From FDR to Barack Obama.* Boulder, CO: Lynne Reinner Publishers.

Squire, P. (2007). Measuring state legislative professionalism: The Squire Index revisited. *State Politics & Policy Quarterly, 7*(2), 211–27.

Supovitz, J., Daly, A., & del Fresno, M. (2015). #CommonCore: How social media is changing the politics of education. *The #Commoncore Project.* Retrieved from: http://repository.upenn.edu/hashtagcommoncore/1.

U.S. Department of Education. (2010). U.S. Secretary of Education Duncan announces winners of competition to improve student assessments. Washington, DC. Retrieved from: www.ed.gov/news/press-releases/us-secretary-education-duncan-announces-winners-competition-improve-student-asse.

Verstegen, D. A. & Knoeppel, R. C. (2012). From statehouse to schoolhouse: Education finance apportionment systems in the United States. *Journal of Education Finance, 38*(2), 145–66.

Wirt, F. & Kirst, M. (1997). *The Political Dynamics of American Education.* Berkeley, CA: McCutchan Publishing.

3

Local School Districts, Citywide Change, and Rural Dilemmas
with Daniella Hall

School Boards

Districts are governed by *school boards*, also known as boards of directors or boards of trustees. Legally, school boards are created and exist at the discretion of the state legislature, and therefore school boards are state and not local officials (Alexander & Alexander, 2015; Briffault, 2005; Ehrensal & First, 2008). Board members serve as public officers on behalf of the state. In practice, however,

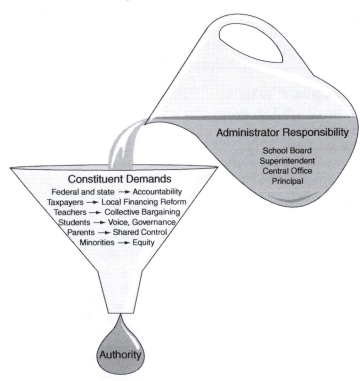

Figure 3.1 School Politics Paradigm. Adapted from Wirt and Kirst (1997, p. 35). Graphical elements used with permission from https://clipartsfest.com.

the board mediates between the needs and concerns of the broader community, standards of professional quality, and expectations from the state (Wirt & Kirst, 1997).

Compositions of School Boards

Three to thirty individuals tend to sit on a school board in three-to-four-year terms. The state legal code determines requirements of candidates, such as minimum age. The composition of school boards is largely similar to demographics of the United States, although somewhat higher socioeconomic status, slightly less diverse, and more educated (Hess & Meeks, 2010). Research shows that eligibility and composition of board members is implicitly determined by social status, political resources, age, and gender. Board members are similar to the turn of the century and tend to be business owners and men (Wirt & Kirst, 1997). Elective school boards account for 94.5 percent of the total (Hess & Meeks, 2010). Most boards are elected for four years. A recent study (Hess & Meeks, 2010) found that school boards are becoming more gender balanced, with 44 percent female and 56 percent male. Thus, the rate of women participating in local government is twice that of women in the U.S. Congress.

School board organization can be town, district, or county-based. Southern states tend to have county boards. Some states, such as Georgia, have school districts within districts. Some Northeastern and Midwestern states have implemented multi-district unions where multiple independent school boards operate within one regional district (Hall & McHenry-Sorber, 2017). Urban cities increasingly have mayoral-appointed boards in urban areas, like Chicago and Philadelphia.

Most school boards are elected by local communities and represent one of the last bastions of localism. Board members campaign on local issues (Ehrensal & First, 2008; Smoley, 1999). The ballots of school district elections tend to be non-partisan since reforms of the Progressive era that sought to reduce corruption by removing politics from elections and professionalizing education (Tyack, 1974). These reforms sought to model school boards on corporations.

All of these reforms sought to *decrease* general public involvement in schools. Reforms also made it harder for citizens to run for school boards by making them citywide elections, while at the same time voter participation was limited by designating school board elections at different times than the general election (Spring, 2011). With few contested seats and low voter turnout, some question the democratic nature of this process (Danzberger, Kirst, & Usdan, 1992; Hess, 2002; Zeigler, Jennings, & Peak, 1974). Additionally, voters who come to the polls are not representative of voters at large (Allen & Plank, 2005; Spring, 2011). In fact, in many school board elections fewer than 5 percent of voters cast ballots (Allen & Plank, 2005, p. 512). Some researchers attribute this decline in participation in school board elections to dissatisfaction theory: people participate in board elections primarily when they want change (Alsbury, 2003, 2008; Lutz & Iannaccone, 1994, 2008).

School Board Responsibilities

School boards have legislative, executive, and judicial powers (Wirt & Kirst, 1997).

- *Judicial.* Bards run hearings about expansions, expulsions, and pupil placements.
- *Executive.* They implement policy from the states.
- *Legislative.* They make policies and control the budget (Glass, Bjork, & Brunner, 2000; Mountford, 2008). Boards may design the policies that the superintendent implements, although boards spend less than one tenth of their time developing and overseeing policy (Hochschild, 2005, p. 325). Instead, boards tend to support policies developed by the superintendent and by state officials, and sometimes by interest groups (Boyd, 1976; Glass et al., 2000; Malen, 2003; Zeigler et al., 1974).
- *Financial.* State law requires each school district to prepare an annual budget, including adopting a budget, collecting revenues, making expenditures, and providing reports and audits to allow for transparency of spending. The school budget is a legal document that limits how much a district can spend. For most states, school districts cannot approve deficit budgets.

Research from the past several decades has criticized the functioning of school boards, citing that many undermined their authority with ineffective or disruptive leadership (Danzberger, 1994; Danzberger et al., 1992; Grady & Krumm, 1998; Wirt & Kirst, 1997; Zeigler, 1973; Zeigler et al., 1974). Some research criticizes the board for micromanaging the superintendent (Conley, 2003; McAdams, 2003) and focusing on narrow self-interest of board members rather than the broader needs of the district (Carver, 1990; Ehrensal & First, 2008).

The *superintendent* is hired by the school board. Superintendents are the chief executive officer of a district. *Central office* staff is the term often used to describe the other administrators that work in the district office. The average tenure of a superintendent is quite low—just three years (Grissom & Mitani, 2016). Additionally, a lack of diversity tends to describe those who fill these positions. Superintendents are 76 percent male and 94 percent white (Kowalski, McCord, Petersen, Young, & Ellerson, 2010).

The work of superintendents and central office staff consists of three spheres of leadership (Cuban, 1998):

- *Political leadership* focuses on coalition building, consensus, buffering, and bridging with the external environment, mediating community needs, and handling fiscal matters.
- *Administrative leadership* responsibilities include increasing efficiency of routine functions, building greater coherence across systems, aligning

curricula, standards, and assessment, managing human resources, including hiring and firing, developing improvement cycles and strategic plans, and managing physical plant activities. They oversee the construction and maintenance of facilities, and implement state requirements regarding issues including certification, curriculum, programming, and regulations.

■ *Professional leadership* activities include professional development, reflective dialogue, enhancing a community of learners, and creating policy focused on teaching and learning.

Superintendents also structure and organize the work of the school board (Dawson & Quinn, 2001; Glass 2001; McAdams 2003; Smoley, 1999). Superintendents act under broad discretion and many policy decisions never reach the board (Wirt & Kirst, 1997). Yet they must also anticipate how the board might react since, ultimately, the board has the power to fire them. Strategic superintendents learn how to actively manage their boards and to create greater power for themselves (Ehrensal & First, 2008).

Historically, superintendents have increased their power in relation to school boards (Callahan, 1962). Often school boards serve a supporting role to superintendents by rubber-stamping district policies and budgets (Boyd, 1976; Malen, 2003). Some states have further delegated authority to superintendents through legislation to focus local governance on "accommodating state priorities ... rather than determining local school priorities and policies" (Malen, 2003, p. 201).

Disempowered school boards then tend to experience role confusion over responsibilities that can create conflict with superintendents and undermine successful governance (Glass et al., 2000; Danzberger et al., 1992; Land, 2002). Role confusion can exacerbate mistrust and weaken collaboration between board members and superintendents (Danzberger et al., 1992; Kirst, 1984; Glass et al., 2000; Mountford, 2008). Glass et al. (2000) conducted a national survey of superintendents and found widespread school board role confusion.

Daniella Hall (2016) found a more complex understanding of role confusion. The study draws on the traditional importance of willingness to act and capacity (resources and skills) to enact reform (McLaughlin, 1991). Hall has found that the strength of the combination of school board capacity and community capacity shapes the scope of possibility for superintendent-board relations. Boards with higher overall capacity are more likely to resist superintendent governance; boards with lower overall capacity are more likely to rely on the superintendent.

● ● ● ● ●

Influencing the Local Level

Despite the increase in national and state policy, research indicates a resurgent role for local actors as well by providing avenues for "non-system" players to

challenge traditional governance arrangements and to implement federal policies (Marsh & Wohlstetter, 2013). The increase of policy at one level is not a
zero-sum game that takes away power from other levels (Bauch & Goldring,
1998; Fuhrman & Elmore, 1990; Marsh & Wohlstetter, 2013; Mitra, 2005). Relations among federal, state, and local levels are also multidirectional. Federal
policy often requires states and districts to alter local politics, and decisions
made by states and districts can also influence federal decisions.

In some states, districts are organized in a pipeline model of many elementary schools leading to one or more high schools. In such states, the number of
districts tends to be quite large. Pennsylvania, for example, has 500 school districts organized in the pipeline model. In other states, districts are aligned based
on grade level. In California, for example, some districts are only elementary
schools, grades K–6. Other districts are only high schools.

In 2013, 29 percent of all students were enrolled in urban districts (NCES,
2013–14b). Students of color and poverty, children of immigrants, and those
with special needs have come to be concentrated within large urban districts
(Sykes, O'Day, & Ford, 2009). In contrast, 34 percent of students are enrolled in
suburban districts, and 36 percent of students are enrolled in town or rural districts (NCES, 2013–14b). One-quarter of all rural students are minorities and
one half of all English language learners are situated in rural schools (Snyder,
Dillow, & Hoffman, 2007).

As federal oversight expanded, district power also expanded, often at the cost of
local school boards (Kirst, 1984; Malen, 2003; Spillane, 1996, 1998). Districts have
increasingly served as policy initiators and policy entrepreneurs including a focus
on learning systems, data analysis, and instructional change (Sykes et al., 2009).
Districts working as "learning organizations" focused on using data for continuous
cycles of improvement can have a range of outcomes. They can improve instruction even in the context of increased accountability of the last 20 years (Berman &
McLaughlin 1977; Spillane 1996; Spillane & Thompson 1997) or they can create
adverse consequences for instruction based on how they design and implement
policies (Bulkley, Fairman, Martinez, & Hicks, 2004; Spillane, 1996).

Building on the concept of *coherence* (O'Day & Smith, 1993), districts have
the ability to align funding, curricula, training, assessment, and related ideas to
create greater reform gains. Research has supported this coherence viewpoint
by finding that when districts do make an impact, they focus on technical
coherence, including: define a vision, align curriculum with standards and
assessment, use data to make decisions and drive instructional change, align
fiscal and human resources with reform priorities, and intervention with struggling schools (Elmore & Burney 1998; Supovitz 2006; Sykes et al., 2009).

Successful coherence often relies on the strength of a professional learning
community (Sykes et al., 2009). Creating a district-wide culture helps to build
trust and legitimacy for reform and instructional mission. This shared vision can
help to shore up collective efficacy and teachers' collective belief that they can
be successful (Tschannen-Moran, Hoy, & Hoy, 1998; Goddard, Hoy, & Hoy,
2000). Developing professional learning communities among teachers has been

shown to be very effective in improving outcomes for children (McLaughlin & Talbert, 2001). Districts can support this work by allowing time for collaboration, complementing learning opportunities with collaborative work, and encouraging teacher leadership (O'Day 2002; Thompson, Sykes, & Skrla, 2008).

●●●●●

District Consolidation

District numbers have consistently declined over time as states press for consolidation in the name of efficiency. Once numbering over 100,000 districts, the nation now has just under 13,500 districts (National Center for Education Statistics, 2013–14a, 2013–14b). California has over 900 districts. The small state of Maine has 242 school districts; Maryland and Delaware have only a handful each (Sykes et al., 2009). North Carolina and Florida, for example, organize districts at the county level, and thus each district comprises a large number of schools. This countywide district structure was sometimes formed as a result of desegregation court rulings after *Brown v. Board of Education of Topeka* (1954); in fact, while desegregation is worse than ever, countywide districts have been shown to reduce segregation (Orfield, Frankenberg, & Lee, 2003).

The benefits of district consolidation are often misconstrued (Hall & Burfoot-Rochford, 2014). Economist studies show that theoretical models of district consolidation could create economies of scale and cost savings (Duncombe & Yinger, 2002, 2005). Yet actual analysis of rural consolidation has not shown these financial findings (Cox & Cox, 2010). Unanticipated costs of consolidation can even raise educational costs, such as transition costs of contract negotiations, restricting facilities, legal fees, and public relationships. Additionally, pay negotiations in centralized districts may "level up" to the highest negotiated pay scale in the contract pool. Educational outcomes of consolidation have been mixed, with students performing lower in large school districts and scores declining in consolidated districts (Howley & Howley, 2010)—and particularly at-risk students (Cotton, 1996; Howley, Johnson, & Petrie, 2011).

District consolidation can be particularly harmful in rural areas due to the school district often being the one community hub in a sparsely populated region. With the school as the focal point of an area, the identity and morale of the community can struggle. Schools serve as markers of social and economic viability and a loss of a school can have unintended consequences in terms of declining property values and reduced business opportunities (Brown & Schafft, 2011; Tieken, 2014).

• • • • •

Community Control

Dissatisfaction theory (Iannaccone & Lutz, 1978; Lutz & Iannaccone, 1994, 2008) argues that a breakdown in approval of local school board actions can lead to a sudden decline in public opinion and sudden and intense attention to board decisions and composition. This shift may occur when newcomers move into the district or due to lack of transparency of decision making or a sudden change in direction of policy making. Dissatisfaction can lead to a protest at a board meeting or removal of board members through elections (Alsbury, 2003, 2008). A new board majority might even be formed that fires the superintendent (Alsbury, 2003, 2008). Local participation then may decline again once the new board is stabilized in congruence with public opinion.

With growing concerns over board governance, some reforms have led to increased local control by devolving decision making to the school level. Some localized reforms have included *site-based decision making* in which schools make hiring and budgetary decisions (Fuhrman, Goertz, & Weinbaum, 2007; Howell, 2005). Sometimes site-based decision making includes parents and teachers in the governance process. Especially popular in the 1980s and 1990s, these site-based reforms have had mixed results. Democratic decision making does not correlate to instructional change, but strong democratic decision making is likely to lead to more restructuring, which in turn can lead to instructional change (Fuhrman et al., 2007).

Expansion of parental authority has ebbed and flowed over the decades. Many community control advocates argue that allowing community members to participate in decision making will allow for greater representation for minority groups. Despite the popularity of increased local control, the parochial interests of local communities can lead to problematic outcomes, such as increased segregation of race, class, and gender, and greater inequities (McDonnell, 2007). Kathryn McDermott's (1999) research found that local control was a barrier to desegregation and efforts to improve learning outcomes in urban areas in New Haven. McDermott found that suburban families viewed poverty as an urban problem and owned no responsibility to help to address it by allowing students to cross district lines to attend wealthier, higher achieving schools.

• • • • •

Consolidation of Power in Cities: Mayoral Control

Mayoral control of cities schools has been a growing trend in beginning in the 1990s. The process consists of mayors taking over the decision making and budget of city school districts.

Mayoral takeover of local districts occurred in a wave of urban areas in the 1990s, led by Boston in 1991. Since then, Chicago, Cleveland, Detroit, Harrisburg, Hartford, Jackson, New Haven, New York City, Oakland, Philadelphia,

Prince Georges County, MD, Providence, Trenton, Washington, DC, and Yonkers have all shifted school control to mayors (Henig, 2013, p. 60). In other cities, mayors have become very active in school district governance, although the structure has not formally changed, including Louisville, Indianapolis, Long Beach Nashville, San Jose, Akron, Columbus, St. Louis, St. Petersburg, and Denver (Spring, 2011). In these cities, mayors have greater control over selecting superintendents, appointing school board members, controlling budgets, and creating charter schools (Henig, 2013). For example, New York City consolidated 32 districts into the power of the mayor in 2002 after the state legislature strengthened mayoral power. Then Mayor Bloomberg had the power to appoint 8 of the 13 board members and to appoint the chancellor of education, Joel Klein (an old friend of Bloomberg), and strongly changed the course of New York educational reform. When members of the board objected to his policies, he fired them (Henig, 2013).

Advantages of mayoral control include a single decision-making point, efficient financial and administrative management, and an integration of services for children (Kirst, 2002). Disadvantages include the removal of democratic voice from school board selection processes. Its ability to change instruction is less clear. Proponents say that mayoral control provides a single point of electoral accountability, improves the management of the school system, and facilitates integration with other children's services (Cibulka & Boyd, 2003; Cuban & Usdan, 2002; Kirst, 2002; Fuhrman et al., 2007; Wong & Shen, 2008; Wong, Shen, Anagnostopolous, & Rutledge, 2007).

Calling it the end of "exceptionalism," Henig (2013) claims that the separate nature of education governance might be changing. He notes education aligning with other domestic policy areas. This shift has been caused by an increase in governors in the 1980s as well as an increase in mayoral control of schools. The mayor assumes a role similar to a CEO in business. This renewed focus on mayoral control indicates an increasing dissatisfaction with education, including concerns of financial corruption in some areas. It also shows the appeal of centralized decision making and the values of efficiency and excellence over equity and local control.

Prior to the Progressive era in the 1920s, mayors often had control of urban districts. Progressives sought to professionalize education and depoliticize schools by moving control to local boards (Tyack, 1974). Mayors believed that having control of school systems was politically risky (Cronin, 1973). The more recent focus on mayoral takeover is re-centralizing power by consolidating policy systems. The arguments for mayoral control include efficiency, stronger management, and closer scrutiny of mayoral races than school board elections (Spring, 2011).

●●●●●

Policy Regimes and Civic Capacity

Local governance may involve the collaboration that occurs in a *policy regime*. This framework focuses on relationships and coalitions formed for specific goals, such as school achievement (Cohen-Vogel & McLendon, 2009; Shipps, 2008). Policy regimes include three dimensions (Wilson, 2000)—the power dynamics between the actors, the way the problems are defined and framed, and the organizational arrangement of how the regime conducts its work. While this broader framework has focused on regulatory policy (Harris & Milkis, 1989) and presidential work (Skowronek, 2008), we focus here on coalitions working in urban areas on school improvement.

To be successful, regimes must possess a unified *purpose* that contains a sense of urgency, adequate resources, and a problem-solving task (Stone 2005, p. 331). This purpose must consist of specific, attainable policy goals (Mossberger & Stoker, 2001). Much research has documented the foci of regimes seeking to improve urban education. *Performance/instrumental regimes* focus on changing teaching and learning and the culture of schools, *progressive/symbolic regimes* seek to improve a community's image, and *employment/organic regimes* attempt to prevent change entirely and preserve the status quo (Mossberger & Stoker, 2001). Shipps (2003) adds two more types of regimes—*enhancement regimes* focus on changing who has a voice in the policy system and *market regimes* focus on increasing economic/market values in educational systems. Bulkley (2007) discusses a specific form of market regime, a *contracting regime*, in which school districts pay private organizations to provide services. Less research examines the process of creating a regime. Cucchiara (2013) has examined how Philadelphia partners with real estate and districts to *re-brand* schools to attract, and retain, professional families to urban public schools.

A key component of regime development is the *engagement* of key stakeholders. Regimes by definition must include a combination of public and private actors (Stone, 2005). While every city has a set of political actors, interest groups, resource patterns, and institutional forces (Shipps, 2003), not every city is a regime.

Civic capacity consists of urban partnership of a coalition of wide-ranging interests to focus on a common problem. These coalitions focus on building relationships between sectors with an emphasis on high degrees of trust and reciprocity, or social capital (Stone, Henig, Jones, & Pierannunzi, 2001; Portz, Stein, & Jones, 1999). While social capital is largely private, interpersonal, and informal, civic capacity is public, and involves major groups and institutions, like CBOs and advocacy organizations, business associations, chambers of commerce, unions, and school districts. Political skill and a focused effort are needed to overcome historical tensions between these groups, including giving a clear definition to the focus of the coalition. The leaders of these groups, often politically elected officials or business leaders, must persuade actors in the coalition that their long-term interests align with the civic vision of the group (Cohen-Vogel & McLendon, 2009; McDonnell, 2009; Sykes et al., 2009).

The research on civic capacity highlights the increasing role of local political institutions in influencing educational change and the need to look beyond local school district governance in cities, especially to understand how current policies are conceptualized and implemented (Sykes et al., 2009). Superintendents and school boards rarely acted as change agents; instead superintendents advocated for educational interests and school boards focused on constituency services. Change can occur in cities with civic capacity (Stone et al., 2001)—a web of community-sector coalitions and structures joined together for a shared purpose, often to improve school achievement. These coalitions included businesses, government officials, foundations, and community-based organizations.

Business interaction and involvement of a wide array of other actors is crucial to successful efforts to mobilize civic capacity, and yet involving businesses can stymie other forms of civic mobilization (McDonnell, 2009). Understanding the extent of mobilization in a community requires an examination of a city's ethnic and racial politics (Henig, Hula, Orr, & Pedescleaux, 1999). Civic capacity can sustain change long term if it is institutionalized in ongoing partnerships and organizations (Shipps, 2006; Stone et al., 2001; Portz et al., 1999). For black leaders in black majority cities, nesting school reform within a broader focus on employment was most successful to keep teachers' unions, black ministers, and community activists aligned with the proposed changes (Orr, 1999).

Box 3.1 Case Study of Civic Capacity in the Rust Belt

Promising strategies from research in Pennsylvania instead consider how to build upon the economic and cultural resources that exist in Rust Belt communities. Abandoned factories, out-migration, and unemployment became the norm in many working-class communities as manufacturers relocated from the Midwestern and mid-Atlantic "Rust Belt" that provided much of the manufacturing resources during the previous century. Over time these regions have succumbed to chronic problems of extended unemployment, increases in substance abuse, and an overall degradation of the quality of life.

When asked how to improve Rust Belt communities, the answer of working-class residents is "jobs, jobs, jobs" (Mitra, Frick, & Movit, 2008). Residents still hold out hope that a megacorporation will ride in like a white knight and employ the community. Research suggests that waiting for employers to come back is not the best way to improve the economic outlook.

Rust Belt citizens tend to have a strong "sense of place'—choosing to live close to family rather than moving away in the hope of promising career opportunities in other locales. Building on the commitment of the community could provide important returns to the economy when coupled with greater awareness of promising local career sectors and alignment of training pathways.

For Rust Belt communities, a coherent strategy combining awareness and alignment strategies could be key to economic growth (Mitra & Halabi, 2012). The awareness of stable careers where young people have a desire to stay local can help to strengthen local economies. Alignment between high schools and post-secondary institutions can provide knowledge, financial incentives, and guidance to attaining proper training to be successful in these careers.

Awareness of Growing Fields

Mitra et al.'s research in a milltown in Pennsylvania (2008) focused on the importance of a strategy focusing on "awareness" of available career opportunities allowing young people information to make better career choices that could keep them close to home while finding a stable career. "There's this old mentality of steel and coal ... If ... the mines are shut down, there is no opportunity. And frankly ... that's the furthest thing from the truth," explains an economic development expert in Johnstown, PA (Mitra et al., 2008, p. 740).

Awareness programs create partnerships with local businesses to introduce secondary students to area careers. Field trips, internships, and job shadowing programs give students greater understanding of what these careers might look like. Rather than career awareness programs that focus solely on the innate talents of youth, these programs educate young people on careers likely to provide local, stable careers.

Responsibility for creating these programs must straddle businesses and schools. Economic development groups have assumed a leadership position as "brokers" between industry and schools. This important role has provided a way for these two sectors to strengthen each other and the community overall. An executive director of an economic development organization explained, "We're starting to see more interaction between educators and employers, but for many ... years there was a wall" (Mitra et al., 2008, p. 748). Through these efforts, Rust Belt communities have experienced some success, most notably in reductions in the ninth-grade dropout rate.

Alignment of Training Pathways

Mitra (2017) describes the story of Derrick—a college graduate with a degree in music education who drove a bread truck after graduating from college. He chose to return to his milltown community outside of Pittsburgh rather than move to Virginia or North Carolina because of his desire to remain close to family.

Derrick's ability to finish college is not the norm in his community. "Even though about 65 percent of our kids were going on to college, only about a fourth of them were finishing," explained a Western Pennsylvania high school principal (Mitra et al., 2008, p. 739; Mitra, 2017). These numbers align with national research stating that the *New Forgotten Half* of the economy are the students that go to college but never finish. Students are rarely warned that they may have years of remedial work before they can begin coursework that counts toward a postsecondary degree. The lack of clear signals about necessary preparation and standards for postsecondary education has a negative impact on student motivation to get the right training.

Promising studies have shown the value of "alignment" with postsecondary preparation as a way to help low-income students gain needed training and enter successful careers. Agreements and working relationships between districts and postsecondary institutions can help traditionally disadvantaged students increase their knowledge about tuition, curricular requirements, placement tests, admissions procedures, and selection criteria.

Connecting high-school curricula with college pre-requisites and college credit is one such example of alignment. Allowing high school students to enroll in college courses provides more seamless pathways into college programs. Dual enrollment options have boosted rates of college degree attainment for low-income students, improved degree progress, and increased college readiness, compared to those who did not earn college credit in high school.

Mitra and Frick (2011) and Mitra (2017) discuss a six-year engineering program in a milltown in Pennsylvania. Students spend two years in each place—high school, community college, and university; a student could receive an engineering degree for just $16,000. The argument also could be made that alignment strategies that entice youth to choose local colleges and universities increase the possibility that they will remain local after they finish their degrees.

● ● ● ● ●

Comprehension Questions

■ What is the role of school districts in educational policy? How has the district vantage point been viewed as leverage for reform and change?

■ Explain the roles of school boards and the role of the superintendent.

■ What is mayoral control and how has it become more significant in educational policy?

● ● ● ● ●

Discussion Questions

■ Compare a school board system versus a mayoral control system—what are the advantages and disadvantages of each? What is the range of governance structures within these two models?

■ How does the concept of civic capacity explain and perhaps give incentives for change across policy silos? How does it make change harder?

■ What are the perceived benefits and concerns of district consolidation?

● ● ● ● ●

Activities

■ Choose a key city/community-wide issue affecting your area. Identify all of the key players who would need to be involved to develop a holistic, cross-sector strategy to address the issue. Who has the most power in your area who could leverage the leadership needed for such a shift in focus to occur? How would civic capacity look in your community to make such a change happen?

■ The Education Commission of the States has a good overview of the diversity of school board structures (it includes governance structures for all levels of education). What are the structures in your area? How do they compare to other states?
Find on the web using the following search terms:

Education Commission States; k-12 governance structures

• • • • •

Further Reading

Brown, D. L. & Schafft, K. A. (2011). *Rural People and Communities in the 21st Century: Resilience and Transformation.* Cambridge, UK: Polity Press.

Hess, F. M. (2002). *School Boards at the Dawn of the 21st Century: Conditions and Challenges of District Governance.* Alexandria, VA: National School Boards Association.

Mossberger, K. & Stoker, G. (2001). The evolution of urban regime theory: The challenge of conceptualization. *Urban Affairs Review, 36*(6), 810–35.

Spillane, J. P. (1998). State policy and the non-monolithic nature of the local school district: Organizational and professional considerations. *American Educational Research Journal, 35*(1), 33–63.

Tieken, M. C. (2014). *Why Rural Schools Matter.* Chapel Hill, NC: UNC Press Books.

Trujillo, T. M. (2013). The disproportionate erosion of local control: Urban school boards, high-stakes accountability, and democracy. *Educational Policy, 27*(2), 334–59.

Tyack, D. B. (1974). *The One Best System: A History of American Urban Education.* Cambridge, MA: Harvard University Press.

• • • • •

Reference List

Alexander, K. & Alexander, M. (2015). *The Law of Schools, Students and Teachers in a Nutshell, 5th Edition.* St Paul: MN: West Academic.

Allen, A. & Plank, D. N. (2005). School board election structure and democratic representation. *Education Policy, 19,* 510–27.

Alsbury, T. L. (2003). Superintendent and school board member turnover: Political versus apolitical turnover as a critical variable in the application of the dissatisfaction theory. *Educational Administration Quarterly, 39*(5), 667–98.

Alsbury, T. L. (2008). School board member and superintendent turnover and the influence on student achievement: An application of the dissatisfaction theory. *Leadership and Policy in Schools, 7*(2), 202–29.

Bauch, P. A. & Goldring, E. B. (1998). Parent-teacher participation in the context of school governance. *Peabody Journal of Education, 73*(1), 15–35.

Berman, P. & McLaughlin, M. W. (1977). *The Management of Decline: Problems, Opportunities, and Research Questions.* Santa Monica, CA: The RAND Corporation.

Boyd, W. (1976). The public, the professionals, and educational policy making: Who governs? *Teachers College Record, 77*(4), 539–78.

Briffault, R. (2005). The local school district in American law. In Howell, W. G. (ed.) *Besieged: School Boards and the Future of Education Politics* (pp. 24–55). Washington, DC: Brookings Institution Press.

Brown v. Board of Education of Topeka, 347 U.S. 483 (1954).

Brown, D. L. & Schafft, K. A. (2011). *Rural People and Communities in the 21st Century: Resilience and Transformation.* Cambridge, UK: Polity Press.

Bulkley, K. E. (2007). Bringing the private into the public: Changing the rules of the game and new regime politics in Philadelphia public education *Educational Policy, 21*(1), 155–84.

Bulkley, K., Fairman, J., Martinez, M. C., & Hicks, J. (2004). The district and test preparation. In Schorr, R. Y., Monfils, L. F., & Firestone, W. A. (eds.) *The Ambiguity of Teaching
to the Test: Standards, Assessments, and Educational Reform* (pp. 113–42). Mahwah, NJ:
Lawrence Erlbaum Associates.

Callahan, R. (1962). *Education and the Cult of Efficiency*. Chicago, IL: University of
Chicago Press.

Carver, J. (1990). *Boards that Make a Difference*. San Francisco, CA: Jossey-Bass.

Cibulka, J. G. & Boyd, W. L. (eds.) (2003). *A Race Against Time: The Crisis in Urban Schooling*. Santa Barbara, CA: Greenwood Publishing Group.

Cohen-Vogel, L. & McLendon, M. (2009). New approaches to understanding federal
involvement in education. In Sykes, G., Schneider, B., & Plank, D. (eds.) *Handbook of
Education Policy Research* (pp. 735–48). New York: Routledge.

Conley, D. T. (2003). *Who Governs Our Schools: Changing Roles and Responsibilities*. New
York: Teachers College Press.

Cotton, K. (1996). Affective and social benefit of small-scale schooling. *ERIC Digest*,
ED401088.

Cox, B. & Cox, B. (2010). A decade of results: A case for school district consolidation.
Education, 13(1), 83–92.

Cronin, J. M. (1973). *The Control of Urban Schools: Perspective on the Power of Educational Reformers*. Ann Arbor, MI: The University of Michigan.

Cuban, L. (1998). How schools change reforms: Redefining reform success and failure.
Teachers College Record, 99(3), 453–77.

Cuban, L. & Usdan, M. (2002). *Powerful Reforms With Shallow Roots: Getting Good
Schools in Six Cities*. New York: Teachers College Press.

Cucchiara, M. B. (2013). *Marketing Schools, Marketing Cities: Who Wins and Who Loses
When Schools Become Urban Amenities*. Chicago, IL: University of Chicago Press.

Danzberger, J. P. (1994). Governing the nation's schools: The case for restructuring local
school boards. *Phi Delta Kappan, 75*(5), 367.

Danzberger, J. P., Kirst, M., & Usdan, M. (1992). *Governing Public Schools: New Times,
New Requirements*. Washington, DC: Institute for Educational Leadership.

Dawson, L. J. & Quinn, R. (2001). Moving boards out of operations, into results. *The
School Administrator, 58*(3), 54.

Duncombe, W. & Yinger, J. (2002). Revisiting economies of size in American education:
Are we any closer to a consensus? *Economics of Education Review, 3*(21), 245–62.

Duncombe, W. & Yinger, J. (2005). How much more does a disadvantaged student cost?
Economics of Education Review, 24(5), 513–32.

Ehrensal, P. & First, P. (2008). Understanding school board politics: Balancing public
voice and professional power. In Cooper, B., Cibulka, J. G., & Fusarelli, L. (eds.) *Handbook of Education Politics and Policy* (pp. 73–88). New York: Routledge.

Elmore, R. F. & Burney, D. (1998). *Continuous Improvement in Community District #2,
New York City (Report to the Office of Educational Research and Improvement)*. Pitts-
burgh, PA: High Performance Learning Communities Project, Learning Research and
Development Center, University of Pittsburgh.

Fuhrman, S. H. & Elmore, R. F. (1990). Understanding local control in the wake of state
education reform. *Educational Evaluation and Policy Analysis, 12*(1), 82–96.

Fuhrman, S. H., Goertz, M., & Weinbaum, E. (2007). Educational governance in the
United States: Where are we? How did we get here? Why should we care? In, Fuhrman,
S. H., Cohen, D., & Mosher, F. (eds.) *The State of Education Policy Research* (pp. 41–61).
Mahwah, NJ: Lawrence Erlbaum Associates.

Glass, T. E. (2001). Superintendent leaders look at the superintendency, school boards, and reform. *ECS Issue Paper,* Denver, CO: Education Commission of the States.

Glass, T. E., Bjork, L., & Brunner, C. C. (2000). *The Study of the American Superintendency, 2000: A Look at the Superintendent of Education in the New Millennium.* Arlington, VA: American Association of School Administrators.

Goddard, R. D., Hoy, W. K., & Hoy, A. W. (2000). Collective teacher efficacy: Its meaning, measure, and impact on student achievement. *American Educational Research Journal, 37*(2), 479–507.

Grady, M. & Krumm, B. (1998). Learning to serve: The state of school board member training. *American School Board Journal, 185,* 36–43.

Grissom, J. A. & Mitani, H. (2016). Salary, performance, and superintendent turnover. *Educational Administration Quarterly, 52*(3), 351–91.

Hall, D. (2016). *Local Control as Resistance: Policy and Practice of Autonomous School Boards.* Unpublished doctoral dissertation. State College, PA: The Pennsylvania State University.

Hall, D. & Burfoot-Rochford, I. (2014). *Vermont Educational Reform: A Balanced Approach to Equity and Funding. Center on Rural Education and Community.* University Park, PA: Penn State University.

Hall, D. & McHenry-Sorber, E. (2017). Politics first: Examining the practice of the multidistrict superintendent. *Education Policy Analysis Archives, 25*(82).

Harris, R. A. & Milkis, S. M. (1989). *The Politics of Regulatory Change: A Tale of Two Agencies.* New York: Oxford University Press.

Henig, J. (2013). *The End of Exceptionalism in American Education: The Changing Politics of School Reform.* Cambridge, MA: Harvard Education Press.

Henig, J. R., Hula, R. C., Orr, M., & Pedescleaux, D. S. (1999). *The Color of School Reform: Race Politics, and the Challenge of Urban Education.* Princeton, NJ: Princeton University Press.

Hess, F. M. (2002). *School Boards at the Dawn of the 21st Century: Conditions and Challenges of District Governance.* Alexandria, VA: National School Boards Association.

Hess, F. M. & Meeks, O. (2010). *School Boards Circa 2010: Governance in the Accountability Era.* The National School Boards Association, The Thomas B. Fordham Institute, and The Iowa School Boards Foundation. Retrieved from: www.nsba.org/sites/default/files/SBcirca2010_WEB.pdf.

Hochschild, J. L. (2005). What school boards can and cannot (or will not) accomplish. In Howell, W. G. (ed.) *Besieged: School Boards and the Future of Education Politics* (pp. 324–38). Washington, DC: Brookings Institution Press.

Howell, W. G. (ed.) (2005). *Besieged: School Boards and the Future of Education Politics.* Washington, DC: Brooking Institution Press.

Howley, C. & Howley, A. (2010). Poverty and school achievement in rural communities: A social-class interpretation. In Schafft, K. A. & Youngblood Jackson, A. (eds.) *Rural Education for the Twenty-First Century: Identity, Place, and Community in a Globalizing World* (pp. 34–50). University Park, PA: Penn State University Press.

Howley, C., Johnson, J., & Petrie, J. (2011). *Consolidation of School Districts: What the Research Says and Means.* Boulder, CO: National Education Policy Center.

Iannaccone, L. & Lutz, F. (eds.) (1978). *Public Participation in School Decision Making.* Lexington, MA: Lexington Books.

Kirst, M. (1984). *Who Controls Our Schools?* New York: Freeman & Co.

Kirst, M. W. (2002). *Mayoral Influences, New Regimes, and Public School Governance.* CPRE Research Report Series RR-049. Consortium for Policy Research in Education, University of Pennsylvania.

Kowalski, T. J., McCord, R. S., Petersen, G. J., Young, I. P., & Ellerson, N. M. (2010). *The American School Superintendent: 2010 Decennial Study*. Lanham, MD: Rowan and Littlefield Education.

Land, D. (2002). Local school boards under review: Their role and effectiveness in relation to students' academic achievement. *Review of Educational Research, 72*(2), 229–78.

Lutz, F. W. & Iannaccone, L. (1994). The crucible of democracy: The local arena. In J. Scribner & D. Layton (eds.) *Politics of Education Association Yearbook* (pp. 39–52). Bristol, PA: Taylor & Francis.

Lutz, F. W. & Iannaccone, L. (2008). The dissatisfaction theory of American democracy. In T. Alsbury (ed.) *The Future of School Board Governance* (pp. 3–24). Lanham, MD: Rowman and Littlefield Education.

Malen, B. (2003). Tightening the grip? The impact of state activism on local school systems. *Educational Policy, 17*(2), 195–216.

Marsh, J. A. & Wohlstetter, P. (2013). Recent trends in intergovernmental relations: The resurgence of local actors in education policy. *Educational Researcher, 42*(5), 276–83.

McAdams, D. R. (2003). Training your board to lead. *School Administrator, 60*(10), 7.

McDermott, K. A. (1999). *Controlling Public Education: Localism versus Equity. Studies in Government and Public Policy.* Lawrence, KS: University Press of Kansas.

McDonnell, L. (2007). The politics of education: Influencing policy and beyond. In Fuhrman, S., Cohen, D., & Mosher, F. (eds.) *The State of Education Policy Research* (pp. 19–40). Mahwah, NJ: Lawrence Erlbaum Associates.

McDonnell, L. (2009). A political science perspective on education policy analysis. In Sykes, G., Schneider, B., & Plank, D. (eds.) *Handbook of Education Policy Research* (pp. 57–70). New York: Routledge.

McLaughlin, M. W. (1991). The RAND change agent study: Ten years later. In Odden, A. R. (ed.) *The Evolution of Education Policy Implementation* (pp. 143–56). Albany, NY: State University of New York Press.

McLaughlin, M. W. & Talbert, J. E. (2001). *Professional Communities and the Work of High School Teaching.* Chicago, IL: University of Chicago Press.

Mitra, D. L. (2005). Adults advising youth: Leading while getting out of the way. *Educational Administration Quarterly, 41*(3), 520–53.

Mitra, D. (2017). Building jobs in the rust belt: The role of education. *The Conversation,* April 11. Retrieved from: https://theconversation.com/building-jobs-in-the-rust-belt-the-role-of-education-72833.

Mitra, D. L. & Frick, W. C. (2011). Civic capacity in educational reform efforts: Finding agency in a time of globalization. *Educational Policy, 25*(5), 810–43.

Mitra, D. L. & Halabi, S. (2012). Paradoxes in policy practice: Signaling post-secondary pathways in the Rust Belt. *Teachers College Record, 114*(1), 1–34.

Mitra, D. L., Frick, W. C., & Movit, M. A. (2008). Brain drain in the Rust Belt: Can educational reform help to build civic capacity in struggling communities? *Educational Policy, 22*, 731–57.

Mossberger, K. & Stoker, G. (2001). The evolution of urban regime theory: The challenge of conceptualization. *Urban Affairs Review, 36*(6), 810–35.

Mountford, M. (2008). Historic and current tensions among board-superintendent teams: Symptom or cause? In T. L. Alsbury (ed.) *The Future of School Board Governance: Relevancy and Revelation* (pp. 81–113). New York: Rowman & Littlefield.

National Center for Education Statistics. (2013–14a). *Number of Public School Districts and Public and Private Elementary and Secondary Schools: Selected years, 1869–70*

Through 2013–14 [Table]. Retrieved from: http://nces.ed.gov/programs/digest/d14/tables/dt14_214.10.asp.

National Center for Education Statistics. (2013–14b). *Number of Public Elementary and Secondary Education Agencies, by Type of Agency and State or Jurisdiction: 2013–14* [Table]. Retrieved from: http://nces.ed.gov/programs/digest/d15/tables/dt15_214.30.asp.

O'Day, J. (2002). Complexity, accountability, and school improvement. *Harvard Educational Review, 72*(3), 293–329.

O'Day, J. A. & Smith, M. S. (1993). Systemic reform and educational opportunity. In Fuhrman, S. (ed.) *Designing Coherent Education Policy: Improving the System* (pp. 250–312). San Francisco, CA: Jossey-Bass.

Orfield, G., Frankenberg, E. D., & Lee, C. (2003). The resurgence of school segregation. *Educational Leadership, 60*(4), 16–20.

Orr, M. (1999). *Black Social Capital: The Politics of School Reform in Baltimore, 1986–1998. Studies in Government and Public Policy.* Lawrence, KS: University Press of Kansas.

Portz, J., Stein, L., & Jones, R. R. (1999). *City Schools and City Politics: Institutions and Leadership in Pittsburgh, Boston, and St. Louis.* Lawrence, KS: University Press of Kansas.

Shipps, D. (2003). Pulling together: Civic capacity and urban school reform. *American Education Research Journal, 40*(4), 841–78.

Shipps, D. (2006). *School Reform, Corporate Style: Chicago, 1880–2000.* Lawrence, KS: University Press of Kansas.

Shipps, D. (2008). Urban regime theory and the reform of public schools: Governance, power, and leadership. In Cooper, B. S., Cibulka, J. G., & Fusarelli, L. D. (eds.) *Handbook of Education Politics and Policy* (pp. 89–108). New York: Routledge.

Skowronek, S. (2008). *Presidential Leadership in Political Time: Reprise and Reappraisal* (pp. 117–49). Lawrence, KS: University Press of Kansas.

Smoley Jr, E. R. (1999). *Effective School Boards: Strategies for Improving Board Performance. The Jossey-Bass Education Series.* San Francisco, CA: Jossey-Bass.

Snyder, T. D., Dillow, S. A., & Hoffman, C. M. (2007). *Digest of Educational Statistics.* Washington, DC: National Center for Education Statistics, Institute of Education Sciences, U. S. Department of Education.

Spillane, J. P. (1996). School districts matter: Local educational authorities and state instructional policy. *Educational Policy, 10*(1), 63–87.

Spillane, J. P. (1998). State policy and the non-monolithic nature of the local school district: Organizational and professional considerations. *American Educational Research Journal, 35*(1), 33–63.

Spillane, J. P. & Thompson, C. L. (1997). Reconstructing conceptions of local capacity: The local education agency's capacity for ambitious instructional reform. *Educational Evaluation and Policy Analysis, 19*(2), 185–203.

Spring, J. (2011). *The Politics of American Education.* New York: Routledge.

Stone, C. N. (2005). Looking back to look forward: Reflections on urban regime analysis. *Urban Affairs Review, 40*(3), 309–41.

Stone, C. N., Henig, J. R., Jones, B. D., & Pierannunzi, C. (2001). *Building Civic Capacity: The Politics of Reforming Urban Schools. Studies in Government and Public Policy.* Lawrence, KS: University Press of Kansas.

Supovitz, J. A. (2006). *The Case for District-Based Reform: Leading, Building, and Sustaining School Improvement.* Cambridge, MA: Harvard Education Press.

Sykes, G., O'Day, J., & Ford, T. (2009). The district role in instructional improvement. In Sykes, G., Schneider, B., & Plank, D. (eds.) *Handbook of Education Policy Research* (pp. 767–84). New York: Routledge.

Thompson, C. L., Sykes, G., & Skrla, L. (2008). *Instructionally-Focused District Leadership: Toward A Theoretical Account.* East Lansing, MI: The Education Policy Center, Michigan State University.

Tieken, M. C. (2014). *Why Rural Schools Matter.* Chapel Hill, NC: UNC Press Books.

Tschannen-Moran, M., Hoy, A. W., & Hoy, W. K. (1998). Teacher efficacy: Its meaning and measure. *Review of Educational Research, 68*(2), 202–48.

Tyack, D. B. (1974). *The One Best System: A History of American Urban Education.* Cambridge, MA: Harvard University Press.

Wilson, C. A. (2000). Policy regimes and policy change. *Journal of Public Policy, 20*(3), 247–74.

Wirt, F. & Kirst, M. (1997). *The Political Dynamics of American Education.* Berkeley, CA: McCutchan Publishing.

Wong, K. K. & Shen, F. X. (2008). Education mayors and big-city school boards: New directions, new evidence. In T. L. Alsbury (ed.) *The Future of School Boards Governance: Relevancy and Revelation* (pp. 319–56). Lanham, MD: Rowman & Littlefield.

Wong, K. K., Shen, F. X., Anagnostopolous, D., & Rutledge, S. (2007). *The Education Mayor: Improving America's Schools.* Washington, DC: Georgetown University Press.

Zeigler, H. (1973). Creating responsive schools. *The Urban Review, 6*(4), 38–44.

Zeigler, L. H., Jennings, M. K., & Peak, G. W. (1974). *Governing American Schools.* North Scituate, MA: Dunbury.

4

• • • • •

Influential Policy Actors

At the national, state, and local levels, a range of policy actors influence the educational system. We begin with a discussion of power more generally. The chapter then highlights some of the key players at each level and discusses their relationship with the formation and implementation of educational policy. The power and prestige/conception of actors will be influenced by the policy windows available (see Chapter 5; Kingdon, 2003) and the power and prestige of the actors (Schneider & Ingram, 1993). The range of problems, solutions, and political contexts swirling about the policy arena helps to determine who has a voice in the process at any given time.

This chapter discusses the range of actors in the educational policy process. Some are perennial actors in decision making and others gain access depending on political contexts, reform waves, and policy cycles. The traditional map for explaining how actors influence the policy system was developed by Marshall, Mitchell, and Wirt (1989). They identified three categories of groups. *Insiders* have actual authority over policy, including legislators and chief state school officers. *Near circle* groups have great influence on the shaping of policy, including education interest groups, teachers' unions, the governor and the executive staff, legislative staff, and the state board. *Far circle* influencers include the School Boards Association, the State Administrator Association, and the courts.

This traditional map of influence is changing as foundations and intermediary organizations are becoming drivers of policy design and implementation. This chapter discusses the formal actors as well as the new power centers in education. These emerging players build upon local relationships to share information, to shape agendas, and to legitimate evidence that preferences ideological positions (Castillo et al., 2015).

• • • • •

National and State Actors

The national and state levels tend to have mirroring sets of formal organizations that lobby and seek input on educational policy. Sometimes referred to as the "Alphabet Soup," these organizations tend to be referred to by their acronyms and initials.

The first set of organizations represents the roles within school systems, including teachers, principals, school board members, superintendents, classified employees, and parents. Some have referred to these organizations as the "big six", including two teachers unions (Spring, 2011; Wirt & Kirst, 1997):

- Classified School Employees Association (AFSCME)
- National/State School Boards Association (NSBA)
- National/State School Administrators Association (NSAA)
- National/State Teachers' Unions (NEA, AFT)
- National/State Parent Teacher Association (PTA)

Teachers' Unions

Looking across the spectrum of local voices, historically, teachers have wanted collective bargaining, parents have wanted shared control, and students have wanted a voice (Wirt & Kirst, 1997, p. 35). Taxpayers want finance reform and disadvantaged groups want more equity. All of these local voices may result in a reduction of the authority of superintendents and school boards (Malen & Cochran, 2008; Wirt & Kirst, 1997).

Teachers' unions in the United States pursue a dual strategy of collective bargaining and political activities, including lobbying and supporting political candidates. These dual purposes can be at odds as the organizations balance innovation with protection of positions, working conditions, and salaries. Strategic choices can depend on local contexts, including historical tensions or trust between unions and district leaders (McDonnell, 2007).

Some states prevent teachers' unions. Called "right to work" states, most are located in the South. Twenty-eight states have "right to work" legislation; five explicitly prohibit teachers' unions—Georgia, North Carolina, South Carolina, Texas, and Virginia. Teachers in these states have been shown to have lower salaries and less of a voice in policy (McHaney, 2015; Cowen, 2009). In most Southern states, collective bargaining is not legalized.

The United States has two main teachers' unions—The American Federation of Teachers (AFT) and the National Educational Association (NEA). The AFT tends to represent urban teachers. Led by Randy Weingartner, and formerly by Albert Shanker, the organization has 1.6 million members (American Federation of Teachers, n.d.). The AFT grew markedly between 1960 and 1975 (Wirt & Kirst, 1997). A union more aligned with organized labor groups such as the Teamsters and AFL-CIO, the AFT has been much more willing to strike than the NEA. The AFT has historically amplified value conflicts between teachers and managers to protect teacher working conditions.

The NEA historically concentrated at state and national levels and little on local teachers' interest groups. It focused on professional issues and finding common ground on controversial issues. The NEA has 3 million members

(National Education Association, 2015). Until the 1960s, it focused on standards and ethics primarily, and lobbied for federal aid and research support.

Teachers' unions gained increasing voice in the policy process by the 1980s, but even then the AFT and NEA at times have taken opposing positions on policy issues. Sometimes state affiliates within the unions take opposing positions, such as when some NEA affiliates supported peer evaluation and other state affiliates opposed it (McDonnell, 2007). In recent years, unions have expanded their research to have positions on college affordability, the implementation of the Elementary and Secondary Education Act, education funding, and civil rights.

Parent Teacher Association

The *Parent Teacher Association* (PTA) represents the most known parental voice in educational policy. It is the largest nonprofessional group interested in policy, with 3.8 million members and 24,334 units (Wirt & Kirst, 1997; PTA, 2016). While the national PTA offers some input into the national education policy process, the organization is most active at the local level. Schools encourage parental involvement on non-controversial issues, such as helping their children with homework, fundraising, and classroom volunteering (Farkas, 1993; McDermott, 1999). The broad and loose confederation of organizations includes diverse political opinions that preclude agreement on controversial issues. Historically, the PTA was referred to in the 1960s as "rarely more than a coffee and cookies organization based on vague good will and gullibility" (Koerner, 1968, pp. 147–8, cited in Wirt and Kirst, 1997, p. 85). Like teachers' unions, the national PTA has increasingly become involved in the policy process as a consumer advocate organization—current issues include revising assessment systems, bridging the gender gap in the sciences, preventing gun violence, offering guidance on reforms related to gender identity guidance, and financing college (Parent Teacher Association, n.d.).

Systematic avenues that allow for parental "voice" in educational policy were once much stronger, including guidelines established in the late 1960s that encouraged parents to volunteer in classrooms (D'Agostino, Hedges, Wong, & Borman, 2001). In the 1970s, the ESEA had parents as core participants in addressing issues of poverty and of educational reform. In the Educational Amendments of 1978, Title One Parent Advisory Councils (TOPACs) and the requirement that parents be involved in decisions about the use of ESEA federal funds (ESEA, 1978) elected parents as advisors. Later, in 1994, President Bill Clinton signed into law the Improving America's Schools Act (IASA), a reauthorization of the ESEA that included a comprehensive model of parent involvement, including the creation of School–Parent Compacts and a requirement that 1 percent of funding must be spent on parent involvement (IASA, 1994).

In the 1970s and 1980s, large numbers of parents became actively involved in special education policy. Prior to the passage of the Education for All Handicapped Children Act in 1975, U.S. public schools accommodated only one in five children with disabilities. With the law, parents now have a right to demand a free education for their children. The law also gives parents the right to participate in the process of determining access and services.

Parental voice has declined, as observed in the 2001 No Child Left Behind legislation (ESEA, Title I, Section 1118, 2001). NCLB provided comprehensive policies on parent involvement, but limited the roles of parents to that of being receivers of information who solely focus on issues relating to their own children. This reframing of parental roles shrank the authority of parents to shape policy at the local level (as is also true for the role of teachers and administrators in the newest SBA policies). Most recently, ESSA has increased parental rights with a greater focus on family engagement in schools and allowing states to permit families to opt their children out of standardized testing (ESSA, 2015). The specifics of implementation are left to the states and ESSA includes provisions that bar the federal government from punishing states based on the number of opt-out families they have.

Parents have increasingly organized to opt their children out of the standardized test process. Across the nation, parents have begun to form opt-out groups to collectively raise concerns about standardized testing, such as *Opt Out of the State Test: The National Movement* (1400 members), *Parents and Kids Against Standardized Testing* (2000 members), and individual opt-out webpages for states including New York, Indiana, Texas, North Carolina, and Colorado—17,000 students on Long Island, New York, alone, in 2014 (Mitra, Mann, & Hlavacik, 2016). The impact of opt-out can be powerful—for example, findings from Pennsylvania show that parental opt-out can influence the outcome of state standardized testing (Beaver, Westmaas, & Sludden, 2014). Parents acting as participants in the educational system have demonstrated the ability to derail some reform efforts (Labaree, 2010; Marsh & Wohlstetter, 2013; Mediratta, Shah, & McAlister, 2009; Vincent, 1996). Although an increasing number of parents are interested in this type of strategy, they often lack information on how to opt out of standardized testing in their states. Research has demonstrated that parents lack information about accountability policies (McDonnell, 2009; Park & Holloway, 2013), and they especially lack information about student obligation to participate in such policies. States do not keep statistics of who is opting out—or at least the opt-out groups have not found any states willing to share this information publicly. Under the previous No Child Left Behind legislation, schools failed to meet Adequate Yearly Progress if fewer than 90 percent of students took the test. ESSA has now given states more flexibility with the opt-out numbers by allowing states to decide whether and how they will count opt-outers in the state numbers.

●●●●●

The New Major Actors

Policy processes are moving. This section examines the shifting policy landscape and its implications to the informal sector. Increasing gridlock in the formal system helps to exacerbate the need to find policy space elsewhere. The consolidation of power in very wealthy foundations contributes to this shift. The systems-changing policy structures that give greater agency to charter-school related organizations and educational management organizations have also contributed to this shift.

Foundations

Increasingly, foundations have become a major source of influence in educational policy at the national and state levels, including the Gates, Lumina, Walton, Broad, Dell, Koch, Ford, and Carnegie Foundations. Foundations privilege research, policy design, implementation, and scaling up based on the ideological priorities of the funders. Through the creation of advocacy networks, they foster deeper learning of these positions and encourage policy growth in the areas endorsed by the philanthropists and their boards (Castillo et. al, 2015; Reckhow, 2013; Reckhow & Tompkins-Stange, 2015).

Philanthropic giving trends include a great interest in structural change, the funding of non-traditional providers such as non-profits and after-school programs, the push for a coordinated reform agenda, and pressure to find ways to measure impact (Hess & Henig, 2015). Sometimes foundations coordinate to dominate a citywide focus on change, such as when the Heinz, Pittsburgh, and Grable Foundations announced a targeted effort toward reform in Pittsburgh in 2002 (Hess & Henig, 2015, p. 3).

Some scholars note the emphasis on a human capital ideology of the big funders, with a focus on competition, efficiency, data, and impact as goals for topics such as charter schools, standardized curricula, and high-stakes testing (Spring, 2011, p. 42). Indeed, it is increasingly common for foundations of donors with new money to hire former Teacher for America employers (an alternative certification route) and people with business degrees. Despite the power of these organizations, they face instability due to ongoing staff turnover. Staff tend to only remain at foundations for an average of three years (Gose, 2012), which could result in a loss of ongoing knowledge and lack of deep understanding of educational issues.

Recent research has stressed that philanthropy works best when funding "high-leverage investments" (Hess & Henig, 2015), focusing on reforms that are promising and strategic but untested and therefore too risky for traditional funding streams to adopt at first. Research refers to these funders as "muscular philanthropy" (Hess & Henig, 2015)—because the funding of projects by these organizations provides a way to test out educational ideas that might not be politically feasible for development through traditional bureaucratic channels. Examples of issues with a high-leverage focus have included the Common Core, teacher evaluation, online education, extended learning time, and charter schools (Hess & Henig, 2015).

Over the years it has been in existence, Gates has donated more dollars to funding education in the United States than just about any other funder. In

2012, the Gates Foundation awarded more than $325 million in education grants, representing more than 6.5 percent of all education grants awarded by foundations worldwide. The sheer size of dollars creates a large influence in the policy conversations that occur since the scope of the work of the foundation is so large. As of 2016, Gates focuses on three areas—teaching, learning, and innovation. More specifically, its efforts have created increased policy interest in technology and gaming in classrooms, student–teacher feedback methods, and Common Core Standards (Gates Foundation, 2016). The Gates Foundation funded McKinsey & Co and other consulting firms to help states with Race to the Top Applications (Kornhaber, Barkauskas, & Griffith, 2016). The Gates Foundation and other foundations have also gained influence as "jurisdictional challengers" (Reckhow & Snyder, 2014, p. 186), who create alliances with state and federal governments, such as Gates Foundation officials being appointed to several key positions in the Obama administration, including the Department of Education (Kornhaber et al., 2016; Mehta & Teles, 2011).

This trend in the power influence of philanthropy also can at times show the flexibility of funders, such as the well-studied pivot of the Gates Foundation away from small schools funding after research showed that it had mixed results. Reckhow and Tompkins-Stange (2015) found another shift from giving directly to providers to increased funding for advocacy by funding education management organizations (see below) and other national organizations who can lobby for particular causes and to public–private partnerships.

Education Management Organizations

Education management organizations (EMOs) are for-profit or non-profit institutions that receive public funds to manage charter or traditional public schools. For-profit EMOs seek a return on investment from these management activities. They create a contract that details how schools are expected to be run and the time frame in which a return on investment is expected based on measurable outcomes. Examples of for-profit EMOs include K12 Inc, National Heritage Academies, Charter Schools USA, Edison Learning, and Imagine Schools. Non-profit EMOs include KIPP. Forty-four percent of charter school students attended EMO-managed schools in 2011–12; students in 37 states and the District of Columbia attend schools managed by EMOs, despite any evidence of positive results (Matthis & Miron, 2013). Those in favor of EMOs support a market-based approach to education (discussed in Chapter 11) and believe that competition will increase educational quality. Critics of EMOs believe that outsourcing educational operations takes limited resources away from students and directs them toward profits and management fees. People also express concern of long-term implications of relinquishing publicly controlled institutions to private organizations.

EMOs have relied upon blogs and social media to disseminate findings and to promote viewpoints (Castillo et al., 2015). Often these corporate-style organizations have media and communication departments to package and distribute ways of understanding education policy concepts. Government officials, traditional researchers, and public citizens lack the capacity and resources to contribute at a similar level. Scott et al. (2017) has referred to "alpha" EMOs who enact a leadership and convening role to bring together networks of EMOs. These organizations have the best funded staff and most sophisticated communication teams.

The *for-profit sector* of educational organizations is growing as testing companies profit from the increase in accountability and assessment. The Biddle Consulting Group, for example, came into existence in the early 1970s to help organizations navigate the challenges presented with the passage of equal opportunity employment and affirmative action laws. Firms such as Biddle provide testing, training, and litigation support (Biddle Consulting Group, LLC, 2015). Other for-profit companies include textbook companies, charter school operators, and organizations (Spring, 2011). Many of these organizations have influenced policy on issues including curriculum, assessment, and school funding.

Business Community

As mentioned in the chapter on local policy (see Chapter 3), business leaders can be instrumental in reform, especially at the local level. The role of business leaders in education dates back to their role in the creation of administrative progressive reforms at the turn of the twentieth century. Changes focused on greater professionalism, centralization, and accountability in public education at the state and local levels (Tyack, 1974).

At the federal level, business involvement historically has largely been limited to the support of vocational education. Business leaders in the 1960s opposed federal involvement in education out of fear of higher taxes and the economic impacts of desegregation (McDonnell, 2007).

Fear of global competition has helped to increase business interest in the educational system since the 1980s, with a focus on issues such as a well-trained workforce and innovation in science, technology, engineering, and mathematics (STEM). The Business Roundtable is an organization representing the CEOs of the largest U.S. corporations. By the 1990s the Business Roundtable visibly supported the Bush administration's *Goals 2000* agenda. More recently, it focused on a campaign promoting programs that they believed would close a perceived skills gap between U.S. workers and those from other nations (Business Roundtable.org, n.d.). Businesses also have been very active in participating in the alignment of Common Core Standards with skills designed for career readiness.

Businesses also have become increasingly involved in cities, and have been considered leaders in catalyzing urban regimes (Stone, Henig, Jones, & Pierannunzi, 2001). The alliance between educational reforms and businesses varies, however, depending on the racial politics of cities. Henig, Hula, Orr, and Pedescleaux (1999) concluded that black-led cities feared becoming enmeshed in racial conflicts or being cast as white nationalists. Depending on previous local contexts, alliances with businesses could harm the political futures of African American political leaders. These leaders were concerned about being portrayed as elitists by grassroots activist organizations.

Think Tanks

Think tanks are organizations that are funded to conduct research and to produce reports. Their influence has even been called "America's shadow government" (Reckhow, 2008; Spring, 2011, p. 95). They consist of a well-funded web of policy actors working in collaboration with free-market organizations (Welner, 2011).

Think tanks tend to produce products of research that are written in more accessible language for policy makers and practitioners than occurs in university settings. The Consortium for Policy Research in Education (CPRE) is an example of a consortium of university scholars who conduct evidence-based research on educational policy, especially at the state level (McDermott, 2009). Since the 1980s, CPRE research has developed one of the most comprehensive long-term examinations of state education policy, including case studies and surveys of state policy assessment and accountability systems. Think tanks are also growing at the state level, such as the Mackinac Center in Michigan, the Buckey Institute in Ohio, The Education Policy and Leadership Center in Pennsylvania, and the Commonwealth Foundation in Pennsylvania (Welner, 2011).

Because of skills at packaging and marketing materials, the work of think tanks tends to receive greater attention by policy makers and practitioners than traditional academic research. The National Education Policy Center also extensively studied the role of think tanks in education. Publications of private think tanks are disproportionately represented in the reporting of educational policy by the media; yet think tanks do not subject their work to the scrutiny of a review process in most cases (Welner, 2011). To evaluate the rigor of research, the Think Tank Twice project was created in 2006 (thinktankreview.org) to apply the academic standards of peer review to the work produced in the think tank sector. The organization has identified think tank reports that attribute policy success to initiatives that have not been implemented and flawed use of data to defend arguments being used regularly by politicians.

Often think tanks have a political perspective. Conservative think tanks focus more on competition and efficiency, with resulting policies focusing on vouchers, charter schools, and morality and religion in schools. Conservative think tanks include the Heritage Foundation, American Enterprise Institute, Hoover Institute, Manhattan Institute for Policy Research, Heartland Institute, and the Cato Institute, each of which focuses on various aspects of free enterprise, limited government, individual freedoms and responsibility, traditional American values, and a strong national defense and foreign presence (American Enterprise Institute, 2017; Cato Institute, n.d.; Heritage Foundation, 2017).

Progressive, left-leaning think tanks tend to focus on issues of equity and access, which turn into policy decisions about wraparound services, desegregation, school funding, and teacher preparation for under-served areas. Progressive think tanks include the Progressive Policy Institute, the Democratic Leadership Council, Commonwealth Fund, Human Rights Watch, Center on Budget and Policy Priorities, Urban Institute, and Economic Policy Institute. Yet, researchers have documented the shift to market-driven reform policies in previously progressive and middle-of-the-road educational think tanks. For example, Brookings Institution and the Center for American Policy Progress often critique market capitalism more broadly, and they tend to champion market-driven reforms in education (Welner, 2011).

While progressive donors tend to support community-based projects, conservative donors have been more willing to donate funds to think thanks. Market-oriented think tanks have benefited from overwhelming financial support by a few targeted funders. Three conservative funders (Lynde and Harr Bradley Foundation, the Sarah Scaife Foundation, and the John Olin Foundation) awarded over $100 million to 15 conservative think tanks (Welner, 2011, p. 42). The result is a tremendous marketing advantage of conservative educational ideas than of progressive reforms.

Box 4.1 The Case of the American Legislative Exchange Council (ALEC)

The American Legislative Exchange Council (ALEC) is a major player in education policy, yet it falls somewhere beyond a traditional think tank or policy organization (Lewis, Mead, & Hall, 2017). ALEC is a non-profit organization that has been in operation since 1973, self-described as "America's largest nonpartisan, voluntary membership organization of state legislators dedicated to the principles of limited government, free markets and federalism" (ALEC, 2015). ALEC's members include conservative state legislators, corporations, foundations, and think tanks, providing opportunities for lawmakers to collaborate with business leaders as they design model legislation, press briefings, and policy agendas for state and federal government (Underwood & Mead, 2012). ALEC's policy work is carried out through taskforces, which are jointly led by a lawmaker and a business leader, ensuring collaboration between the legislative and corporate sides of the organization (Ujifusa, 2012; Underwood & Mead, 2012). The organization has a wide reach, and ALEC claims responsibility for 20 percent of all legislative bills passed in recent years (ALEC, 2015). Although ALEC has extensive influence on state and federal policy making, the organization has operated largely in secret until a 2012 whistle-blower complaint by Common Cause (Common Cause, 2016; Center for Media and Democracy, 2015).

In educational policy, ALEC's primary contribution is through the creation of model bills that are shared with legislators. The model bills are often proposed unchanged and without attribution to ALEC by state legislators (Anderson & Donchik, 2014; Underwood & Mead, 2012). These bills promote a neoliberal model of education that prioritizes privatization of public schools through charters, vouchers, and parent trigger laws; privatization of student data collection; expanding standardized testing; reducing the power of teachers' unions; and increasingly privatizing the teaching workforce (Barbosa, 2015; Dannin, 2012; Underwood &

Mead, 2012). ALEC is also behind the controversial annual Report Card on American Education, a critical examination of each state's education policies, on which the National Education Policy Center (NEPC), after evaluating the Report Card, concluded, "The report's purpose appears to be more about shifting control of education to private interests than in improving education" (Lubienski & Brewer, 2013, p. 2).

ALEC's expansive influence on policy making in many regards is synonymous with a lobbying institution, a claim which ALEC itself denies (Common Cause, 2016; Dannin, 2012). Anderson and Donchik (2014) explain:

> ALEC represents a unique combination of "statework," corporate lobbying, and think tank. While ALEC is in many ways more in the tradition of a lobby group promoting corporate interests in education, it provides a legally legitimate space for corporations to co-write (not merely influence) model bills that, in turn, insert a business and market logic, discourse and ideology into the public sector, promoting both the financial and ideological interests of the corporate sector.
>
> (p. 27)

In blurring the line between lobbying and policy work, ALEC enables corporations to have greater access and voice in legislation, effectively bypassing the democratic process of governance (Anderson & Donchik, 2014; Kammer, 2013). ALEC has a significant impact on legislative and judicial policies, and in acting as a lobbying institution, undermines democratic participation in the legislative process (Barkan, 2013; Kammer, 2013; Lewis et al., 2017).

Research-Practice Partnerships

Research-practice partnerships (RPPs) are longer term relationships between practitioners and researchers designed to investigate ways to improve teaching and learning (Coburn & Penuel, 2016). The concept extends beyond education to other social science fields such as mental health, criminology/community policy, and health care. Extending beyond one project, they consist of dedicated relationship building focused on dilemmas emerging from the field and the original collection of data. This shift redefines notions of researchers as staying neutral and apart from the process. Continuous improvement in an RPP model intentionally involves researchers as a part of the process. The collaboration is the knowledge generation engine. The practitioners are also in a different role, sharing in the research and analysis (Cannata, Cohen-Vogel, & Sorum, forthcoming).

Coburn and Penuel (2016) explain that the research indicates that, RPPs can improve educational outcomes when working well (Donovan, 2013; Fishman, Penuel, Allen, & Cheng, 2013) through greater use of research (Tseng, 2012) and drilling deep into problems of practice (Coburn, Penuel, & Geil, 2013). *Networked improvement communities* (NICs) are one form of partnership closely associated with improvement science and originated by the Carnegie Foundation for the Advancement of Teaching (LeMahieu, Grunow, Baker, Nordstrum,

& Gomez, 2017). The intention through networks is for learning to be not only about one's own context, but about the other participating learning organizations. The NIC provides a common language and ideas for conceptualizing problems of practice and models of change and ways to communicate and distribute learning across the network (Bryk, Sebring, Allensworth, Easton, & Luppescu, 2010; Cannata et al., forthcoming). Other widely-known RPPs include the Chicago Consortium for Chicago School Research (Bryk et al., 2010), the Houston Education Research Consortium (López Turley & Stevens, 2015), and the Strategic Action Research Partnership (Donovan & Pellegrino, 2003).

Professional organizations include discipline-focused organizations that promote research, policy, and practice ideas focused on narrower topics, such as the National Council of Social Studies, the National Council of Teachers of Mathematics, and the American Educational Research Association (AERA). These professional organizations serve as a convening mechanism for the creation of fields of research and scholars. Through conferences, journals and other publications, committees, and social media, professional organizations share the research of the field, discuss current policy issues of importance to the field, and offer a way to build the community and share ideas. AERA's mission, for example, states its role in the creation and sharing of knowledge, improving methods and measures, and encouraging the application of research results in real-world settings (AERA, n.d.).

●●●●●

Comprehension Questions

■ How has the role of private foundations increased in educational policy and what are the implications?

■ How has the role of parents changed over time?

■ What are education management organizations and how have they become involved in educational policy?

■ What is ALEC and why has it been so influential in recent times?

■ How can RPPs help to foster educational change?

●●●●●

Discussion Questions

■ What is the purpose of interest groups in educational politics and policy? How can they be helpful and how do they hinder the democratic process?

■ Who are the most influential actors currently in the federal and state educational systems? Why do you say so?

■ Discuss the new ways in which media amplifies the ability of an interest group to make an impact.

● ● ● ● ●

Activities

■ Many videos are available online about interest group formation, including videos from the Crash Course Government and Politics series on YouTube, including "Interest Groups #42" and "Interest Group Formation #43." Find on the web using the following search terms:

YouTube; "Interest Groups #42"; "Interest Group Formation #43"

■ Research one of the main foundations supporting education and/or one of the think tanks to learn about their priorities and political viewpoint.

● ● ● ● ●

Further Reading

#CommonCore. (2017). *How Twitter Works.* Center for Policy Research in Education. Retrieved from: www.hashtagcommoncore.com/#0-5.

Callahan, D. (2017). *The Givers: Wealth, Power, and Philanthropy in a New Guilded Age.* New York: Knopf.

Fielding, M. (2001). Students as radical agents of change. *Journal of Educational Change, 2*(2), 123–41.

Hess, F. M. & Henig, J. R. (2015). *The New Education Philanthropy.* Boston, MA: Harvard Education Press.

Marsh, J. A. & Wohlstetter, P. (2013). Recent trends in intergovernmental relations: The resurgence of local actors in education policy. *Educational Researcher, 42*(5), 276–83.

McDermott, K. (2009). The expansion of state policy research. In Sykes, G., Schneider, B., & Plank, D. (eds.) *Handbook of Education Policy Research* (pp. 749–66). New York: Routledge.

Mediratta, K., Shah, S., & McAlister, S. (2009). *Community Organizing for Stronger Schools: Strategies and Successes.* Boston, MA: Harvard Education Press.

Mitra, D., Mann, B., & Hlavacik, M. (2016). Opting out: Parents creating contested spaces to challenge standardized tests. *Education Policy Analysis Archives,* March.

Mitra, D., Serriere, S., & Kirshner, B. (2014). Youth participation in U.S. contexts: Student voice without a national mandate. *Children & Society, 28*(4), 292–304.

Reckhow, S. & Snyder, J. W. (2014). The expanding role of philanthropy in education politics. *Educational Researcher, 43*(4), 186–95.

United Nations. (1989). *Convention on the Rights of the Child.* Geneva: United Nations.

● ● ● ● ●

Reference List

American Educational Research Association. (n.d.). Retrieved from: www.aera.net/About-AERA.

American Enterprise Institute. (2017). Retrieved from: www.aei.org/about/.

American Federation of Teachers. (n.d.). Retrieved from: www.aft.org/about.

American Legislative Exchange Council. (2015). Retrieved from: www.alec.org.

Anderson, G. L. & Donchik, L. M. (2014). Privatizing schooling and policy making: The American Legislative Exchange Council and new political and discursive strategies of education governance. *Educational Policy, 30*(2), 322–64.

Barbosa Jr, F. (2015). Unfulfilled promise: The need for charter school reform in New Jersey. *Seton Hall Legislative Journal, 39*(2), Article 5.

Barkan, J. (2013). Plutocrats at work: How big philanthropy undermines democracy. *Social Research, 80*(2), 635–52.

Beaver, J., Westmaas, L., & Sludden, J. (2014). *The Potential Effects of Opting out of State Tests in Pennsylvania.* Philadelphia, PA: Research for Action.

Biddle Consulting Group, LLC. (2015). *About Us.* Retrieved from: www.biddle.com/about-biddle.php.

Bryk, A. S., Sebring, P. B., Allensworth, E., Easton, J. Q., & Luppescu, S. (2010). *Organizing Schools for Improvement: Lessons from Chicago.* Chicago, IL: University of Chicago Press.

Business Roundtable.org. (n.d.). Retrieved from: http://businessroundtable.org/issues/education-workforce/committee.

Cannata, M., Cohen-Vogel, L., & Sorum, M. (forthcoming). Partnering for improvement: Improvement communities and their role in scale up. *Peabody Journal of Education.*

Castillo, E., Lalonde, P., Owens, S., DeBray, E., Scott, J., & Lubienski, C. (2015, April). E-advocacy among intermediary organizations: Brokering knowledge through blogs. Paper presented at the annual meeting of the American Educational Research Association, Chicago, IL.

Cato Institute. (n.d.). Retrieved from: www.cato.org/about.

Center for Media and Democracy. (2015). *ALEC Exposed.* Madison, WI: Center for Media and Democracy. Retrieved from: www.prwatch.org/topics/alec-exposed.

Coburn, C. & Penuel, W. (2016). Research-practice partnerships in education: Outcomes, dynamics and open questions. *Education Researcher, 45*(1), 48–54.

Coburn, C. E., Penuel, W. R., & Geil, K. (2013). *Research-Practice Partnerships at the District Level: A New Strategy for Leveraging Research for Educational Improvement.* New York: William T. Grant Foundation.

Common Cause. (2016). *ALEC,* January 3. Retrieved from: www.commoncause.org/issues/more-democracy-reforms/alec/.

Cowen, J. M. (2009). Teacher unions and teacher compensation: New evidence for the impact of bargaining. *Journal of Education Finance, 35*(2), 172–93.

D'Agostino, J. V., Hedges, L. V., Wong, K. K., & Borman, G. D. (2001). Title I parent-involvement programs: Effects on parenting practices and student achievement. In Borman, G. Stringfield, S., & Slavin, R. (eds.) *Title I: Compensatory Education at the Crossroads* (pp. 117–36). Mahwah, NJ: Lawrence Erlbaum Associates.

Dannin, E. (2012). Privatizing government services in the era of ALEC and the great recession. *University of Toledo Law Review, 43*(503), Spring.

Donovan, M. S. (2013). Generating improvement through research and development in educational systems. *Science, 340,* 317–19.

Donovan, M. S. & Pellegrino, J. W. (eds.) (2003). *Learning and Instruction: A SERP Research Agenda.* Washington, DC: National Academies Press.

Elementary and Secondary Education Act of 1965, Pub. L. No. 95–561, 92 Stat. 2143 (1978).

Every Student Succeeds Act (ESSA) of 2015. P.L. 114–95, 20 U.S. C. 6301 (2015).

Farkas, G. (1993). *Divided Within, Besieged Without: The Politics of Education in Four American School Districts.* New York: Public Agenda Foundation.

Fishman, B. J., Penuel, W. R., Allen, A.-R., & Cheng, B. H. (eds.) (2013). Design-based implementation research: Theories, methods and exemplars. *National Society for the Study of Education Yearbook.* New York: Teachers College Press.

Gates Foundation. (2016). What we do. Retrieved from: www.gatesfoundation.org/What-We-Do/US-Program/K-12-Education.

Gose, B. (2012). Turnover of program officers causes problems for charities. *Chronicle of Philanthropy, 24*(8), 7.

Henig, J. R., Hula, R. C., Orr, M., & Pedescleaux, D. S. (1999). *The Color of School Reform: Race Politics, and the Challenge of Urban Education.* Princeton, NJ: Princeton University Press.

Heritage Foundation. (2017). Retrieved from: www.heritage.org/about-heritage/mission.

Hess, F. M. & Henig, J. R. (2015). *The New Education Philanthropy.* Boston, MA: Harvard Education Press.

Improving America's Schools Act of 1994, Pub. L. 103–382 (1994).

Kammer, A. S. (2013). Privatizing the safeguards of federalism. *Journal of Law and Politics, 29*(1), 69–150.

Kingdon, J. W. (2003). *Agendas, Alternatives, and Public Policies.* New York: Longman Publishing Group.

Koerner, J. (1968). *Who Controls American Education?* Boston, MA: Beacon Press.

Kornhaber, M. L., Barkauskas, N. J., & Griffith, K. M. (2016). Smart money? Philanthropic and federal funding for the Common Core. *Education Policy Analysis Archives, 24*(93).

Labaree, D. (2010). *Someone Has to Fail: The Zero-Sum Game of Public Schooling.* Cambridge, MA: Harvard University Press.

LeMahieu, P. G., Grunow, A., Baker, L., Nordstrum, L. E., & Gomez, L. M. (2017). Networked improvement communities: The discipline of improvement science meets the power of networks. *Quality Assurance in Education, 25*(1), 5–25.

Lewis, M., Mead, J., & Hall, D. (2017). The American Legislative Exchange Council as a "friend of the court" in education cases. *Journal of Law and Social Change, 21.*

López Turley, R. N. & Stevens, C. (2015). Lessons from a school district-university research partnership: The Houston Education Research Consortium. *Educational Evaluation and Policy Analysis, 37*(1S), 6S–15S.

Lubienski, C. & Brewer, T. J. (2013). *Review of "Report Card on American Education: Ranking State K-12 Performance, Progress, and Reform."* Boulder, CO: National Education Policy Center. Retrieved from: http://nepc.colorado.edu/thinktank/review-report-card-ALEC-2013.

Malen, B. & Cochran, M. V. (2008). Beyond pluralistic patterns of power: Research on the micropolitics of schools. In Cooper, B. S., Cibulka, J. G., & Fusarelli, L. D. (eds.) *Handbook of Education Politics and Policy* (pp. 148–78). New York: Routledge.

Marsh, J. A. & Wohlstetter, P. (2013). Recent trends in intergovernmental relations: The resurgence of local actors in education policy. *Educational Researcher, 42*(5), 276–83.

Marshall, C., Mitchell, D., & Wirt, F. (1989). *Culture and Education Policy in the American States.* London: Falmer.

Matthis, W. & Miron, G. (2013). *Private Education Management Organizations Running Public Schools Expand.* 14th edition. Boulder, CO: National Education Policy Center.

McDermott, K. A. (1999). *Controlling Public Education: Localism Versus Equity. Studies in Government and Public Policy*. Lawrence, KS: University Press of Kansas.

McDermott, K. (2009). The expansion of state policy research. In Sykes, G., Schneider, B., & Plank, D. (eds.) *Handbook of Education Policy Research* (pp. 749–66). New York: Routledge.

McDonnell, L. (2007). The politics of education: Influencing policy and beyond. In Fuhrman, S., Cohen, D., & Mosher, F. (eds.) *The State of Education Policy Research* (pp. 19–40). Mahwah, NJ: Lawrence Erlbaum Associates.

McDonnell, L. M. (2009). 2009 Presidential address: Repositioning politics in education's circle of knowledge. *Educational Researcher, 38*(6), 417–27.

McHaney, S. (2015). Is right-to-work the kiss of death for labor unions? *PBS Newshour,* March 9. Retrieved from: www.pbs.org/newshour/rundown/right-work-kiss-death-labor-unions/.

Mediratta, K., Shah, S., & McAlister, S. (2009). *Community Organizing for Stronger Schools: Strategies and Successes*. Boston, MA: Harvard Education Press.

Mehta, J. & Teles, S. (2011). Jurisdictional politics: A new federal role in education. In Hess, F. M. and Kelly, A. P. (eds.) *Lessons from a Half-Century of Federal Efforts to Improve America's Schools* (pp. 217–30). Cambridge, MA: Harvard Education Press.

Mitra, D., Mann, B., & Hlavacik, M. (2016). Opting out: Parents creating contested spaces to challenge standardized tests. *Education Policy Analysis Archives*, March.

National Education Association. (2015). Retrieved from: www.nea.org/home/2580.htm.

Parent Teacher Association. (n.d.). Retrieved from: www.pta.org/about/.

Parent Teacher Association. (2016). *2016 Annual Report*. Retrieved from: www.pta.org/about/content.cfm?ItemNumber=1508&navItemNumber=554.

Park, S. & Holloway, S. D. (2013). No parent left behind: Predicting parental involvement in adolescents' education within a sociodemographically diverse population. *The Journal of Educational Research, 106*(2), 105–19.

Reckhow, S. (2008). A shadow bureaucracy: How foundations circumvent politics to reform schools. Paper presented at the American Political Science Association, Boston, MA, August 28–30.

Reckhow, S. (2013). *Follow the Money: How Foundation Dollars Change Public School Politics*. New York: Oxford University Press.

Reckhow, S. & Snyder, J. W. (2014). The expanding role of philanthropy in education politics. *Educational Researcher, 43*(4), 186–95.

Reckhow, S. & Tompkins-Stange, M. (2015). "Singing from the same hymnbook" at Gates and Broad. In Hess, F. & Henig, J. (eds.) *The New Education Philanthropy: Politics, Policy, and Reform* (pp. 55–77). Cambridge, MA: Harvard Education Press.

Schneider, A. & Ingram, H. (1993). Social construction of target populations: Implications for politics and policy. *American Political Science Review, 87*(2), 334–47.

Scott, J., DeBray, E., Lubienski, C., Lalonde, P., Castillo, E., & Owens, S. (2017). Urban regimes, intermediary organization networks, and research use: Patterns across three school districts. *Peabody Journal of Education, 92*, 16–28.

Spring, J. (2011). *The Politics of American Education*. New York: Routledge.

Stone, C., Henig, J., Jones, B., & Pierannunzi, C. (2001). *Building Civic Capacity: The Politics of Reforming Urban Schools*. Lawrence, KS: University Press of Kansas.

Tseng, V. (2012). *Partnerships: Shifting the Dynamics Between Research and Practice*. New York: William T. Grant Foundation.

Tyack, D. B. (1974). *The One Best System: A History of American Urban Education*. Cambridge, MA: Harvard University Press.

Ujifusa, A. (2012 April 20). Controversial policy group casts long K-12 shadow. *Education Week*. Retrieved from: www.edweek.org/ew/articles/2012/04/20/29alec_ep.h31.html.

Underwood, J. & Mead, J. F. (2012). A smart ALEC threatens public education. *Phi Delta Kappan, 93*(6), 51–5.

Vincent, C. (1996). Parent empowerment? Collective action and inaction in education. *Oxford Review of Education, 22*(4), 465–82.

Welner, K. G. (2011). Free-market think tanks and the marketing of education policy. *Dissent, 58*(2), 39–43.

Wirt, F. & Kirst, M. (1997). *The Political Dynamics of American Education*. Berkeley, CA: McCutchan Publishing.

II

The Policy Process

This section details how the policy process as a political system wages battle about ideas and values. While problematizing a linear model of policy, this section addresses issues of power and the relation to parts of the policy process—problem formation/agenda setting, policy formation, implementation, sustainability, and scale.

5

●●●●●

Public Policy and Power

*P*ublic policy is the process by which a political system develops laws, regulations, and rules. It is a process that defines problems, proposes solutions, incites action, and can ultimately lead to changes that affect individuals and communities. Scholars study policy to understand the processes of educational change and the intention of policies; it is also studied for practical reasons to understand how it affects schools and the educational process (Cochran et al., 2015).

In addition to those working in the three branches of government, a large cadre of individuals and organizations have full-time jobs trying to influence the policy system. Lobbyist organizations include corporations, unions, and other interest groups explicitly seeking to influence candidates and elected officials about specific issues. Non-profit organizations and advocacy organizations are not allowed to officially lobby for an issue, but serve as "advocates" of issues and are constantly trying to influence the conversation on policy by providing issue briefs, research, and information that align with their positions on issues such as educational testing, child welfare, the budget, and more.

Educational researchers and policy analysts seek to describe and understand the policy process and how change might affect individuals and groups, with an assumption of a smaller level of bias than advocates and lobbyists. They can influence the policy conversation by sharing research in a format that is accessible to policy makers and lobbyists. They also can testify before law making bodies to provide expert opinions on policy issues.

Reform is change. Reform includes big ideas and attempts to address long-standing problems such as educating children, caring for the sick and elderly, and encouraging economic growth. Reform movements historically can take decades and include a wide range of policies that may occur as a society shifts. Such reform shifts could include shifts toward greater equality based on race, class, gender, and sexual identity. Or a shift could be from a socialist to a capitalist economic system. *Reform cycles* tend to occur in often slow and steady work (Elmore & McLaughlin, 1988); at other times, it occurs in great bursts (Baumgartner & Jones, 1993). Policy is the vehicle by which reform can happen, often in the form of legislation and protocols.

Policy cycles are much faster than reform cycles (Tyack & Cuban, 1995). They tend to align with elections and shifts in national mood based on important events. Often pressures from the duration of legislation sessions to the shifting of a national mood can heighten the speed at which policy passes, or prevent important rules from being enacted. Within this process is ongoing compromise, debate, and consensus (Fowler, 2013).

Public policy is officially made by government bodies. In the United States, the legislature, the courts, and the executive branches all make policy, discussed in Section I. The legislature makes policy through laws. The judicial system makes policy through court decisions. The executive makes policy through regulation and, at the federal level, through treaties. These three bodies can also appoint other bodies to make policy. For example, state legislatures and executives often delegate much of the rule and regulatory authority of schools to a state board of education comprised of officials appointed by the executive. For education, the local school board often has great power for designing, implementing, and blocking policy.

⊛ ⊛ ⊛ ⊛ ⊛

Rational Decision-Making Process

A traditional decision-making model assumes rationality. It assumes that public decisions are made in the best interests of all. It assumes sufficient information and time to gather data and to assess options. Until the 1980s, most policy textbooks described public policy as a *decision-making process.* In a classic textbook of policy, Stokey and Zeckhauser (1978) outline a five-step rational decision-making process as the basis of policy.

1. Identifying the problem
2. Laying out the alternative courses of action
3. Predicting the consequences
4. Valuing the outcomes
5. Making a choice

This model assumed that the decision maker has the information to evaluate the options and to make a high-quality decision (Gregory, 1989; Lindblom & Woodhouse, 1980). Even with perfect information, the decision-making model assumes that we all share the same values and beliefs that would lead to the same decision. It also assumes that a policy process can be neutral and objective when making political decisions. Policy research since the 1980s has called this logic into question.

⊛ ⊛ ⊛ ⊛ ⊛

Policy as a Political Process

Since the 1980s, policy research has emphasized that policy making is a political process based on negotiation and compromise. It involves deliberation and a discussion of ideas. In democratic contexts, the political context assumes a *polis*—a community that must come together to sort out what the community believes as a collective and how they will create a shared spaced of governance based on those beliefs (Stone, 1997). It is a battle of ideas and values rather than facts. As Dunn (1994, p. 137) states:

> Many people believe that policy problems are objective conditions whose existence may be established simply by determining that the facts are in a given case. This naïve view of the nature of policy problems fails to recognize that the same facts—government statistics on crime—are often interpreted in markedly different ways by different policy stakeholders. Hence the same policy relevant information can and often does result in conflicting definitions and expansions of a problem. This is not so much because the facts of the matter are inconsistent (and often they are) but because policy analysts, policy makers and other stakeholders hold competing assumptions about human nature, government, and opportunities for social change.

Policy making is the craft of assessing what others need and how to negotiate compromise. It is a process of understanding context and how the political and social events of a community, nation, and world influence the space in which discussions can occur (McLaughlin, 1987), and how crises and unexpected events can shift the focus of policy making dramatically and often irrationally.

● ● ● ● ●

Policy as Power

An understanding of politics would not be complete without a discussion of power. Joel Spring (2002, p. 33) defines *power* as "The ability to control the actions of other people and the ability to escape from the control of others, including attempt to gain economic advantages." Spring speaks of connections between knowledge and power and ability of knowledge to lead to freedom from the power and control of others.

Scholars seeking to question authority and to challenge the dominant paradigm have constructed multiple images and frameworks for understanding this paradoxically illusive and central concept. Freire (1970), Habermas (1971), Foucault (1982), and Deleuze (1988) offer some of the more commonly discussed paradigms. Even work that does not explicitly discuss power includes assumptions about it, and Youdell (2006) argues of the importance to make them visible to be able to interrogate how they influence policy and practice. This book elaborates further on issues of power in other chapters, especially in the chapter focusing on equity (Chapter 12).

● ● ● ● ●

Policy as Argument

Creating policy can be considered a struggle over ideas and underlying values. In the best cases, it is a deliberation in which participants in the political process are open to hearing other viewpoints. It involves considering how to meld together deeply held beliefs into creative solutions to longstanding concerns. In the worst case, it is entrenched political warfare in which opposing parties are unwilling to budge on issues and the focus is on the differences between groups rather than the common ground.

Most matters of public policy are *ill-structured problems* (Dunn, 1994, p. 146), that is, problems that have many decision makers with varying and often unknown values. Effective policy makers understand the role of argument and persuasion in their task. If the policy arena is a battle over ideas, then the goal of a policy maker is to persuade, to clarify, and to convince. Giandomenico Majone (1989) describes this work as a "craft" in which the policy makers choose from a palette of data to design persuading arguments. Combining story telling with carefully chosen facts and research, a skilled policy maker weaves together a narrative of a compelling and creative path toward addressing a problem. A carefully chosen statistic or a photograph taken during a crisis event can focus attention on a problem. Effective policy making includes an awareness of timing, attention to detail, awareness of limitations, and creative and effective persuasion (Stone, 1997).

Compare this vision of policy with the rational decision-making model in which all facts and research are obtained and the most accurate and strongest data are brought forward. A rational decision-making model assumes that all values have been stipulated before a decision-making process occurs; a political model assumes that the formation and articulation of value is in fact at the heart of what policy making is. Often a policy maker already has made a decision about a position and then sets out to find the most compelling narratives to support this belief. In this case, policy is about persuasion and inciting action rather than making a decision based on the best information. Deborah Stone (1997) contrasts these two perspectives, as shown in Table 5.1.

The policy maker might find research and facts that support a chosen position, even if more rigorous research exists for the other side. Ideas and beliefs shape policy. Rigorous research can sway ideas and beliefs—but only if the research itself is presented in a compelling and thoughtful way to policy makers.

Table 5.1 Contrasting Political Models

Rational Model	Political Model
Discovering a solution	Justifying a solution
Objectivity	Advocacy
Knowing "that"	Knowing "how"

Source: Stone (1997, p. 138)

Often this messaging is a missing link for researchers—finding ways to share findings in a format that is accessible to policy makers and is timely.

⬤ ⬤ ⬤ ⬤ ⬤

Process Matters

How a policy is made matters as much as what the policy says in many cases. The art and craft of policy making requires understanding that policy making is about building relationships, negotiating positions, and compromise. Policy is about relationships between individuals and organizations. Many of these relationships are nurtured over years and decades. This background of relational context is often invisible to someone not enmeshed in a particular policy context and yet these relationships can determine potential pathways for policy making and roadblocks.

Because the relationships are usually longer lasting than any given policy, the process of how any policy is developed can affect future policies. Trust can be strengthened or weakened. Alliances can be formed or broken.

Policies can also be more about setting up opportunities for future opportunities, rather than accomplishing intended goals at one time. Policy makers with a longer strategy in mind may compromise on a current issue in the hope of achieving greater gains later. In this way, politics is much like a chess game. Sometimes intentional defeat in the immediate context could lead to greater victories later.

⬤ ⬤ ⬤ ⬤ ⬤

The Importance of Ethical Policy

Understanding that policy ideas are cobbled together also brings an awareness that deception can also be a big part of the policy process. In the name of getting policy passed, often information is deliberately withheld that could favor an opposing view. Special interests might even intentionally seek to obstruct public opinion on an issue.

Box 5.1 Case Study: Policy Framing and Symbols

Bill Moyers (*Free Speech for Sale*, 1999) created a documentary that describes in detail ways in which John McCain sought to create a cigarette tax in the 1990s that would provide revenue for cigarette-related health problems and children's programs. Using images of cuckoo clocks (Washington has gone "cuckoo"), Christmas trees (Congress spending too much money), and using a soccer mom with a mug of coffee on a front porch to name a few, these sets of ads set to reframe how the public conceived of a piece of legislation through a million-dollar ad campaign. The cigarette companies used these images to draw attention away from a bill aimed at taxing smokers to help address the medical costs of smoking, and to reframe the bill as a problematic tax and spend policy targeted at working-class Americans (when it actually targeted *smoking* Americans, many of whom happen to also be working class).

Given the potential for obstruction, some scholars argue that a political process must contain a shared sense of ethical conduct for a democracy to work effectively. Majone (1989) refers to such a process as providing standards of argument and structures. Good policy, according to Majone (1989):

■ begins with plausible premises

■ clarifies controversial issues

■ educates citizens to become "informed"

■ provides a source for mutual learning—debate is a two-way (or more) interchange.

In recent times in U.S. history, national policy making has been marked by gridlock and a lack of progress in many policy arenas. Thus policy making can often be about preventing policy as much as making change possible. The extent to which preventing policy is ethical is a matter of great discussion in current policy debates.

The role of the media in amplifying powerful voices and silencing others has also been a critical concern of political ethicists in recent decades. Diana Mutz (2015) discusses the "in your face" politics of media outlets through amplifying coverage of those that watchers dislike and by encouraging a lack of civility in dialogue across positions during discussions/debates and rants on television. Mutz finds that this incivility reduces respect and willingness to understand opposing viewpoints and reduces trust in politicians and the political process.

● ● ● ● ●

Defining the Policy Process

Overall, the text emphasizes the intersection of ideas/values, groups of individuals, and political opportunity to formulate and implement policy. With the constraints of a linear textbook, the chapters provide components of the policy process, most commonly associated with the work of Kingdon (1984). These components are problem formation, agenda setting and framing, implementation, scaling and sustainability.

Marcus Weaver-Hightower (2008) provides an alternative framework of policy knowledge that argues against a linear conception of policy. It builds upon the work of Firestone's (1989) ecology of games that discusses the metaphor of policy as a series of overlapping games with winners and losers and Mazzoni's (1991) arena model. Weaver-Hightower presents an ecological model that highlights the complexity of the political policy system—a system that includes actors, relationships, environments/structures, and processes (2008, p. 156). This emphasis moves beyond policy as an artifact (often a written document) and instead to conceive of policy as a relational process. Examining policy with an ecological model involves looking at the movement of discourse and resource among actors. Policy is also not solely centrally occurring in formal actors anymore, but also through private sector actors, and increasingly foundations and ideological interest groups, as discussed in Chapter 4 (Reckhow, 2013). Local issues can become symbols and battlefields for policy debates, such as funding of local school board elections by national interest groups (Reckhow, Henig, Jacobsen, & Alter Litt, 2016). For example, the Los Angeles Unified School District School Board candidates were largely funded either by charter school lobbyists or teachers' unions (Scott et al., 2017).

Figure 5.1 redesigns these Kingdon components in an ecological shape to stress the ways in which the concepts from each chapter in this section occur at every point in the policy process. This book therefore offers the Kingdon categories as the way to deliver the information in the textbook while stressing that it is also important to problematize the conception of policy as an orderly and linear process. However, we adapt the Kingdon model into an ecological shape to stress the disorderly nature of policy.

We discuss:

- *Problem formation, agenda setting, and framing* (Chapter 6). Not all problems get onto a policy agenda at any given time. One of the first steps in a policy process is an awareness of a problem that needs to be solved, and a political willingness to tackle that issue at that time.

- *Policy formation* (Chapter 7). Policy ideas must be narrowed into a concrete document that can be shared and interpreted—a legislative bill, an executive order, a court decision. The target population of a policy matters, as some groups have more power and prestige than others. Policy tools shape the intent of policies in large part based on the target populations. Some policies are designed to punish. Other policies are designed to encourage.

- *Policy implementation* (Chapter 8). The policy process does not stop when the policy is adopted. Instead, many scholars of policy study how policy adoption is just the beginning of understanding how a policy idea is translated into practice. Often the enacted policy looks very different from the intended idea.

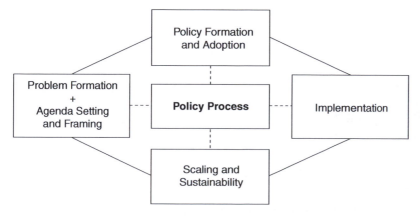

Figure 5.1 Policy Process. Adapted from Kingdon (1984).

■ *Sustainability and scale* (Chapter 9). As policies settle into use, researchers, practitioners, and policy makers must take stock of how well they are working and establish conditions that can set reforms up for success. Sustaining a beloved reform to other contexts can be a challenge because of shrinking resources and competitive needs. Spreading the idea also might fail because it does not have the capacity to thrive in other environments.

●●●●●

Comprehension Questions

■ How are Stone and Majone's descriptions of the policy process different from Stokey and Zeckhauser's?

■ How, according to Majone, is policy an art and a craft?

■ What is power? How does it influence education?

■ Stone talks about ideas behind policies—what are some of these fundamental ideas?

●●●●●

Discussion Questions

■ How does the conception of policy as a linear policy versus a matrix change your understanding of what the policy process is like?

■ Building off of the criteria for ethical policy discussed in this chapter, do you believe that the policy process occurs in an ethical way? How does this conception vary when comparing federal, state, and local examples?

●●●●●

Activities

■ On a sheet of paper make two columns and label them "rational decision-making model" and "political model." Sort the words below into one of the two columns.

Discovering a solution
Predicting the consequences
Policy window
Identifying alternatives
Identifying a target audience
Outcomes focused
Persuasion
Inciting action

Neutrality

Battle of ideas

Evidence

Timing

Target audience

Problem solving

Context matters

Valuing the outcomes

Based on individual thinking

Based on collective negotiating

Moral ideas

Craft

Decisionism

Argument

Positivism

Objectivity

Paradox

■ Visit factcheck.org to review independent analysis of the factual accuracy of politicians' speeches. Discuss the implications of the inaccuracies and if you believe they were intentional or accidental.

●●●●●

Further Reading

Kingdon, J. W. (1984). *Agendas, Alternatives, and Public Policies* (Vol. 45). Boston, MA: Little, Brown.

Lindblom, C. E. (1959). The science of "muddling through". *Public Administration Review, 19*(2), 79–88.

Weaver-Hightower, M. B. (2008). An ecology metaphor for educational policy analysis: A call to complexity. *Educational Researcher, 37*(3), 153–67.

●●●●●

Reference List

Baumgartner, F. R. & Jones, B. D. (1993). *Agendas and Instability in American Politics.* Chicago, IL: University of Chicago Press.

Cochran, C. E., Mayer, L. C., Carr, T. R., Cayer, N. J., McKenzie, M., & Peck, L. (2015). *American Public Policy: An Introduction.* Independence, KY: Cengage Learning.

Deleuze, G. (1988). *Spinoza: Practical Philosophy* (R. Hurley, Trans.). San Francisco, CA: City Lights Books.

Dunn, W. N. (1994). *Public Policy Analysis: An Introduction* (2nd ed.). Englewood Cliffs, NJ: Prentice Hall.

Elmore, R. F. & McLaughlin, M. W. (1988). *Steady Work. Policy, Practice, and the Reform of American Education*. Santa Monica, CA: The RAND Corporation.

Firestone, W. A. (1989). Educational policy as an ecology of games. *Educational Researcher, 18*(7), 18–24.

Foucault, M. (1982). The subject and power. *Critical Inquiry, 8*(4), 777–95.

Fowler, F. C. (2013). *Policy Studies for Educational Leaders: An Introduction*. Upper Saddle River, NJ: Merrill.

Freire, P. (1970). *Pedagogy of the Oppressed*. New York: Seabury Press.

Gregory, R. (1989). Political rationality or "incrementalism"? Charles E. Lindblom's enduring contribution to public policy making theory. *Policy & Politics, 17*(2), 139–53.

Habermas, J. (1971). *Knowledge and Human Interests*. (J. J. Shapiro, Trans.). Boston, MA: Beacon.

Kingdon, J. W. (1984). *Agendas, Alternatives, and Public Policies* (Vol. 45). Boston, MA: Little, Brown.

Lindblom, C. E. & Woodhouse, E. J. (1980). *The Policy-Making Process*. Englewood Cliffs, NJ: Prentice Hall.

Majone, G. (1989). *Evidence, Argument, and Persuasion in the Policy Process*. New Haven, CT: Yale University Press.

Mazzoni, T. L. (1991). Analyzing state school policymaking: An arena model. *Educational Evaluation and Policy Analysis, 13*(2), 115–38.

McLaughlin, M. W. (1987). Learning from experience: Lessons from policy implementation. *Educational Evaluation and Policy Analysis, 9*(2), 171–8.

Moyers, B. (1999). *Free Speech for Sale: A Bill Moyers Special*. Produced by Public Affairs Television, Inc. (originally aired on PBS).

Mutz, D. (2015). *In-Your-Face Politics: The Consequences of Uncivil Media*. Princeton, NJ: Princeton University Press.

Reckhow, S. (2013). *Follow the Money: How Foundation Dollars Change Public School Politics*. New York: Oxford University Press.

Reckhow, S., Henig, J. R., Jacobsen, R., & Alter Litt, J. (2016). Outsiders with deep pockets: The nationalization of local school board elections. *Urban Affairs Review*, Online First, 1078087416663004.

Scott, J., DeBray, E., Lubienski, C., Lalonde, P., Castillo, E., & Owens, S. (2017). Urban regimes, intermediary organization networks, and research use: Patterns across three school districts. *Peabody Journal of Education, 92*, 16–28.

Spring, J. (2002). *Conflict of Interests: The Politics of American Education*. Boston, MA: McGraw Hill.

Stokey, E. & Zeckhauser, R. (1978). *Primer for Policy Analysis*. New York: W. W. Norton.

Stone, D. A. (1997). *Policy Paradox: The Art of Political Decision Making*. New York: W. W. Norton.

Tyack, D. B. & Cuban, L. (1995). *Tinkering Toward Utopia*. Cambridge, MA: Harvard University Press.

Weaver-Hightower, M. B. (2008). An ecology metaphor for educational policy analysis: A call to complexity. *Educational Researcher, 37*(3), 153–67.

Youdell, D. (2006). *Impossible Bodies, Impossible Selves: Exclusions and Student Subjectivities*. Dordrecht, Netherlands: Springer.

6

●●●●●

Problem Formation, Agenda Setting, and Framing

●●●●●

Problem Formation

The process of developing and improving governance consists of identifying and addressing fundamental dilemmas of society. These dilemmas include helping those that are struggling due to poverty, disability, inequity, and poor health. They also involve aspiring to excellence and helping talented individuals gain the skills and resources that can lead to innovation, excellence, and creative solutions. Societies must balance the freedom of individuals to live in ways that align with their own values and beliefs, while also preserving safety of the population by controlling dangerous behaviors.

The list of potential policy problems in a society is far longer than any individual decision-making body can tackle at one time. Kingdon (1984) describes the difference between conditions and problems. Abundant numbers of *conditions* create stress and discord, but only *policy problems* raise to the surface to demand public attention, often due to the influence of policy stakeholders. These problems reflect the unrealized desires, values, and opportunities for change and action. They may involve comparisons between populations or a battle over differing values.

Problem structuring involves a focus on a subset of unrealized needs (Dunn, 1994). Problems are prioritized within particular political conditions and contexts. Problem structuring matters because policy makers often define the problem in a way that prevents a solution and blocks creative thinking. For example, Wedell-Wedellsborg (2017) gives two examples of this mindshift. One is the problem of finding homes for stray dogs. Another way of framing the problem would be to reduce the number of dogs needing a home. By reducing the number of people who give up their pets to shelters, the number of dogs in shelters would be reduced dramatically. In a second example, Wedell-Wedellsborg talks about the problem of elevators being too slow. Rather than improving the speed of elevators, mirrors were placed at every floor. People became so engrossed in their own images that complaints about the elevator speed dropped dramatically. These examples demonstrate that framing of a problem in an unsolvable way is often the true struggle for policy rather than the creativity and quality of the solution (Dunn, 1994, p. 137).

Ill-structured problems tend to involve multiple changemakers with competing values. Often these values are unknown or immeasurable. Most of the big longstanding problems of public society are ill-structured (Dunn, 1994, p. 140)—problems such as poverty, educational excellence, taxation, and equity.

Choosing which problems to address at the present moment is the focus of this chapter. The variation of ethical and ideological perspectives influences how problems are defined and approached (Cochran, Mayer, Carr, & Cayer, 1982, 1986). There are great stakes when it comes to problem definition. Some populations and issues are favored over others. There are winners and losers. Some are helped and some are hurt (Kingdon, 1984).

To understand the selection of problems at a given point and time, and why some periods in time are marked by greater change than other times, we consider many components of problem formation in this chapter. We consider how policy makers define problems and how this problem definition influences the policies that can be constructed by exploring the concept of framing, target populations, timing, policy windows, and punctuated equilibrium.

●●●●●

Framing Ideas

How a problem is framed affects what policy solutions are available. It narrows the scope of what is on the table in a political negotiation. Problem structuring does not begin with clear ideas but instead with a vague set of conditions, worries and stressors in the environment (Dunn, 1994). Policy problems are created from these environmental conditions through a process of framing.

Framing consists of the strategic decisions made to amplify a policy problem to garner support and attention to the concerning conditions. To understand the concept of framing, consider how a picture frame might crop a larger image. Choosing what part of the image to frame and what to cut involves decisions of what matters most for where that picture will be hung. If all of the vision can't be shared, strategic decisions must be made regarding what to emphasize, and what to de-emphasize.

The design of policy problems is only possible when policy makers engage in the craft of problem formation (Majone, 1989). Policy problems are therefore socially constructed and maintained based on subjective human judgment (Dunn, 1994). Complicated problems must be simplified in a political space to pass policies of reasonable length and scope. Getting people to agree to a new problem or to see an old problem in a new light is the essence of politics (Kingdon, 1984). Problems are simplified to facilitate the communication and discussion of them aloud and on paper. They are also simplified to make passage more possible—to reduce the number of policy actors involved in a conversation and to narrow the scope of the debate (Kingdon, 1984; Rosen, 2009; Stone, 1997).

Contexts affect which problems are elevated to a level of concern. Contexts can overwhelm and drive the nature of change (Talbert & McLaughlin, 1994; McLaughlin, 1990). Contexts include technical concerns (demographics and economics), cultural values, and political conditions (Olssen, Codd, & O'Neill, 2004). The demographic context includes the salient characteristics of stakeholders, particularly those with voting or financial power, such as age, ethnicity, and socioeconomic status, among other identities. Cultural values consist of ideological beliefs predominant at the time, such as fiscal conservatism, environmentalism, and libertarianism. Political conditions include election results and the fluctuation of political indicators such as polls and the relationship between political parties. Political conditions also include bodies of government in a particular time period, such as stalemates within Congress and between the legislative and executive branches post-2000 in the United States. History also determines how policy is shaped (Kofod, Seashore Louis, Moos, & van Velzen, 2012).

Box 6.1 Framing a Complex Problem

Combatting poverty is a complex and longstanding problem. It consists of many issues, including employment, housing, health care, education, substance abuse, public safety, and more. While one might espouse reducing poverty as a policy goal, the creation of policies, it is usually considered too broad to tackle all at once. Policy will likely only tackle one piece of the issue—housing subsidies or job growth strategies. Even within those smaller ideas, the scope needs to be narrowed to a particular strategy at a particular time. So instead, poverty is shrunk down to a sub-issue. For example, the original money for the Elementary and Secondary Education Act was a poverty strategy based on the premise that helping poor children to perform better in school could reduce poverty. So the entire issue of poverty was shrunk into school achievement.

Defining a Target Audience

Framing also includes narrowing the scope of individuals discussed in a policy problem. Creating a target audience is part of the narrowing process. A *target audience* is the body of individuals who are the object of either the policy itself or the people who are being identified as potential supporters in a political context.

Target audiences are often transparent in political campaigns. In a primary, Republicans and Democrats are talking mostly to their own parties—the target audience is an individual likely to vote in that party election. Therefore, the candidates speak to issues important to party voters. Republicans tend to speak about taxes, the relaxing of gun laws, family values, and stopping immigration, while Democrats tend to speak about poverty, accessible health care, tougher gun laws, and equitable distribution of resources.

Once political parties select their candidates, the target audience for a general political election changes dramatically. These same candidates must then position themselves to capture the middle—independent or swing voters, mostly moderates, who are willing to consider both Republican and Democratic candidates. The framing of conversation shifts from partisan issues of guns and equity to more centrist issues, such as jobs and education. Looking at the websites of the same candidates during a primary and then again during a general election can show this shift over time. Trump's campaign was unusual in that it did not swing to the center during the general election but instead focused on increasing its base on the periphery.

●●●●●

Agenda Setting

The concept of *agenda setting* explains, why this policy at this time? Gradually a social give-and-take converges into a shared societal perception that a particular problem is pressing. Then, agenda formation begins (Cochran et al., 1982). The various demands and perspectives create an agenda of alternative proposals for dealing with the issue. Some proposals and demands never make it to the agenda and others are put on the agenda in alternated form.

Anthony Downs (1972) provides a model of the *issue attention cycle*—a process for understanding how and why some problems rise to the level of policy development while most do not. Downs (1972) stresses that not all problems rise to the level of the issue attention cycle. The problems that do rise to this level tend to occur because a problem that is otherwise lacking its own intrinsic interest has been manufactured to become dramatic and exciting. The direct effort to draw attention might also require a shift of perspective, moving the majority from feeling that they do not suffer from the problem to feeling that addressing the issue would bring significant benefits to the majority.

Finding the Policy Window

A *policy window* is a conceptual way of thinking about how and why some conditions become policy problems and others do not. John Kingdon (1984) offers a framework for understanding when policy windows are open for change (see Figure 6.1).

Essentially, policy formation is a combination of problems needing to be solved, solutions looking for a problem, and political context that filters what is allowed on the agenda. All of these pieces consist of the "policy soup." Kingdon (1984) describes these three components as:

> *Political stream*: the contexts in which policy sit and the lens through which problems and solutions will be viewed. This includes what party is in power in official elections, the economic outlook for a country, perceived threats

from other nations, the national mood, and recent crises, scandals, and natural disasters.

Agenda stream: this stream consists of problems looking for a solution; the problems on the agenda at any time.

Alternatives stream: in this stream are solutions looking for problems. Advocates look for opportunities to leverage solutions. Advocates are looking to insert their solutions into the policy system Such advocacy ideas could be more funding to children's programming, restricting access to abortion, and increasing privatization of schools.

Mazzoni (1991) offers another way of conceptualizing this process through describing arenas of conflict and change. Arenas provide a way of legitimating people and concepts, and establishing rules. As policy travels between arenas, it is subject to new rules and contexts that can be dramatically different from previous conditions. Mazzoni's model captures the volatility and irregularity of the political system.

Assessing audience and introducing the evidence requires an awareness of *timing*. The current contexts affect what can be discussed on the political agenda. What issues fit onto a policy agenda—what problems get on the table— often depends on what is happening in the world locally, regionally, nationally, and internationally. Shifts in events can open up new opportunities for changing policy. Some of these events are planned, such as national elections and planned announcements of economic figures. Others are unplanned, such as natural disasters, scandals, and wars.

Having solutions ready for problems may sound irrational, and it can be. It is important to remember that policy cycles happen quickly. Particularly in times of crisis, policy makers are expected to identify and pass solutions quickly— often too fast for an even-handed decision-making process. Indeed, some of the most illogical policy decisions have occurred in times of crisis.

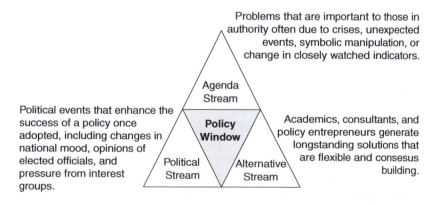

Figure 6.1 Kingdon's Policy Window. Adapted from Kingdon (1984).

Sociologists James March and Johan Olsen (1986) refer to this process as the *garbage can model*—instances in which policy problems and proposed solutions are paired together with little fit between them. The garbage can model amplifies the inherent ambiguity of policy design. The agenda setting component of policy often includes tethering problems and solutions together in an irrational, unorganized process, one that March and Olsen call "organized anarchy." Such a situation often includes: "1) problematic preferences, 2) unclear means, 3) fluid participation" (Cohen-Vogel & Ingle, 2007; March & Olsen, 1986).

Box 6.2 Garbage Can Theory

One example of the garbage can theory could be the U.S. decision to go to war with Iraq after the 9/11 tragedy. While the nation was in crisis, mourning the loss of 5000 people in the World Trade Center bombings, the United States wanted to strike back immediately to do "something" to fight against terrorism. Despite the fact that the terrorist attacks were not instigated by Saddam Hussein at all but instead by Al-Qaeda terrorists, President Bush declared war against Hussein and Iraq. The troubles with Iraq had been longstanding problems, stemming from unfinished business from the original Gulf War conducted by his father, George H. W. Bush. Clinton also indicated an interest in capturing Hussein. The events of 9/11 created political conditions, a political stream as Kingdon (1984) would say, that permitted the longstanding solution of capturing Saddam Hussein to be attached to the problem of the 9/11 attacks.

Social Media and Framing

Social media can help to influence agenda setting and problem formation.

In the previous generation, the news tended to be dominated by the three main television networks and most individuals received information from common sources that purported to give a balanced view of current events. Problem definition and agenda setting were controlled by almost a monopoly of news sources, but also with the goal of reaching a broad audience. Increasingly, media outlets have proliferated, including television, talk radio, and social media.

Social media can be a democratic tool that can increase the ability for anyone to share opinions and to allow for grassroots mobilization (Boullianne, 2015). Within the realm of education policy, social media has become the primary source of legitimation and translation of viewpoints. Educational policy makers and influencers are increasingly turning to blogs and Twitter to legitimate and translate research findings and to emphasize viewpoints (Castillo et al., 2015).

The power of social media can be seen in Twitter Revolution refers to protests and movements that occurred during 2009–2013 in the Middle East and surrounding regions. The activists used Twitter as a primary mode of communication to mobilize change. Twitter has over 328 million active users worldwide as of 2016 (Statista, 2017). With only 140 characters per message, but the ability to add images and links, Twitter has catapulted to the forefront of knowledge exchange in politics and the educational policy industry. Twitter users create social networks by "following" one another and "retweeting" liked messages. Mentioning using the "@" symbol in the tweet is a way to give credit and build a networking relationship with other Twitter users. Hashtags (#) create a way to develop keywords and threads of messages. Yet, Tweetbots can manipulate the democratic nature of Twitter. These automated computer systems can generate large volumes of tweets from a range of addresses, making it seem like an idea is "trending" or a popular item even though it is coming from only a few central sources (#CommonCore, 2017).

Behavioral Economics

The emerging field of *behavioral economics* examines how individuals make irrational decisions. Previous assumptions that humans are inherently rational are not proving to be true. Instead, individuals tend to make skewed decisions and these skewed choices have patterns that can be identified. Drawing on economics and psychology, behavioral economists study how humans are "predictably irrational" over and over again (Ariely, 2008). Rather than acting rationally, predicting options and following a best possible course of action, individuals systematically repeated irrational behaviors.

People often have little idea about how much they like, or how to value, goods and experiences (Lowenstein, 2014). Individuals assess risk markedly differently than the real dangers. Individuals also gain satisfaction from revenge even when it damages people materially (Wheelan, 2011).

Ariely's (2008) bestselling book, *Predictably Irrational*, describes his years of experiments documenting how forces, such as emotions and cultural norms, influence individual behavior, and how humans underestimate the influence of these forces on our decision making.

Applying these concepts to policy, Thaler and Sunstein (2008, p. 3) talk about how individuals can play the role of *choice architect*. These individuals can selectively organize and present information to help to influence the choices that individuals make. Such decisions could be made on ethical grounds of the best interests of the individuals or financial grounds of how to make the most money.

People also tend to make decisions based on personal experience rather than what the research tells them. For example, recent research on charter schools (see Chapter 11) shows decision makers will ignore strong research showing limited effects of charter schools in favor of local success (Scott et al., 2017).

Steady Work and Punctuated Equilibrium

The process of change has been characterized as slow and difficult most of the time. A famous piece by Elmore and McLaughlin (1988) calls this process "steady work." Policy problems are chronic rather than acute; the process of change is slow and difficult. Educational problems are rarely solved but instead evolve (McLaughlin, 1987). Often this slower change is for the best, because disruptive change can damage a system more often than help it (Meyer & Rowan, 1977).

Making changes in a stable system requires maintaining a "systems orientation" (McLaughlin, 1991, p. 154). Teachers need support, such as time, training, and coaching. Removing constraints such as poor equipment and faulty facilities is not enough—it is necessary to focus on schoolwide enablers as well, such as a shared mission, feedback structures, and schoolwide goals.

Despite the steady work of policy, change can occur and in great bursts. The policy window helps us to understand how policies can happen in bursts rather than incrementally. The concept of *punctuated equilibrium* also helps. The term is defined as a change model in which a policy system is mostly change averse—change rarely occurs. The long view of public policy development is not one of gradual adjustment but episodic and disjointed bursts of change (Baumgartner & Jones, 1993). When change occurs, many contexts change all at once.

Originally derived from the research of evolutionary biologists Niles Eldredge and Stephen Jay Gould (1972), the concept of punctuated equilibrium does not view change as "steady work" (Elmore and McLaughlin, 1988) or as incremental change that involves a slow muddling through (Lindblom, 1959). Instead, the overall picture of the policy environment is resistant to change and exists in relative stasis. Stasis in the policy world can be envisioned as gridlock and incrementalism (Kelly, 1994; McLendon & Cohen-Vogel, 2008). Often during such times of stasis or lack of change, policy decision making does not occur in grand fashion but more quietly at the subsystem level of each of the branches of government (Baumgartner & Jones, 1993).

During periods of *incremental change*, policy makers adjust the status quo in limited, reversible ways (Lindblom, 1959). In an entrenched system of opposition, groups seek to gain and regain political advantage, much like a pendulum slightly swinging back and forth in a self-correcting system. This tough-to-change system leads to self-correcting counter-moves that create a dynamic equilibrium (Baumgartner & Jones, 1993). Research from the field of improvement science increased the use of the idea of "rapid-change" cycles to the work of educational reform. Discussed in greater detail in Chapter 9, the idea of smaller efforts in greater quantity, assuming many will fail and some will succeed, is one effort to counteract this strong tendency toward stasis and stability in educational systems.

Incremental drift and periods of stability can end suddenly and dramatically. Change when it does occur is sudden, abrupt, and dramatic. It can even be considered revolutionary. The rare moments of dramatic change create equilibrium in which gridlock monopolies are challenged or overthrown (Baumgartner & Jones, 1993). For example, the 1960s is a recent time in history of great social and political change in which many policies and systems changed all at once.

Public Idea

When shifting public opinion or drawing attention to a policy, a public idea is created. A *public idea* is a concept that has captured the attention of policy makers and the public. Mark Moore (1988) explains that public ideas help to shape the way in which the public discusses a policy problem. In creating an idea, evidence is selectively used to create a vision of the problem, often in new and innovative ways that hold the attention of the public.

Often a problem is framed with the solution of "Who can we blame?" (Rosen, 2009). While politicians seek allies in a problem, they may also seek to create enemies to galvanize emotion around an issue. By creating villains and scapegoats, the emotion of outrage and anger can increase public support and pressure to encourage political action on an issue.

Box 6.3 The Rhetoric of *A Nation at Risk*

The famous report *A Nation at Risk*, published in 1983 by the U.S. Department of Education (National Commission on Excellence in Education, 1982), sought to galvanize concern for education in the United States. The report used rhetoric such as, "If an unfriendly foreign power had attempted to impose on America the mediocre educational performance that exists today, we might as well have viewed it as an act of war." During the Cold War, the report blamed schools as one of the reasons that the United States might not be keeping up with the Soviets. The publication sought to evoke fear and concern and to shift the perspective of U.S. schools from doing well to failing to compete with other nations. The report built upon fear and suspicion to create doubts about the successes of U.S. schools, despite subsequent research that failed to align the rhetoric of failing schools with evidence from school performance (Berliner & Biddle, 1995).

● ● ● ● ●

Framing a Problem

Creating public interest in a problem focuses greatly on the craft of policy making (Majone, 1989), as discussed earlier. While the world faces a myriad of problems at any given time, the policy world simplifies this list to a handful of ideas at any time. People filter the information and experiences that they receive to create order and logic about the world that they see. By creating scripts (Goffman, 1978), symbols (Rosen, 2009; Stone, 1998), and patterns, humans give meaning to their lives. Policy making builds out of this meaning-making process.

In Figure 6.2, any problem could lead to a range of public ideas, and each public idea could lead to a range of policy solutions. The choices are often based upon the creativity of the policy makers as well as the contexts of the time.

Scripts are created so that we do not have to exert conscious effort for repeated patterns of behavior. For example, when we drive to a familiar place

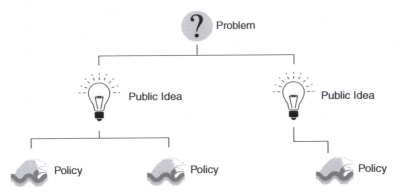

Figure 6.2 Policy Wave Amplification. Adapted from Baumgartner and Jones (1993, p. 16).

but don't remember getting there or we engage in the routine of getting ready in the morning, we are often not fully present in our experiences. These scripts help to ease the processing of our brain.

When translated into policy, some policies seek to institutionalize social status, including legitimizing some groups and delegitimizing others (Rosen, 2009). For example, the Defense of Marriage Act in 1996 sought to define marriage as one man, one woman and, in the process, delegitimized the status of LGBTQ communities by preventing same-sex couples from acquiring the status of marriage. Another example is the set of federal and state laws known as "Megan's Law" enacted in 1994 and soon after. These pieces of legislation created rules in which sex offenders must register with local officials and sought to strengthen the criminalization of sex offenders as a lifetime status.

Box 6.4 Stereotyping in the Famous Blue Eyes/Brown Eyes Experiment

These scripts can also lead to prejudice and bias when we categorize individuals and groups (Stone, 1998), such as a famous experiment in which a teacher, Jane Elliot, treats children differently based on eye color. The teacher developed the exercise to help to explain to students why Martin Luther Kind was assasinated. The teacher decided that experiencing racism would be more powerful than talking about it. Within a day of separating children based on eye color, the children started treating one another differently, giving privilege to one eye color and creating stigma for the other eye color. The experiment helped to teach what happens when we stereotype and stigmatize.

Rosen discusses this categorization as a *constitutive* aspect of policy. It is work that creates or changes meaning. Symbols can also create social action and incite change, including politics of representation. Symbols are the focal point of the argument and persuasion that frame public ideas. They simplify a concept and in doing so can develop and sustain a public idea. Rhetorical devices in policy making often depend heavily on metaphor. Some words focus on danger, such as slippery slope, wedge, financial cliff. Others focus on disease, such as dying cities, urban blight. The use of numbers and data can also provide a strong anchor to draw attention to an idea. Numbers make an idea feel "valid" and "real." They can clarify; they can also mislead and confuse. Visual symbols include the use of famous spokespeople. Still photos and video clips, such as first responders rescuing victims, children as signs of hope, and examples of bravery and of corruption, can dramatically change and sustain public opinion.

The most compelling public ideas diagnose what is already present in innovative ways, such as history and social relations (Majone, 1989; Moore, 1988). They respect existing ideas and yet also manage to provide a new, innovative way of presenting a longstanding problem so that the public is willing to discuss it anew.

Symbols can be especially compelling in education policy because of the role of education as the nation's cultural faith. The public nature of education and the universal experience of schools also increase the ability of the average citizen to understand and feel engaged, and even feel like an expert on the topic. Since Horace Mann at the turn of the twentieth century, education has been purported to serve as the great equalizer that can take a person from rags to riches. Whether or not it is true in fact, this purpose of education has shaped strategy for addressing a myriad of social problems, including child poverty and the assimilation of immigrants. Schools have become a focal point for improving society in large part due to this symbol of education as the savior of all.

Education, therefore, is a source of a great deal of public ideas and symbolism. The focus of education as a symbol highlights the expressive role of policy (Rosen, 2009). Competing goals embedded in these symbols include individual attainment, promoting democracy, cultivating the talents of individuals, and meeting the needs of disadvantaged groups.

Policy Entrepreneurs

Key to the success of idea-based policy making is *policy entrepreneurs.* These actors in the policy system promote innovation. They can sculpt compelling symbols out of words and visual images. Others have strong and deep networks to help a policy idea diffuse quickly (McDonnell, 2007).

Greater involvement in policy networks improved the likelihood of getting on a policy agenda (Mintrom & Vergari, 1998). The external networks of advocates from other states increased the likelihood of education policy ideas grasping the issue attention phase of policy making. However, the ideas of neighboring states did not influence the likelihood of legislative approval. Once on the agenda, legislative approval was more likely influenced by internal networks of support, such as the support of teachers' unions.

The activities of neighboring policy actors and governments can also influence getting a policy on the agenda. At the state-level, "gate keepers" control the agenda and confer great advantages in shaping policy outcomes (Cobb & Elder, 1983, cited in Cohen-Vogel & Ingle, 2007). Cohen-Vogel and Ingle (2007) studied policy adoption and diffusion across state contexts. They found that the influence of neighboring states is most pronounced during the agenda-setting policy phase and much less so as the policy moves toward the adoption phase.

Timing

Public ideas can come at any point in the policy process. They help to focus attention onto a new problem. They can also help to justify a solution that has been developed for a longstanding problem. In creating an idea, alternative problems and frames of problems are then kept off the agenda as well.

Public ideas might come before a problem is on the agenda. *Softening up* is a process of introducing ideas once unthinkable. But over time with consistent repetition, and the help of symbolism and persistence, the public starts to consider them feasible. The removal of the teaching of evolution in science classrooms and the development of creationist science is an example.

Box 6.5 Case Study: What is the Purpose of School Lunches?

The National School Lunch Program (NSLP) provides hot meals to the majority of public school students across the United States, serving 31 million children each day in 2012 (United States Department of Agriculture, 2013). The lunches must meet nutrition standards published by the U.S. Department of Agriculture (USDA). The government subsidizes the lunches for low-income students, who can purchase lunch at a reduced cost or get a free lunch based on their parents' income levels. The federal program, run through the USDA, also helps to relieve farmers of surplus meat, vegetables, and fruit to needy children. Some schools also provide breakfast and after-school snacks.

The lunch program has become a focus of many policy goals, and childhood obesity has drawn the lunch program into the spotlight since the George W. Bush administration. Nearly one-third (31.3 percent) of children aged 10–17 are overweight or obese (State of Obesity, 2017). The Secretary of Agriculture under Bush, Ann Veneman, was quoted as saying that most of the eating done by children is not at schools and "the bulk of the eating decisions, or the buying, is done by the parents" (Gersema, 2003).

The USDA under the Bush administration claimed that the NSLP was not making kids more obese. During the Obama administration, Michelle Obama's Let's Move Program targeted childhood obesity and issued a recommendation that the quality of food should be improved in schools, including a need to update the nutritional standards. This change led to the passage of the Healthy, Hunger-Free Kids Act in 2010, which led to new standards for food sold in schools for the first time in 30 years, including requirements for more servings of fruits, vegetables, and whole grains, a decrease in sodium and sugar, and a ban on trans-fats, as well as labelling requirements giving the number of calories in foods (Johnson, 2016).

While the Physicians Committee for Responsible Medicine argues that school lunch is partly to blame for young people being overweight during the Bush administration, citing fatty and unhealthy food choices like chicken nuggets and pepperoni pizza (Gersema, 2003), it was also felt that the Let's Move Campaign did not do enough on limiting consumption of cheese, meat, and grains (Johnson, 2016).

The National Pork Producers Council (NPPC) views this take as an attack on meat. They have stated that increasing research is showing the value of meat in the diet because of the high protein levels. The NPPC has suggested that pork entrees are being served and still meeting nutritional goals. They also recommend that the USDA extends the use of commodities to include low-fat pork products for breakfast since they are a good source of protein (Vansickle, 2003).

The Food Research and Action Center (FRAC) is a non-profit organization focusing on eradicating hunger and undernutrition. Expanding the school lunch program has been one of the key strategies urged by FRAC to help to address undernutrition and hunger in the United States. Rather than attacking the lunch program as the cause of obesity, FRAC has suggested that the main problem is fast foods, super-sized portions, and cheap snack foods (Gersema, 2003). Blaming the food industry has been exacerbated by movies such as *Super Size Me* (2004), which documented the changes in Director Morgan Spurlock's body when he subsisted only on food from McDonald's for a month. The food companies and fast food restaurants in turn blame individuals who have chosen not to exercise and are choosing to overeat.

Choose one of the following roles:

Ann Veneman, USDA secretary under George Bush
Michelle Obama, founder of the Let's Move Program
Physicians Committee for Responsible Medicine
National Pork Producers Council
Food Research Action Center
McDonald's
High school student
High school parent

Given the documented problems with childhood obesity, how would your group/person frame the problem?

1. What are the reasons for this problem?
2. Who is to blame?
3. What policy recommendations would your group/person make to solve the problem?
4. What allies might you make with other groups/people?
5. What types of solutions are the most easily passed?

● ● ● ● ●

Comprehension Questions

■ What is the difference between defining a problem and the subsequent formation of a public idea?

■ How does the field of behavioral economics help to explain the lack of rationality in the policy process?

■ How does the concept of punctuated equilibrium explain big changes in political systems? What is an example of punctuated equilibrium? How does the example demonstrate the core ideas?

●●●●●

Discussion Questions

■ We have seen in the previous chapter how Majone talks about creativity in the policy process. Choose a current policy issue and identify the ways that creativity influenced the development of the public idea.

■ Choose a current policy and apply the Kingdon policy windows framework to it. Identify the political, alternative, and agenda streams of your chosen policy.

●●●●●

Activities

■ Organize a National Issues Forum discussion on the topic of "What is the twenty-first-century mission for our public schools?" The three positions are: prepare students for the workplace; prepare students to be active and responsible citizens; help students to discover and develop their talents.
Find on the web using the following search terms:

> *preparing-todays-kids-tomorrows-jobs; NIFI*

●●●●●

Further Reading

#CommonCore. (2017). *The Evolution of Social Media in Politics.* Retrieved from: www.hashtagcommoncore.com/#0-2.

Ariely, D. (2008). *Predictably Irrational.* New York: HarperCollins.

Baumgartner, F. & Jones, B. (1993). *Agendas and Instability in American Politics.* Chicago, IL: University of Chicago Press.

Kingdon, J. W. (1984). *Agendas, Alternatives, and Public Policies* (Vol. 45). Boston, MA: Little, Brown.

Majone, G. (1989). *Evidence, Argument, and Persuasion in the Policy Process.* New Haven, CT: Yale University Press.

March, J. G. & Olsen, J. P. (1986). Garbage can models of decision making in organizations. In March, J. G. & Weissinger-Baylon, R. (eds.) *Ambiguity and Command* (pp. 11–35). Marshfield, MA: Pitman Publishing.

Moore, M. (1988). What sort of ideas become public ideas? In Reich, R. (ed.) *The Power of Public Ideas* (pp. 55–84). Cambridge, MA: Ballinger Publishing Company.

Rosen, L. (2009). Rhetoric and symbolic action in the policy process. In Sykes, G., Schneider, B., & Plank, D. (eds.) *Handbook of Education Policy Research* (pp. 267–85). New York: Routledge.

● ● ● ● ●

Reference List

#CommonCore. (2017). *The Evolution of Social Media in Politics*. Retrieved from: www.hashtagcommoncore.com/#0-2.

Ariely, D. (2008). *Predictably Irrational*. New York: HarperCollins.

Baumgartner, F. & Jones, B. (1993). *Agendas and Instability in American Politics*. Chicago, IL: University of Chicago Press.

Berliner, D. C. & Biddle, B. J. (1995). *The Manufactured Crisis: Myths, Fraud, and the Attack on America's Public Schools*. Reading, MA: Addison-Wesley.

Boullianne, S. (2015). Social media use and participation: A meta-analysis of current research. *Information, Communication, & Society, 18*(5), 523–38.

Castillo, E., Lalonde, P., Owens, S., DeBray, E., Scott, J., & Lubienski, C. (2015). E-advocacy among intermediary organizations: Brokering knowledge through blogs. Paper presented at the annual meeting of the American Educational Research Association, Chicago, IL, April.

Cochran, C., Mayer, L., Carr, T., & Cayer, N. (1982). *American Public Policy: An Introduction*. New York: St. Martin's Press.

Cochran, C. E., Mayer, L. C., Carr, T. R., & Cayer, N. J. (1986). *American Public Policy*. New York: St. Martins Press.

Cohen-Vogel, L. & Ingle, W. K. (2007). When neighbors matter most: Innovation, diffusion and state policy adoption in tertiary education. *Journal of Education Policy, 22*(3), 241–62.

Defense of Marriage Act (DOMA) Pub. L. 104–199, 110 Stat. 2419, enacted September 21, 1996, 1 U.S.C. § 7 and 28 U.S.C. § 1738C.

Downs, A. (1972). Up and down with ecology: The issue attention cycle. *Public Interest, 20*, 39–50.

Dunn, W. (1994). *Public Policy Analysis: An Introduction*. Englewood Cliffs, NJ: Prentice Hall.

Eldredge N. & Gould, S. J. (1972). Punctuated equilibria: An alternative to phyletic gradualism. In Schopf, T. (ed.) *Models in Paleobiology* (pp. 82–115). San Francisco, CA: Freeman, Copper and Company.

Elmore, R. F. & McLaughlin, M. W. (1988). *Steady Work. Policy, Practice, and the Reform of American Education*. Santa Monica, CA: The RAND Corporation.

Gersema, E. (2003). Don't blame school lunches for overweight kids, says agriculture secretary. *Wall Street Journal*, January 11.

Goffman, E. (1978). *The Presentation of Self in Everyday Life*. Harmondsworth: Penguin Books.

Johnson, S. (2016). Gauging the public health value of Michelle Obama's "Let's Move" Campaign. *Modern Healthcare*. Retrieved from: www.modernhealthcare.com/article/20160823/NEWS/160829986.

Kelly, S. Q. (1994). Punctuated changes and the era of divided government. In Dodd, L. & Jillison, C. (eds.) *New Perspectives on American Politics* (pp. 162–90). Washington, DC: Congressional Quarterly Press.

Kingdon, J. W. (1984). *Agendas, Alternatives, and Public Policies* (Vol. 45). Boston, MA: Little, Brown.

Kofod, K., Seashore Louis, K., Moos, L., & van Velzen, B. (2012). Historical perspectives on educational policy and political cultures. In Seashore Louis, K. & van Velzen, B.

(eds.) *Educational Policy in an International Context: Political Culture and Its Effects* (pp. 29–48). New York: Palgrave Macmillan.

Lindblom, C. E. (1959). The science of "muddling through". *Public Administration Review, 19*(2), 79–88.

Lowenstein, G. (2014). Foreword, In Samson, A. (ed.) *The Behavioral Economics Guide.* Retrieved from: www.behavioraleconomics.com.

Majone, G. (1989). *Evidence, Argument, and Persuasion in the Policy Process.* New Haven, CT: Yale University Press.

March, J. G. & Olsen, J. P. (1986). Garbage can models of decision making in organizations. In March, J. G. & Weissinger-Baylon, R. (eds.) *Ambiguity and Command* (pp. 11–35). Marshfield, MA: Pitman Publishing.

Mazzoni, T. L. (1991). Analyzing state school policymaking: An arena model. *Educational Evaluation and Policy Analysis, 13*(2), 115–38.

McDonnell, L. (2007). The politics of education: Influencing policy and beyond. In Fuhrman, S., Cohen, D., & Mosher, F. (eds.) *The State of Education Policy Research* (pp. 19–40). Mahwah, NJ: Lawrence Erlbaum Associates.

McLaughlin, M. W. (1987). Learning from experience: Lessons from policy implementation. *Educational Evaluation and Policy Analysis, 9*(2), 171–8.

McLaughlin, M. W. (1990). The RAND change agent study revisited: Macro perspectives and micro realities. *Educational Researcher, 19*(9), 11–16.

McLaughlin, M. W. (1991). The RAND change agent study: Ten years later. In Odden, A. R. (ed.) *The Evolution of Education Policy Implementation* (pp. 143–56). Albany, NY: State University of New York Press.

McLendon, M. K. & Cohen-Vogel, L. (2008). Understanding education policy change in the American states: Lessons from political science. In Cooper, B. S., Cibulka, J. G., & Fusarelli, L. D. (eds.) *Handbook of Education Politics and Policy* (pp. 30–51). New York: Routledge.

Meyer, J. W. & Rowan, B. (1977). Institutionalized organizations: Formal structure as myth and ceremony. *American Journal of Sociology, 83*(2), 340–63.

Mintrom, M. & Vergari, S. (1998). Policy networks and innovation diffusion: The case of state education reforms. *The Journal of Politics, 60*(01), 126–48.

Moore, M. (1988). What sort of ideas become public ideas? In Reich, R. (ed.) *The Power of Public Ideas* (pp. 55–84). Cambridge, MA: Ballinger Publishing Company.

National Commission on Excellence in Education. (1983). *A Nation at Risk: The Imperative of Educational Reform.* Washington, DC: U.S. Government Printing Office.

Olssen, M., Codd, J., & O'Neill, A. M. (2004). *Education Policy: Globalization, Citizenship, Democracy.* London: Sage.

Rosen, L. (2009). Rhetoric and symbolic action in the policy process. In Sykes, G., Schneider, B., & Plank, D. (eds.) *Handbook of Education Policy Research* (pp. 267–85). New York: Routledge.

Scott, J., DeBray, E., Lubienski, C., La Londe, P. G., Castillo, E., & Owens, S. (2017). Urban regimes, intermediary networks, and research use: Patterns across three school districts. *Peabody Journal of Education, 92*, 16–28.

Spurlock, M. (2004). *Super Size Me.* Samuel Goldwyn Films.

State of Obesity. (2017). *Fast Facts.* Trust for America's Health and the Robert Wood Johnson Foundation. Retrieved from: www. stateofobesity.org/childhood.

Statista. (2017). Number of monthly active Twitter users worldwide from 1st quarter 2010 to 1st quarter 2017 (in millions). Retrieved from: www.statista.com/statistics/282087/number-of-monthly-active-twitter-users/.

Stone, D. (1998). *Policy Paradox: The Art of Political Decision Making.* New York: Addison-Wesley Longman.

Talbert, J. E. & McLaughlin, M. W. (1994). Teacher professionalism in local school contexts. *American Journal of Education, 102*(2), 123–53.

Thaler, R. & Sunstein, C. (2008). *Nudge: Improving Decisions about Health, Wealth, and Happiness.* New Haven, CT: Yale University Press.

United States Department of Agriculture. (2013). *National School Lunch Program Fact Sheet.* Retrieved from: www.fns.usda.gov/sites/default/files/NSLPFactSheet.pdf.

Vansickle, J. (2003). Pork's school lunch value. *National Hog Farmer.* Retrieved from: www.nationalhogfarmer.com/news/farming_porks_school_lunch.

Wedell-Weddellsborg, T. (2017). Are you solving the right problems? *Harvard Business Review*, January/February. Retrieved from: https://hbr.org/2017/01/are-you-solving-the-right-problems.

Wheelan, C. J. (2011). *Introduction to Public Policy.* New York: W. W. Norton & Company.

7

●●●●●

Policy Formation

This chapter considers what happens during the drafting and passing of legislation. It focuses on the intersection of policy instruments and target populations, including how power influences options in the political process.

The construction of policy is a lesson in incentives and punishment. Most policies either encourage positive behavior or discourage negative behavior. A common metaphor used to describe this difference is of training a donkey. Either we can dangle a carrot in front of him to encourage him to move forward or use a stick from behind to punish him if he does not move.

It should be mentioned, though, that not all policy decisions are driven by a clear and immediate outcome. Some policy efforts are a result of political compromises that end up in policy outcomes that no one desired. Sometimes they are steps toward a bigger goal, much like moves in a chess game. For example, the No Child Left Behind Act (2001), discussed in detail in Chapter 1, required all states to develop assessment systems to measure whether students could reach a proficient score. The percentage of students receiving proficient scores had to increase every year, and after ten years, *all* students had to be proficient—an impossible feat. The most cynical critics believed that this strict mandate was designed to fail—a way to show that public schools are not up to the challenge. If public schools cannot meet the standards set for them, then policy space might be created for alternatives, such as privatization and vouchers.

Box 7.1 Riding the Subway in Sweden

The monitoring of mandates relates to cultural values in a society. The United States possesses within it an individualistic culture that seeks to "buck the system" (Steers, Nardon, & Sanchez-Runde, 2013, pp. 60–6). It means that often in U.S. society, people tend to enjoy finding ways to figure out the loopholes to get out of mandates, and therefore monitoring is an even greater cost. I notice this difference most greatly when I travel to other nations such as Sweden and Japan, where cultural cohesion is generally more stable, due to a more homogenous population and a shared societal value of fraternity rather than individualism. Thinking of the security in place to enter the subway system in New York City or Washington DC, I was quite surprised to find that in Stockholm, Sweden, many stations have no gates or barricades to enter the subway. The ticket booth is off to the side and it is expected that all will buy a ticket. Monitors occasionally patrol the system to ensure compliance. But for the most part, passengers do comply. When I asked fellow subway travelers why everyone complied and paid instead of "trying to get away with it," most Swedes seemed puzzled by the question. They spoke of it being in everyone's interest to follow the rules and pay for a ticket. Otherwise, they would all be subjected to greater inconvenience of higher subway fares to pay for the monitoring, the inconvenience of barricades, and that lack of civility and respect for one another.

●●●●●

Policy Tools

Policy tools can set the tone and design of policy and can punish or reward. They can also realign systems. McDonnell and Elmore (1987) introduced the concept with a discussion of mandates, inducements, systems changing, and capacity building, as noted in Table 7.1. Hortatory strategies (McDonnell, 1994) will also be discussed in this chapter. One written policy might contain many policy tools or just one.

In policy language, punishments are often described as *mandates,* or "sticks." These types of policies place a sanction, rule, or other method of force intended to create a stigma about something and to punish those who do not obey. The punishments could be minor, such as a loss of privileges and opportunity, public shaming/loss of status, and fines. They can even be as drastic as jail and death, depending on how strongly the idea within the policy aligns with public values.

An assumption of mandates is that the public must be forced to do something that they would not otherwise do, and that it is worth the energy, money, and political capital to force behavior in this manner. Mandates are often the most expensive policy tool because of the cost of monitoring and enforcement necessary to monitor compliance of mandates.

The consequences must be strong enough for people to fear them and obey the mandate. Consequences make people pay attention. Mandates force a focus on that policy over others. Educational leaders face a stream of unending demands from local, state, and federal levels. These leaders are given too many rules and mandates to possibly follow all of them—a key problem with the public policy process. Part of this discretion is discerning what matters effectively. Successful leaders will naturally follow any mandates that align with their own values—they share a will to follow the policy. For other issues for which they do not see the merit for themselves or their schools, administrators must make strategic decisions on what demands must be addressed. Successful administrators learn how to discern which mandates will actually be monitored and which will not. For example, if principals are told that they must develop a database to track all students on multiple measures, and the principal does not find value for her school in such a system, the sanctions for not completing this task must be clear to her in order for it to rise above the many other priorities.

Table 7.1 Policy Typologies

	Elements	Optimal Effects	Costs	Advantages	Examples
Mandates	Rules	Consent	Enforcement	Benefits to individuals and society	Traffic laws EPA regulations
Incentives	Money	Create value with short-term returns	Oversight	Control of funds and direct value to individuals	Block grants EnergyStar rebates
Capacity Building	Long-term investment	Enhance latent abilities	Short-term investment	Long-term impact across society	Historical preservation Foundational research
System Change	Change in authority	Increased effectiveness	Power shift causes instability and resistance	New pathways for policy development	Energy deregulation School vouchers
Hortatory	Informative Uses symbolism Appeals to values	Targets audience motivated to act	Communication	Bypasses gridlock in the direct policy process	First Lady Laura Bush's effort to promote reading

Source: Adapted from McDonnell and Elmore (1987 p. 137), McDonnell (1994), and Fowler (2013).

Another example is ignoring parking tickets on a university campus. In a case where the parking office is a university office, it does not always have authority to impound a car or otherwise enforce payment. Faculty members have been known to stack the parking tickets on their dashboards rather than pay them, because there is no mechanism to enforce the mandate. Faculty cannot lose their jobs for ignoring the rule.

Mandates assume that the behavior and values in question are worthy of public scorn. Relatedly, they assume that individuals cannot be encouraged to do the right thing, and therefore they must be punished when they do the wrong thing (Schneider & Ingram, 1990). This distinction could be cultural, such as the individualistic nature of Americans making it difficult to have unmonitored systems, such as the subway discussed above. They also could be related to power, such as professors not paying for parking tickets because they could not be fired.

Incentives or *inducements* are policy tools that encourage positive behavior, often money or privileges. Recipients receive rewards such as grants, tax breaks, and public acknowledgement. Incentives require that encouragement is enough to change behavior. It may be that people really want to change the behavior and just need an opportunity to do so, or it might be that the reward is so great that they change their behaviors even if they do not want to do so. Alternatively, if the reward is not great enough, it might not be perceived as worth the effort to change one's behavior. This policy tool works best when it is designed such that people are aware of the opportunities available to them. They have adequate information and the capacity to understand how to maximize the benefit of the policy. The incentive also must be substantial enough to make the change required (Schneider & Ingram, 1990).

Capacity-building policy tools are a provision of support in terms of money, training, and services. They are designed when incentives/inducements are preferred, but that target population is not able yet to do what the policy wants them to do. They might lack training, infrastructure, or knowledge. It is assumed that the policy target has the will to enact the idea behind the policy but they lack the skills to do so. Examples of capacity-building strategies include providing professional development for teachers and offering money through incentive grants to encourage schools to buy new technology.

As with incentives, capacity-building policy design must be enticing enough for participants to want to participate. Either the idea is compelling and people are just seeking whatever training they can, or the training and investment is big enough that people are willing to learn about something that they otherwise would not do. The training and opportunity then need to be compelling enough to change viewpoints to ensure that the change might endure beyond the policy itself. Participants also need the resources to participate (Schneider & Ingram, 1990). Hidden or uncovered costs of participation must be considered as they impact ability to participate, as they should for incentive policies.

Systems-changing policies are a very different type of policy tool. They allow for the transfer of governance or authority from one organization, agency, or individual to another. Rather than punishing or rewarding behavior, these tools seek to change structural arrangements of a policy. An example of system changes is the creation of a cabinet level position on Homeland Security after 9/11. With a mission of focusing on security, anti-terrorism, immigration, cyber security, and disasters, the new department consolidated the work occurring in several cabinet departments, including Treasury (U.S. Secret Service; Customs), Justice (Immigration and Naturalization Service; Office for Domestic Prepared- ness; Domestic Energy Support Teams, National Infrastructure FBI), Agriculture (Animal and Plant Inspection; Animal Disease Center), Transportation (Coast Guard; Transportation Security Administration), Energy (Nuclear Incident Response Team; Countermeasures Programs; Energy Security), Defense (National Communication Systems; National Biological Warfare Defense Ana- lysis), Health and Human Service (Strategical National Stockpile; National Dis- aster), General Services Administration (Federal Computer Incident Response Center, and the Federal Emergency Management Agency).

Sometimes this systems-changing strategy is aimed at increasing efficiency, such as folding two structures together that do similar work. It could also be to reduce conflict caused by political or ideological changes, or on a positive note, to recognize synergies that have occurred conceptually. For example, in Penn- sylvania, former Governor Rendell sought to create a new position in the Penn- sylvania executive branch that sought to bridge the Department of Education and Health to address early education (birth to age five). Since preschools are not a public system, they are located in the Health and Public Welfare part of the government, while the rest of the school systems are in the Education department. The governor hoped that a person could provide a structural bridge between the two systems to help to coordinate and encourage alignment and innovation for birth to five learning.

Other times systems changes occur when we do not know how to solve a problem, but it looks like we are "doing something." Reconstitution of failing schools can fit under this category. Research indicates that we know little about how to turn around a failing school, and especially at the high school level. The idea of "closing" a school and opening it up again the next year in the same place, with the same students, but with different administrators and teachers is an example of a systems-changing policy that rarely leads to better results, but is a dramatic example of "doing something."

Hortatory strategies are rhetorical policy devices used by governmental offi- cials who have the power to express opinions that can sway public opinion and potentially other governmental units (McDonnell, 1994). Sometimes considered the "bully pulpit" the president, governors, and other influential politicians can use their status to make speeches to sway public opinion. Governmental agen- cies can also publish reports. The famous Department of Education report *A Nation at Risk* (National Commission on Excellence in Education, 1983), for example, used inflammatory language to reshape public opinion to believe that the educational system was in crisis.

Hortatory tools are often used when gridlock or political opposition prevents stronger policy channels from being used. If a president can't get legislation passed through Congress, he can still hold a press conference to raise awareness about issues, as well as issue reports from the executive branch and host White House conferences to discuss issues of importance.

Hortatory tools are also often used in areas in which you cannot force people to change, such as parenting behaviors. We cannot force parents to read to their children or to feed their children healthier foods, but we can engage in public relationship campaigns to encourage such behaviors. The question is, does a movie star on a commercial encourage someone to change their behavior? In an hortatory device, the person must be influential enough to cause the public to reflect and consider new ideas. Oprah Winfrey is an example of a public figure who has great influence among a portion of women especially. This policy strategy aligns closely with key principles from advertising and public relations. The more compelling the message, the more enticing or memorable the visual and rhetorical devices, the more impact it might have.

In times of policy alignment, a state or federal legislature might pass a series of individual laws with the intent of a bigger vision of change. This broader vision can be considered *metapolicy*.

Box 7.2 Case Study of Metapolicy

Janet Chrispeels (1997) wrote of such a process that occurred in California in the 1990s. The example provides a way to understand how policy messages with a coherent, consistent, long-term vision can have a greater impact on change. The California legislature oversaw the passage of several pieces of educational legislation aimed at coherent education policy. The legislation included laws about: curriculum frameworks, textbook selection, subject matter reform, assessment, and charter school legislation, among other issues. This vision of educational change required an alignment of viewpoint of the governor, legislature, and Department of Education. According to Chrispeels, this successful development of metapolicy allowed for legislation with a range of policy tools to offer layers of reinforcing messages. The variation of policy tools also helped to leverage pressure and support across the system, with a special focus on multiple instances of capacity building to provide training and shared understanding of the legislation.

This California example also draws upon the value of bottom-up policy reform. Bottom-up policy presumes that the implementers of policy possess wisdom and knowledge essential for policy to work effectively. Policy is thus written loosely to allow for agency for local-level actors to influence the design, implementation, and enforcement of policy. Teachers and administrators are involved in framework development, textbook selection, program quality reviews, subject matter projects, school restructuring, networks, and piloting class. Recursivity, or mutual learning, between policy makers and local educators provided symbiotic sources of learning and professionalism throughout the legislative and implementation process.

By drawing on networks of teacher leaders and administrators to help to design the legislation and building in multiple opportunities for these educators to provide feedback during the development and substantive implementation (see Chapter 4), the policy system built capacity and support of the ideas behind the change process.

● ● ● ● ●

Policy Targets

Policy design is not just a matter of tools but also who the target of the policy is. Schneider and Ingram (1993) provide a compelling framework for considering how social perception and power of individuals can affect how policy is designed.

As Table 7.2 indicates, the Schneider and Ingram framework is a grid based on two axes. The horizontal axis consists of the social construction of the target population—do we as a society have a positive or negative impression of this group? Do we discriminate against this category of people or offer extra favors and the benefit of the doubt? The purpose of this framework is not to question the bias inherent in our policy system but rather to make the bias explicit as a way to understand how it impacts policy design. For example, we as a society tend to think favorably regarding mothers, children, the elderly, the military, scientists, and business people. We tend to think disparagingly about other groups, and we are much more uncomfortable talking about when we do not think highly about groups. But categories of people who have been viewed as unfavorable include the very wealthy and the very poor, drug addicts, Muslim Americans, immigrants, gangs, unions, and even youth.

The vertical spectrum of this framework focuses on people who have power in our society, based on money and social status. Some people have power regardless of who is in office, such as people who vote more (including the elderly) and people with lots of money and influence, such as business people. Other people have power and influence based on who is in office. When a Democrat is president or the Democrats hold the majority in the House and Senate, for example, unions and cultural elites might have greater influence and receive more policy benefits. When Republicans are in power in the legislative or executive, wealthy business owners and key members of the religious right might have greater influence.

Table 7.2 includes a few examples of people that fit each quadrant of the grid. People with high social construction and high power are considered *Advantaged* in this framework, including scientists and the elderly. The people in this category tend to receive inducements more than others, and perhaps more than they truly deserve—a direct provision of resources, training, and knowledge. Little regulation is built into policy targeted at these groups because of high societal trust. When punishment must occur, it is much less than deserved often and tends to focus on "standards" and "charges" rather than stigma (Schneider & Ingram, 1993). These policy decisions are justified with the arguments that they are instrumental in nature—helping these target populations benefits everyone, according to the commonly held views in a society. These viewpoints include the beliefs that scientists find cures to societal problems. Business officials keep our economy strong. The military protects our nation.

Table 7.2 Social Constructions and Political Power

		CONSTRUCTIONS	
		Positive	Negative
POWER	Strong	**Advantaged** Examples: Elderly, business, scientists Tools: Inducements and capacity building Justification: Benefits the public good	**Contenders** Examples: Unions, the Christian Right Tools: Hidden inducements, limited and overly symbolic mandates Justification: Hidden, try not to discuss
	Weak	**Dependents** Examples: Children, mothers Tools: Capacity building and mandates/use of authority Justification: Justice oriented (equality and equity) and paternalistic	**Deviants** Examples: Criminals, gangs Tools: Mandates and limited capacity building Justification: Public safety

Source: Adapted from Schneider and Ingram (1993, p. 336).

The other quadrant easiest to understand is the bottom right quadrant, labeled as *Deviants*. These are individuals who have little power and who are not viewed favorably, including criminals and gangs. Burdens and punishment are overprescribed to this quadrant, and the punishments can be very severe—jail, death, deportation, and other forms of social exclusion. Few benefits are given to these categories, even when they benefit society. For example, educating and giving job training to prisoners greatly reduces the likelihood of further acts of crime and violence once released, but despite the societal benefit, such programs are poorly funded and often unavailable.

The other two quadrants are more difficult to conceptualize due to the dissonance between one positive and one negative category. *Dependents* have a positive social construction, but little power. Children and mothers fit into this category, and often justice-oriented values are used to argue for support of these groups, such as equality, equity, needs, and rights (Schneider & Ingram, 1993). Yet often the supports of this group are insufficient and involve labels and stigma. Burdens and punishments are often paternalistic in nature, suggesting that such individuals need protection from themselves.

The final quadrant is even harder to conceptualize. *Contenders* have political power but potentially have a negative social construction. Whether they fit in this box depends on who is in power. Unions might fit in this category if Democrats are in power; wealthy business people and the Christian Right might fit here if Republicans are in power. Contenders are owed political favors and yet the broader public might not think highly of those favors being offered. Therefore, they tend to occur *sub rosa*, in a fashion in which they are hidden from public view and portrayed as less than they actually are (Schneider & Ingram, 1993). Benefits are said to be for the public good when they are offered. In contrast, benefits are exaggerated. Punishments are rarely as extreme. For example, the sentences of business executives and "white collar crime" have much lower jail time and punishment than typical sentences.

●●●●●
Comprehension Questions

■ What are policy problems? How do contexts and conditions define these problems?
■ How do target audiences change the scope of a policy problem?
■ What is metapolicy?
■ Make a table describing the purposes and consequences of each policy tool.

●●●●●
Discussion Questions

■ Discuss the role of power and how it influences policy options and outcomes for groups of individuals.
■ Discuss the trade-offs been choice of policy tool when designing legislation.

●●●●●
Activities

■ Design a brief policy designed to reach each of the following goals. Each policy should use a different policy instrument.
    ☐ Improve standardized test scores for a low performing school
    ☐ Increase the enrollment of students of color at a charter school
    ☐ Increase state participation in a federal voucher program
    ☐ Reduce bullying in middle schools
■ List the policy tool(s) most likely used for each of the following policies:
    ☐ A federal preschool program for poor children
    ☐ A school board policy for dealing with the procedure for expelling children
    ☐ A legal requirement that minority teachers be hired to staff an inner-city dropout prevention program
    ☐ A bill to require all children in grades K–6 to study the dangers of drugs
    ☐ A law requiring the development of state content standards in all major subjects, grades K–12

■ Using the Schneider and Ingram framework, place the following target populations on the framework grid:

Exercise 7.1

Advantaged	Contenders
Dependents	Deviants

Homeless
General Motors
Juvenile delinquents
Immigrants
Refugees
Illegal immigrants
Muslim Americans
Irish Americans
Elementary school teachers
WalMart
Lesbians
Transgender individuals
Soccer moms
College professors
New York Times
Fox News

☐ How does the position in the box change during different presidential
administrations? What would it be like in the Obama administration? The
Trump administration? The George W. Bush administration?

☐ How does the extent to which a group is in flux in societal norms versus
settled influence where they fit in the boxes?

●●●●●

Further Reading

Chrispeels, J. H. (1997). Educational policy implementation in a shifting political climate: The California experience. *American Educational Research Journal, 34*(3), 453–81.

McDonnell, L. M. & Elmore, R. F. (1987). Getting the job done: Alternative policy instruments. *Educational Evaluation and Policy Analysis, 9*(2), 133–52.

Schneider, A. & Ingram, H. (1993). Social construction of target populations: implications for politics and policy. *American Political Science Review, 87*(2), 334–47.

●●●●●

Reference List

Chrispeels, J. H. (1997). Educational policy implementation in a shifting political climate: The California experience. *American Educational Research Journal, 34*(3), 453–81.

Fowler, F. C. (2013). *Policy Studies for Educational Leaders: An Introduction.* Upper Saddle River, NJ: Merrill.

McDonnell, L. M. (1994). Assessment policy as persuasion and regulation. *American Journal of Education, 102*(4), 394–420.

McDonnell, L. M. & Elmore, R. F. (1987). Getting the job done: Alternative policy instruments. *Educational Evaluation and Policy Analysis, 9*(2), 133–52.

National Commission on Excellence in Education. (1983). *A Nation at Risk: The Imperative for Educational Reform: A Report to the Nation and the Secretary of Education, United States Department of Education.* Washington, DC: The Commission.

No Child Left Behind (NCLB) Act of 2001, 20 U.S.C.A. § 6301 *et seq.*

Schneider, A. & Ingram, H. (1990). Behavioral assumptions of policy tools. *The Journal of Politics, 52*(2), 510–29.

Schneider, A. & Ingram, H. (1993). Social construction of target populations: Implications for politics and policy. *American Political Science Review, 87*(2), 334–47.

Steers, R. M., Nardon, L., & Sanchez-Runde, C. J. (2013). *Management Across Cultures: Challenges and Strategies.* Cambridge: Cambridge University Press.

8

●●●●●

Policy Implementation

Implementation has become one of the main topics of education policy research in the past three decades. The chapter focuses on the framework of the relationships policy and practice, including the difference between a top-down approach to policy making and a bottom-up view that includes grassroots and teachers' perspectives. It considers the research on sensemaking, garbage can theory, co-adaptation, will and capacity, metapolicy, and street-level bureaucrats in the new era of accountability. We will discuss in greater detail in Chapter 9 ways in which implementation and scale are no longer considered to be separate but instead are both more effectively considered together. That is, adaptation of the design to deepen and spread a reform should be incorporated into all discussions of how to implement a design from the beginning (Redding, Cannata, & Taylor Haynes, forthcoming).

Implementation—what happens after a policy is passed and how it makes its way into practice—has proven to be as important as the quality of the legislation, if not more so. This chapter focuses on the importance of understanding the contexts and conditions of educational implementation and their crucial role in the policy process. The main headline from implementation research is that *implementation dominates outcome* (McLaughlin, 1991). Local responses dominate any unified vision of a reform.

Consider the carnival game Plinko (see Figure 8.1), featured on the game show The Price is Right. Contestants place chips at the top of a peg board with the goal of the chips sliding their way down the board and into the prize slot. Often on either side of the grand prize are slots for no prize at all. Why a chip chooses one path versus another in the game seems to be quite arbitrary, and often policy makers face the same level of befuddlement regarding why an intended policy did not make the impact that it was expected to make.

In implementation, local variability is the rule; uniformity is the exception (McLaughlin, 1990). As important as this statement might be in policy research, understanding variability matters. Some variability is intentional. Other times it is random.

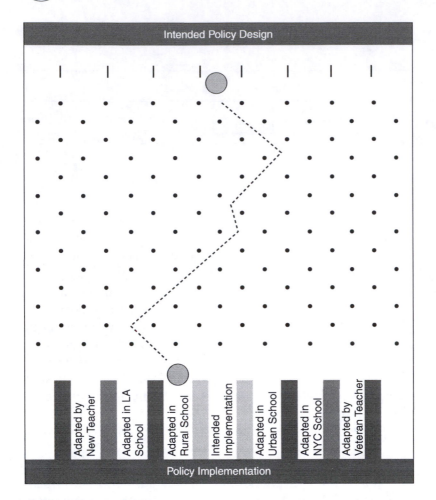

Figure 8.1 Policy Plinko.

●●●●●

Relating the Top and the Bottom

The first step in understanding implementation is to recognize that translation takes place. Scholars have used the term *mutual adaptation* (Datnow & Park, 2009; McLaughlin, 1991) to explain how the design of the policy and the behavior of the implementers must coalesce to achieve successful implementation. Also called *co-invention* (Darling-Hammond, 1990), this concept discusses the give and take between policy and practice. How a policy is written rarely is what a policy looks like at the practitioner level. This process consists of merging intended policy with local contexts. For example, how an elementary teacher might incorporate the idea of a morning meeting in the classroom could depend on the size of the classroom, the number of children, a space to sit, the amount of time the teacher has in the day, the ideas and values that the teacher wants to emphasize in the classroom, the current events happening in the world and in the lives of the children in the room, among other concerns. Variation across local educational systems can lead to a distortion of the policy message (Spillane, 1998, 1999).

Central to this understanding of implementation is an understanding of top-down and bottom-up perspectives. *Top-down* takes the perspective of a policy maker, such as a state agency, looking at how a policy from the top might reach a classroom. *Bottom-up* instead provides a perspective on how practitioners view the policy system.

Some policy research defines this difference as the *macro–micro* connection. A *macro* view of policy looks at the regularities of the policy process and structures that create stability. Looking from the macro level provides insufficient guidance on understanding outcomes, alternatives, and how policies operate in practice.

Backward mapping (Elmore, 1985) provides a way of encouraging policy makers to begin with the practitioners and work backward to predict the supports and training needed to help to enable the success of a policy. The work of McLaughlin (1991) argues that backward mapping is still a top-down approach because it assumes that a top-level view of the policy process takes into account all of the networks across teachers at the ground level.

A *micro perspective* focuses on the individual level, emphasizing unique contexts and interpretations of policy (Malen, 2006). When asking teachers how they make sense of a policy, they do not create the same map a policy maker might. Rather than pointing to formal hierarchies of principals, district leaders, state intermediate units, and state agencies, teachers point to horizontal linkages for support.

Through *horizontal ties*, teachers talk about other teachers that they have met at professional conferences or through online training; teachers from pre-service and summer programming, and non-profits and intermediary organizations working in partnership with schools (Talbert & McLaughlin, 1994; Lieberman, 1995). They have the opportunity to deepen learning and to amplify connections between theory and informed practice (Dalton & Moir 1996; Miller & O'Shea 1996).

Previous research on teacher networks has shown the power of professional opportunities that extend beyond school builds to connect teachers to one another (Talbert & McLaughlin, 1994; Lieberman, 1995). The Research-Practice Partnerships and Networked Improvement Communities (long-term relationships between practitioners and teachers discussed in Chapter 4) are examples of types of professional communities. Networks can help teachers to deepen classroom expertise and develop new leadership roles (Lieberman & McLaughlin, 1992). They also help teacher morale and leadership (Darling-Hammond & McLaughlin, 2011). Furthermore, teacher empowerment and student empowerment are symbiotic mechanisms. The more teachers feel empowered, the greater their willingness to give students voice and leadership opportunities as well (Bauch & Goldring, 1998; Mitra, 2007; Muncey & McQuillan, 1991). The bottom-up view of policy supports, then, often looks very different than someone from the top could predict. Such research therefore calls on the importance of building on natural networks of teachers (McLaughlin, 1991; McLaughlin & Talbert, 2001) and otherwise involving teachers in the policy making and implementation processes rather than presuming to know what they might need.

● ● ● ● ●

Loose Coupling

The U.S educational system is fragmented institutionally (Cohen & Spilane, 1992; McDonnell, 2007). Due to the constitution as well as the nation's history and culture, the system contains multiple levels that share authority and power. It is also fragmented due to recent historical trends, such as federal *categorical funding*—meaning that funding must be used for specific purposes at specified levels of the system rather than giving districts and states flexibility to make decisions on how to use the funds.

To understand the implications of fragmented power and decision making, we will explore the concepts of tight and loose coupling. Let's first consider the characteristics of a *tightly-coupled system*. McDonald's, Disney World, the Catholic Church, special operations of the military—all of these are examples of tightly coupled systems. Such organizations have a centrally held clear vision and tight linkages between units within the organization. Clarity of mission and a strict adherence to uniformity are important components of such organizations. When one steps into a McDonald's, no matter where in the country or the world, one expects a McDonald's French fry to have a similar flavor, texture, and taste. The setup of the store is very common regardless of location and the experience of dining also is quite similar. In fact, it is considered a fun part of traveling in our family, to note the differences in McDonald's across the world. Fried cheese is served in Germany. A second kind of potatoes, in addition to French fries, is served in Ireland. No beef products of any kind are served in McDonald's in India. Yet despite these differences, the quintessential experience that defines a McDonald's feels very much the same.

Such a tightly-coupled system has distinct advantages. It provides a uniform level of quality. It also allows for a clear channel of communication throughout the organization. McDonald's establishes a clear brand with the expectation that you will receive the same service and same food regardless of where you are in the world. Panera Bread provides maps of how to arrange the pastries so that every store has them in the same order.

For special operations in the military, a quick chain of command provides a way for directives to be communicated and executed, from command to the soldiers on the ground. For targeted missions, clear communication and shared understanding of the task are central to the goals of the organization.

In contrast to these examples, a *loosely-coupled* organization does not have such straightforward communication (Shulman, 1983; Weick, 1976). It has often been said that teachers can close their classroom door and have a large amount of control over how students learn. Undoubtedly, parents can document the differences in student experience and enjoyment of school from year to year depending on the teacher. Even in an era of accountability, which essentially has led to a tighter coupling between classrooms, schools, and state governments, teachers still have a great deal of flexibility regarding how to deliver content. A lack of communication between structures can also influence policy implementation. It could also lead to a delay of implementation or even a local resistance to the perceived changes.

Increased policy activity from the state level (the top of a system) could increase state activity at a local level rather than thinking of a zero-sum game (Fuhrman & Elmore, 1990). States might mobilize public and professional reactions to issues. Other times, the use of a new policy might be used to leverage personal agendas and other local needs and interests (Patashnik & Zelizer, 2013).

Reforms to "teacher-proof" a curriculum rest in the belief that a more tightly coupled system of education would be in the best interest of students. In such curricula, teachers read a script provided by the curriculum company and are expected to follow directions and implement a curriculum out of a box instead of using teacher discretion to teach individuals. This type of a vision has been shown to have some positive impact in areas in which teacher quality is known to be extremely low. For example, the program *Success for All* is a reading program in which teachers work from scripted lesson plans. While scripted plans might be the best of a few options in under-resourced areas with teachers who do not have proper training, the majority of teacher researchers believe in the value of teachers having professional discretion to meet the needs of students (Slavin, 1996; Quint et al., 2013; Klinger, Cramer, & Harry, 2006).

Indeed, the benefits of a loosely-coupled system include that it provides a sensing mechanism to its environment and thus allows for the adaptation of principles to local contexts. Therefore, a teacher in a small private school in Beverly Hills might teach very differently than a teacher of 30 students in inner-city Philadelphia due to the materials, the facilities of the classroom, the expertise of the teacher, and the needs of the students present.

In addition to adaptability, a loosely-coupled system seals off failure. Much like an egg carton, a loosely coupled system protects pieces of an organization from other pieces (Weick, 1976). While these buffers and lack of communication make it hard to spread innovation in schools, it also means that failures and unsuccessful reforms also do not cause widespread damage. Loosely-coupled systems therefore have great stability.

Loosely-coupled systems allow for innovation. At times, corporations with a traditional leadership structure might intentionally decouple a unit from the main tightly coupled structure to encourage creativity and innovation. For example, General Motors intentionally decoupled the Saturn group in 1985 to encourage a new way of thinking about cars. This idea led to initial increases in profits and a culture very different from the main organization. When Saturn's profitability began to wane in the late 1990s and was ultimately discontinued in 2009, it also did not lead to the destruction of General Motors (Krisher & Thomas, 2009).

Decoupling a part of an organization, or running a system in a decoupled fashion, can also make it less expensive to run. Compliance and monitoring of quality control are expensive and not as necessary if individual units have greater autonomy of purpose and function. Relatedly, organizations in which the mission and vision of an organization are harder to measure benefit from a loosely coupled system. In the field of education, success of a "school" or a "teacher" proves to be hard to measure since the students come into a classroom with such a wide range of previous experiences. The value-added impact of one particular teacher is therefore hard to assess.

Systems that are hard to measure tend to eschew inspection systems and focus instead on certification (Shulman, 1983). Inspection systems attempt to assess the quality of implementation. They often look for a uniform standard and the meeting of criteria of excellence. Certification systems instead tend to use inputs as measurements instead of outputs. They look at the years of service and the degrees that teachers hold to compensate teachers, instead of how instructors teach students. It is very expensive and difficult to examine how instruction happens in school and easier to talk about what can be controlled—topics taught, years of experience, and so on.

When considering policy design for a loosely coupled system, mandates discussed in the previous chapter are much less effective since they require a level of monitoring and compliance that is hard to accomplish in a loosely coupled system. Instead, policy tends to include moral and political imperatives that orient individuals and institutions toward shared values. Yet the specific procedures for implementation are variable. These moral and political imperatives will compete with other values already within the policy system (Weick, 1976).

With the increased expectations of accountability and attention to theories of knowledge management (Nonaka & Takeuchi, 1995) and learning organizations (Seeley-Brown & Duguid, 2000; Senge, 1994) prevalent since the 1990s, educational leadership has taken a more tightly coupled approach to management (Dieter-Meyer, 2002). Nevertheless, the attributes of loosely coupled systems remain prevalent in school systems. Shulman (1983, p. 490) has described some specific reasons why mandates and strict control of schools are very difficult given the contexts of education (see Table 8.1).

●●●●●

Street-Level Bureaucrats

Often individuals working in bureaucracies must interpret policy with insufficient guidance. In loosely coupled systems, there is greater expectation for such interpretations. *Street-level bureaucrats* (Weatherley & Lipsky, 1977) describe individuals for whom demands of their services are higher than they can

Table 8.1 Difficulties of Mandates and Control in the Educational Context

Inconsistencies Among Mandates
Policies passed by legislatures regarding education are often contradictory. For example, the Federal Individuals with Disabilities Education Act (IDEA) legislation (1975) cites that each student must have his or her individual needs met in alignment with ability and disability. The Elementary and Secondary Education Act, now ESSA of 2015,) says that all students must be tested every year from grades 3–8. Very few students are exempted from the test and few can receive accommodations. As a result, most students are expected to take the test in the same fashion as all other students, regardless of disability. Variability across states also occurs. Pennsylvania offers little flexibility for special needs students, whereas Maine offers a broader range of accommodations.

Limits on Resources, Time, or Energy
Policies often try to add on additional responsibilities to teachers and administrators without taking into account what demands already exist. Policies also often do not build in funding for additional expectations but assume that school personnel can find additional time and training to complete additional demands.

Limitations of Teacher Expertise
Many policies fail to include sufficient training to implement a new idea. For example, it is common to send one teacher from a building to attend training and expect that the teacher will come back and share what is learned with everyone else in the building, and the idea will be shared and diffused to everyone.

Limitations of Working Conditions
Much that affects teaching and learning is beyond teacher control. Students come to school hungry, scared, worried, sleepy. Some kindergarteners come to school reading books and others have not learned their letters yet. All of these factors influence if and when a child is ready to learn.

The Self-Defeating Mandate
"How" matters as much as "what"—the manner in which policy is designed will influence its ability to be implemented.

Source: Shulman (1983, p. 490).

provide. They interact directly with the public and often have to make on-the-job decisions on how to implement directives.

Nurses, police officers, teachers, and the person who answers the phone—these individuals must make on-the-spot decisions regarding when to enforce a policy strictly and when to grant discretion. In the context of young people, implementers also include people outside of formal education, including after-school organizations, mayors, business leaders, and school reform designers/support providers. These individuals must create procedures and protocols to make their job feel rational, including prioritizing or limiting clientele, shrinking policy goals, and creating routine procedures. A range of contexts influence what kinds of incentives and constraints guide the decisions of these street-level bureaucrats (Evans, Rueschemeyer, & Skocpol, 1985; McLaughlin, Scott, Deschenes, Hopkins, & Newman, 2009). The work of street-level bureaucrats is highly discretionary. It includes vague work objectives and performance measures.

Box 8.1 Street-Level Bureaucrat Case Study: Opting Out

The experiences of parents trying to opt their children out of state-mandated policies provide a useful extended example of how street-level bureaucrats interpret policy. Mitra, Mann, and Hlavacik (2016, p. 11) interviewed and documented the experiences of parents calling a state Department of Education (DOE) to ask how they could opt their student out of standardized testing. Because few states had written an opt-out policy during the NCLB era, the actual decision about opting out often became the decision of street-level bureaucrats. As a result, the implementation of opt-out policy often became variable and a problem for the smallest unit (McLaughlin, 1987). In the case of opt-out, the people answering the phones in the DOE were forced to interpret policy, including creating new policies or even reversing policies.

Most states have adopted informal processes that are shared with only the most inquisitive parents, such as those who write to state officials—a chief focus of state discussion forums on the United Opt Out website. For example, a participant shared a conversation between a parent and DOE official. The DOE response to a parent request for information on how to opt out was (United Opt Out website, West Virginia data):

> The obvious answer to your question is just not to send the student to school on the day(s) of the testing and the makeup days. If you would like another option, I will need the information above before I can answer your question.

This response reflected the ability of a front-line employee to create or even reverse policy.

In Pennsylvania and Arizona, families must have a religious reason for opting out. Despite this narrowly codified policy, the implementation of this law is widely defined to include any moral or ethical concerns about the test. For example, one family in Pennsylvania told the state's DOE that they were opting out for health reasons. The department official asked the family to please use the religious exemption to avoid undue hassle, as a parent in the family active on the website elaborated on her experiences in a follow-up interview (October, 2010):

> I called the Department of Education ... in Harrisburg and ended up talking to ... the Director of the Department of Assessments ... I explained to him the situation with my son ... who has extreme test anxiety and was scratching his legs at night before the tests to the point that he was bleeding ... [I asked if], there was a medical exception that we could take. And he says, "...I advise you take the religious exemption." And I said, "Well it's not really a religious issue. It's a medical issue..." And he says, "Just do it," you know. "That's what it's for. It's a catchall thing. Just go for it."

The chasm between the law as written and the law as enforced was considerable in this parent's experience. However, this particularly dramatic policy ambiguity and the agency it granted this family, and presumably all families in Pennsylvania, only became clear when this parent took the initiative to contact the state DOE. In this way, policy variability depends in part on each parent's ability or willingness to contact his or her state DOE.

●●●●●

Policy Feedback, Layered Policy, and Sensemaking

Policies land on top of other policies. The importance of history is relevant in policy making. No policy lands in a vacuum. Successful policy implementation considers what has come before and builds upon it, rather than tries to destroy it. Policies are "layered" (Patashnik & Zelizer, 2013, p. 1077) on pre-existing practice. Like in the videogame *Tetris*, a popular computer game, puzzle pieces fall from the sky. Winning the game involves rotating the pieces to fit what lies beneath the puzzle pieces. Aligning the pieces with what lies beneath, including local political cultures and beliefs about school, can help to remove implementation obstacles and creates more room to manipulate future ideas.

The political science concept of "policy feedback" (McDonnell & Weatherford, 2016; Mettler & Soss, 2004) explains how new policies that do not align with previous values, beliefs, and rules will shift the benefits and costs of a system for interest groups and influential individuals. These people will decide whether the shifts are enough of a threat or motivation to actively engage in facilitating or blocking an implementation process.

The lens of *sensemaking* has grown in its use in implementation research (Weick, 1995). Research on sensemaking examines the process of how teachers' pre-existing knowledge and practices transform and synthesize their understanding of new policy messages and subsequent policy implementation (Coburn, 2005a). Sensemaking provides a way to analyze the experiences of teachers and other street-level bureaucrats by putting their understanding of a policy change at the center of analysis. It provides a way of thinking about how contexts, conditions, networks, and resources influence the ways that new ideas are integrated into practice. Teachers with shared goals in collaborative environments who trust their peers are more likely to enact changes in their classroom practice (Newmann, King, & Youngs, 2000).

Peer networks matter, especially for teachers, as they seek to integrate new ideas. Teachers adapt their practice in part through communication with school leaders and others in formal and informal interchanges (Brezicha, Bergmark, & Mitra, 2015; Spillane, 1999). By exchanging ideas and interpretations of policies, they construct shared understandings and adjust their own professional stance on their teaching goals and practice (Coburn & Talbert, 2006; Copland, 2003). Other social interactions and trusting relationships also enable or constrain reform (Bryk & Schneider, 2003; Smylie & Evans, 2006).

Leaders play an important role in shaping the availability of social networks that can either facilitate or hinder reforms. Principals can help create environments that facilitate collegiality and growth through collaborative opportunities (Louis, Marks, & Kruse, 1996). Principals can increase a teacher's sense of trust and security by helping to provide a supportive, fair, and cooperative environment (Tarter, 1995; Tschannen-Moran, 2001). In addition, the structure of the school settings can also support the implementation process by facilitating teachers' understandings and policy perceptions through established time for collaboration and reflection (Louis, 1994; Spillane, Reiser, & Reimer, 2002). How teachers learn about policy problems and designs also influences how reforms become implemented in practice (Honig, 2009; O'Day, 2002). Lastly, the extent of teacher participation with the school's decision-making process can heavily influence a teacher's own sensemaking of policy messages (Spillane et al., 2002).

● ● ● ● ●

Will, Capacity, and Fidelity

From 1973 to 1978, the RAND Corporation carried out a study of the implementation of the Elementary and Secondary Education Act (Berman & McLaughlin, 1974, 1978; Berman, Greenwood, McLaughlin, & Pincus, 1975). They found that ineffective change included excessive use of external consultants, one-shot training, packaged approaches, and comprehensive projects. What worked better was concrete, teacher-specific training, classroom support, teacher participation in project decisions, and principal participation (McLaughlin, 1984).

McLaughlin (1991, p. 147) is famous for emphasizing that policy "can't mandate what matters." Will and capacity matter most in terms of effective implementation. Local responses depend upon individual incentives and beliefs (McLaughlin, 1987).

Will consists of the extent to which practitioners want to implement the policy because they share the value of the policy. *Capacity* is the tools and training needed to implement a policy. Even if a practitioner believes in a policy, that person may not have the training, the resources, or the time to do so (Spillane & Thompson, 1997). Capacity can also be considered more broadly to include

---

Box 8.2 Math Implementation Gone Awry

One of the most famous studies to demonstrate this importance of fidelity is the case of Ms. Oublier (Cohen, 1990). The article documents an enthusiastic teacher who has wholeheartedly embraced the elementary mathematics reforms of the district. Indeed, the evaluator visited her room because she was considered the poster-child of the reform for the school. She embraced the ideals of the reform and sought to change her classroom instruction based on these ideals. Upon observation of the classroom, however, the evaluator determined that the teacher did not understand the concepts fully and her interpretation of the reforms did not embrace the key concepts that the math reform was embracing. For example, rather than emphasizing that there are many ways to understand and compute a math problem, the teacher emphasized one correct way to a solution. Instead of focusing on the how and why of the problem, she focused on memorization and the right answer. The article raises important questions regarding the types of training and support that Oublier and others like her would need to ensure that fidelity is maintained. Visiting the classrooms of others, ongoing training rather than a summer-only institute, coaches who come in to observe and give feedback are some ways that the problem of Oublier can be helped.

professional preparation, duration of leadership tenure, and civic capacity and social capital (Hall, 2016).

Fidelity to a policy is an important part of capacity. It involves ensuring that how a practitioner understands a policy aligns with the core principles at the heart of the policy goals (McLaughlin & Mitra, 2001). An understanding that co-adaptation must occur for policy to apply to local contexts becomes the exception rather than the rule (McLaughlin, 1991). Yet within such variability, change can be so drastic that the "deal breakers" of a policy get violated such that the policy goals cannot be fulfilled.

While the first generation of RAND research emphasized the importance of an aligned belief between practitioners and the policy, practice can change beliefs (McLaughlin, 1991, p. 149). To accomplish such a change in practice, policy must be communicated well to be understood well. Teachers need discussion and professional development at all levels of the system. Teachers teach from what they know. To influence content, policy cannot just change curriculum; it must also change teacher education and certification, and provide ongoing professional development, supervision, and evaluation to influence teaching.

Political support of a policy can change dramatically during the implementation phase of a policy process. McDonnell and Weatherford (2016) discuss how policy enactment tends to occur in a narrow window of time, within few decision venues and with a national set of interest groups. In controls, implementation of the same policy often occurs at multiple state and local venues over a longer time period, in a much more diverse set of venues and with state and local actors who may not agree with national officials on the intentions of the policy. As implementation was expected to begin in these states, support for the policy faded (McDonnell & Weatherford, 2016).

●●●●●

Intermediaries as Facilitators of Change

Recent research on educational implementation has focused on the role of *intermediaries*—the nodes of a system that connect the policy makers with the practitioners. Often these intermediaries or non-system actors (Coburn, 2005b) are professional organizations, issue driven non-profits, and for-profit support agencies. The importance of policy being initiated by a school district central office has been found (Honig, 2004). Also, if policy is counter-normative, it is most likely to encourage innovation (Paquin Morell & Coburn, 2017) and to persist (Mitra, 2009) if partnership occurs with organizations outside the system to keep a normative focus on the reform. Others have looked at the ways in which districts can form intermediary partnerships to promote instructional improvement (Marsh, Kerr, Ikemoto, & Darilek, 2006).

Related research has looked at the role of "brokers" who serve as connectors between actors and organizations. They have extensive social networks and span gaps between others' networks (Burt, 1992, 2007; Gould & Fernandez,

1989; Paquin Morell, & Coburn, 2017). They can access information and resources, and build relationships. They can also control information and interpretation of policy (Burt, 1999; Fernandez & Gould, 1994; Kellogg, 2014; Paquin Morell, & Coburn, 2017; Stovel & Shaw, 2012).

District as Intermediary

Research increasingly points to the school district as an important intermediary actor in the design and implementation of educational reform (Hightower, Knapp, Marsh, & McLaughlin, 2002b; Spillane, 1996). Studies have examined the district role in many reforms, including: new teacher induction programs (Kapadia, Coca, & Easton, 2007), the formation of teacher learning communities (McLaughlin & Talbert, 2001), teacher recruitment (Darling-Hammond & Sykes, 2003; Useem, Offenberg, & Farley, 2007), and instructional reform (Cohen & Barnes, 1993; Elmore & Burney, 1997; Firestone & Mayrowetz, 1998; Grossman, Thompson, & Valencia, 2002; Hightower, Knapp, Marsh, & McLaughlin, 2002a; Marsh et. al., 2005; Newmann, Smith, Allensworth, & Bryk, 2001; Spillane, 1998; Spillane et al., 2002; Spillane & Thompson, 1997). Research also has examined how districts learn and become learning organizations to better utilize their resources and capacities (Coburn & Talbert, 2006; Honig, 2007; Spillane & Callahan, 2000; Stein & Coburn, 2008).

As is true with other organizations, districts must balance innovation and improvement with efforts to maintain district legitimacy and self-preservation. The current context of high-stakes testing increases the district's need to focus on preserving image, and therefore legitimacy, in a time of possible instability. School districts face increasing challenges of compliance, capacity, and credibility. State and federal accountability systems have increased compliance pressures on central office leadership; how districts interpret these pressures and respond to the scrutiny of stakeholders and publicity from local media holds significance for understanding the design and implementation of reform policy. High-stakes accountability has raised the stakes for student, teacher, principal, and district, with consequences such as student retention (Roderick, Nagaoka, & Allensworth, 2005), teacher and administrator demotion (Rice & Malen, 2016), decreased funding from state and federal sources, public shaming strategies such as publishing names of failed schools, and, ultimately, school closure, restructure, or reconstitution. Some districts lost decision-making control as states and mayors removed elected school boards, appointed superintendents, and disbanded local school councils (Cuban & Usdan, 2003; Kirst, 2002; Wong & Shen, 2001).

●　●　●　●　●

Comprehension Questions

■ What are some of the reasons that it is difficult to implement policy in schools?

■ What is loose coupling, and why is it important for understanding implementation in schools?

■ What is a street-level bureaucrat and why is this concept important in understanding policy implementation?

●●●●●

Discussion Questions

■ How can teachers influence the policy system?

■ What types of supports might have prevented implementation problems, such as a loss of fidelity of the reform in the case of Ms. Oublier?

■ Generate examples of tight and loose coupling and explain why you choose these examples.

■ When is loose coupling advantageous? How is it problematic?

■ When and why might different levels of a system have different levels of coupling within the same organization?

■ Why are will and capacity critical concepts for understanding implementation? How can policy be designed to accommodate both?

■ Play the telephone game of passing on a message throughout the class. Identify where the message changed and why it might have. Discuss the parallels to loose coupling.

●●●●●

Activities

■ Provide a specific example for each of Shulman's (1983) reasons why contexts in education make it difficult to implement mandates:

☐ Inconsistencies among mandates

☐ Limits on resources, time, or energy

  • Can't keep adding to an already full load

☐ Limitations of teacher expertise

  • Lack of capacity building or overall training

☐ Limitations of working conditions

  • Much is beyond teacher control

☐ The self-defeating mandate

  • "How" matters as much as "what"

● ● ● ● ●

Further Reading

Coburn, C. E. (2005). Shaping teacher sensemaking: School leaders and the enactment of reading policy. *Educational Policy, 19*(3), 476–509.

Marsh, J. A., Kerr, K. A., Ikemoto, G. S., & Darilek, H. (2006). Developing district-intermediary partnerships to promote instructional improvement. In Wong, K. K. & Rutledge, S. A. (eds.) *Systemwide Efforts to Improve Student Achievement* (pp. 241–70). Charlotte, NC: IAP.

McLaughlin, M. W., Scott, R., Deschenes, S., Hopkins, K., & Newman, A. (2009). *Between Movement and Establishment: Organizations Advocating for Youth.* Stanford, CA: Stanford University Press.

Mitra, D. L. (2009). The role of intermediary organizations in sustaining student voice initiatives. *Teachers College Record, 111*(7), 1834–68.

Redding, C., Cannata, M., & Taylor Haynes, K. (2017). With scale in mind: A continuous improvement model for implementation. *Peabody Journal of Education.*

Weick, K. E. (1976). Educational organizations as loosely coupled systems. *Administrative Science Quarterly, 21*(1), 1–19.

● ● ● ● ●

Reference List

Bauch, P. A. & Goldring, E. B. (1998). Parent-teacher participation in the context of school governance. *Peabody Journal of Education, 73*(1), 15–35.

Berman, P. & McLaughlin, M. W. (1974). *Federal Programs Supporting Educational Change: A Model of Educational Change, Vol. I.* Santa Monica, CA: The RAND Corporation.

Berman, P. & McLaughlin, M. W. (1978). *Implementing and Sustaining Innovations, Vol. 8.* Santa Monica, CA: The RAND Corporation.

Berman, P., Greenwood, P., McLaughlin, M. W., & Pincus, J. (1975). *Federal Programs Supporting Educational Change, Vol. IV (Abridged), A Summary of the Findings in Review.* Santa Monica, CA: The RAND Corporation.

Brezicha, K., Bergmark, U., & Mitra, D. L. (2015). One size does not fit all: Differentiating leadership to support teachers in school reform. *Educational Administration Quarterly, 51*(1), 96–132.

Bryk, A. S. & Schneider, B. (2003). Trust in schools: A core resource for school reform. *Educational Leadership, 60*(6), 40–5.

Burt, R. S. (1992). *Structural Holes: The Social Structure of Competition.* Cambridge, MA: Harvard University Press.

Burt, R. S. (1999). Entrepreneurs, distrust, and third parties: A strategic look at the dark side of dense networks. In Thompson, L. L., Levin, J. M., & Messick, D. M. (eds.) *Shared Cognition in Organizations: The Management of Knowledge* (pp. 213–43). New York: Psychology Press.

Burt, R. S. (2007). *Brokerage and Closure: An Introduction to Social Capital.* Oxford: Oxford University Press.

Coburn, C. E. (2005a). Shaping teacher sensemaking: School leaders and the enactment of reading policy. *Educational Policy, 19*(3), 476–509.

Coburn, C. E. (2005b). The role of nonsystem actors in the relationship between policy and practice: The case of reading instruction in California. *Educational Evaluation and Policy Analysis, 27*(1), 23–52.

Coburn, C. E. & Talbert, J. E. (2006). Conceptions of evidence use in school districts: Mapping the terrain. *American Journal of Education, 112*(4), 469–95.

Cohen, D. K. (1990). A revolution in one classroom: The case of Mrs. Oublier. *Educational Evaluation and Policy Analysis, 12*(3), 327.

Cohen, D. K. & Barnes, C. A. (1993). Conclusion: A new pedagogy for policy. In Cohen, D. K., McLaughlin, M. W., & Talbert, E. (eds.) *Teaching for Understanding* (pp. 240–76). San Francisco, CA: Jossey-Bass.

Cohen, D. K. & Spillane, J. P. (1992). Policy and practice: The relations between governance and instruction. *Review of Research in Education, 18*(1), 3–49.

Copland, M. A. (2003). Leadership of inquiry: Building and sustaining capacity for school improvement. *Educational Evaluation and Policy Analysis, 25*(4), 375–95.

Cuban, L. & Usdan, M. D. (eds.) (2003). *Powerful Reforms With Shallow Roots: Improving America's Urban Schools.* New York: Teachers College Press.

Dalton, S. & Moir, E. (1996). Symbiotic support and program evaluation: Text and context for professional development of new bilingual teachers. In McLaughlin, M. W. & Oberman, I. (eds.) *Teacher Learning: New Policies, New Practices.* New York: Teachers College Press.

Darling-Hammond, L. (1990). Instructional policy into practice: The power of the bottom over the top. *Educational Evaluation and Policy Analysis, 12*(3), 339–47.

Darling-Hammond, L. & McLaughlin, M. W. (2011). Policies that support professional development in an era of reform. *Phi Delta Kappan, 92*(6), 81–92.

Darling-Hammond, L. & Sykes, G. (2003). Wanted, a national teacher supply policy for education: The right way to meet the "highly qualified teacher" challenge. *Education Policy Analysis Archives, 11*, 33.

Datnow, V. & Park, A. (2009). Conceptualizing policy implementation: Large-scale reform in an era of complexity. In Sykes, G., Schneider, B., & Plank, D. (eds.) *Handbook of Education Policy Research* (pp. 348–61). London: Routledge.

Dieter-Meyer, H. (2002). From "loose coupling" to "tight management"? Making sense of the changing landscape in management and organization theory. *Journal of Educational Administration, 40*(6), 515–20.

Elmore, R. F. (1985). Forward and backward mapping: Reversible logic in the analysis of public policy. In Hanf, K. I. & Toonen, T. A. J. (eds.) *Policy Implementation in Federal and Unitary Systems* (pp. 33–70). Dordrecht, Netherlands: Springer.

Elmore, R. F. & Burney, D. (1997). *Investing in Teacher Learning: Staff Development and Instructional Improvement in Community School District #2, New York City.* Columbia University, New York: National Commission on Teaching & America's Future.

Evans, P. B., Rueschemeyer, D., & Skocpol, T. (eds.) (1985). *Bringing the State Back in.* Cambridge, UK: Cambridge University Press.

Every Student Succeeds Act (ESSA) of 2015, P. L. 114–95, 20 U.S.C. § 6301 (2015).

Fernandez, R. M. & Gould, R. V. (1994). A dilemma of state power: Brokerage and influence in the national health policy domain. *American Journal of Sociology, 99*(6), 1455–91.

Firestone, W. A., Mayrowetz, D., & Fairman, J. (1998). Performance-based assessment and instructional change: The effects of testing in Maine and Maryland. *Educational Evaluation and Policy Analysis, 20*(2), 95–113.

Fuhrman, S. H. & Elmore, R. F. (1990). Understanding local control in the wake of state education reform. *Educational Evaluation and Policy Analysis, 12*(1), 82–96.

Gould, R. V. & Fernandez, R. M. (1989). Structures of mediation: A formal approach to brokerage in transaction networks. *Sociological Methodology, 19,* 89–126.

Grossman, P., Thompson, C., & Valencia, S. W. (2002). Focusing the concerns of new teachers: The district as teacher educator. In Hightower, A. M., Knapp, M. S., Marsh, J. A., & McLaughlin, M. W. (eds.) *School Districts and Instructional Renewal* (pp. 129–42). New York: Teachers College Press.

Hall, D. (2016). *Local Control as Resistance: Policy and Practice of Autonomous School Boards.* Unpublished doctoral dissertation. State College, PA: The Pennsylvania State University.

Hightower, A. M., Knapp, M. S., Marsh, J. A., & McLaughlin, M. W. (eds.) (2002a) *School Districts and Instructional Renewal.* New York: Teachers College Press.

Hightower, A. M., Knapp, M. S., Marsh, J. A., & McLaughlin, M. W. (2002b). The district role in instructional renewal: Setting the stage for dialogue. In Hightower, A. M., Knapp, M. S., Marsh, J. A., & McLaughlin, M. W. (eds.) *School Districts and Instructional Renewal* (pp. 1–6). New York: Teachers College Press.

Honig, M. I. (2004). The new middle management: Intermediary organizations in education policy implementation. *Educational Evaluation and Policy Analysis, 26*(1), 65–87.

Honig, M. I. (2007). *Policy Implementation and Learning: How Organizational and Socio-Cultural Learning Theories Elaborate District Central Office Roles in Complex Educational Improvement Efforts.* Washington, DC: Center for the Study of Teaching and Policy.

Honig, M. I. (2009). No small thing: School district central office bureaucracies and the implementation of new small autonomous schools initiatives. *American Educational Research Journal, 46*(2), 387–422.

Individuals with Disabilities Education Act (1975), 34 CFR § 300.1.

Kapadia, K., Coca, V., & Easton, J. Q. (2007). *Keeping New Teachers: A First Look at the Influences of Induction in the Chicago Public Schools.* Chicago, IL: Consortium on Chicago School Research, University of Chicago.

Kellogg, K. C. (2014). Brokerage professions and implementing reform in an age of experts. *American Sociological Review, 79*(5), 912–41.

Kirst, M. W. (2002). *Mayoral Influences, New Regimes, and Public School Governance.* CPRE Research Report Series RR-049. Consortium for Policy Research in Education, University of Pennsylvania.

Klinger, J., Cramer, E., & Harry, B. (2006). Challenges in the implementation of success for all in four high-need urban schools. *The Elementary School Journal, 106*(4), 333–49.

Krisher, T. & Thomas, K. (2009). GM seeks up to $30B in aid, will cut 47,000 jobs, February 17, *Associated Press.* Retrieved from: www.sandiegouniontribune.com/sdut-gm-bailout-021709-2009feb17-story.html.

Lieberman, A. (1995). Practices that support teacher development: Transforming conceptions of professional learning. *Innovating and Evaluating Science Education: NSF Evaluation Forums, 67* (1992–94).

Lieberman, A. & McLaughlin, M. W. (1992). Networks for educational change: Powerful and problematic. *Phi Delta Kappan, 73*(9), 673.

Louis, K. S. (1994). Beyond "managed change": Rethinking how schools improve. *School Effectiveness and School Improvement, 5*(1), 2–24.

Louis, K. S., Marks, H. M., & Kruse, S. (1996). Teachers' professional community in restructuring schools. *American Educational Research Journal, 33*(4), 757–98.

Malen, B. (2006). The micropolitics of education: Mapping the multiple dimensions of power relations in school polities. *Journal of Education Policy, 9*(5), 147–67.

Marsh, J. A., Kerr, K. A., Ikemoto, G. S., & Darilek, H. (2006). Developing district-intermediary partnerships to promote instructional improvement. In Wong, K. K. & Rutledge, S. A. (eds.) *Systemwide Efforts to Improve Student Achievement* (pp. 241–70). Charlotte, NC: IAP.

Marsh, J. A., Kerr, K. A., Ikemoto, G. S., Darilek, H., Suttorp, M., Zimmer, R. W., & Barney, H. (2005). *The Role of Districts in Fostering Instructional Improvement Lessons from Three Urban Districts Partnered with the Institute for Learning.* Santa Monica, CA: The RAND Corporation.

McDonnell, L. (2007). The politics of education: Influencing policy and beyond. In Fuhrman, S., Cohen, D., & Mosher, F. (eds.) *The State Of Education Policy Research* (pp. 19–40). Mahwah, NJ: Lawrence Erlbaum Associates.

McDonnell, L. M. & Weatherford, M. S. (2016). Recognizing the political in implementation research. *Educational Researcher, 45*(4), 233–42.

McLaughlin, M. W. (1984). Teacher evaluation and school improvement. *Teachers College Record, 86*(1), 193–207.

McLaughlin, M. W. (1987). Learning from experience: Lessons from policy implementation. *Educational Evaluation and Policy Analysis, 9*(2), 171–8.

McLaughlin, M. W. (1990). The RAND Change Agent study revisited: Macro perspectives and micro realities. *Educational Researcher, 19*(9), 11–16.

McLaughlin, M. W. (1991). The RAND Change Agent study: Ten years later. In Odden, A. R. (ed.) *Education Policy Implementation* (pp. 143–55). Albany, NY: State University of New York Press.

McLaughlin, M. W. & Mitra, D. L. (2001). Theory-based change and change-based theory: Going deeper, going broader. *Journal of Educational Change, 3*(1), 301–23.

McLaughlin, M. W. & Talbert, J. E. (2001). *High School Teaching in Context.* Chicago, IL: University of Chicago.

McLaughlin, M. W., Scott, R., Deschenes, S., Hopkins, K., & Newman, A. (2009). *Between Movement and Establishment: Organizations Advocating for Youth.* Stanford, CA: Stanford University Press.

Mettler, S. & Soss, J. (2004). The consequences of public policy for democratic citizenship: Bridging policy studies and mass politics. *Perspectives on Politics, 2*(1), 55–73.

Miller, L. & O'Shea, C. (1996). Partnership: Getting broader, getting deeper. In McLaughlin, M. W. & Oberman, I. (eds.) *Teacher Learning: New Policies, New Practices.* New York: Teachers College Press.

Mitra, D. L. (2007). The role of administrators in enabling youth-adult partnerships in schools. *NASSP Bulletin, 91*(3), 237–56.

Mitra, D. L. (2009). The role of intermediary organizations in sustaining student voice initiatives. *Teachers College Record, 111*(7), 1834–68.

Mitra, D., Mann, B., & Hlavacik, M. (2016). Opting out: Parents creating contested spaces to challenge standardized tests. *Education Policy Analysis Archives.* March.

Muncey, D. & McQuillan, P. (1991). *Empowering Nonentities: Students in Educational Reform.* Working paper #5. Providence, RI: School Ethnography Project, Coalition of Essential Schools, Brown University.

Newmann, F. M., King, M. B., & Youngs, P. (2000). Professional development that addresses school capacity: Lessons from urban elementary schools. *American Journal of Education, 108*(4), 259–99.

Newmann, F. M., Smith, B., Allensworth, E., & Bryk, A. S. (2001). *School Instructional Program Coherence: Benefits and Challenges. Improving Chicago's Schools.* Chicago, IL: Consortium on Chicago School Research.

Nonaka, I. & Takeuchi, H. (1995). *The Knowledge-Creating Company*. New York: Oxford University Press.

O'Day, J. (2002). Complexity, accountability, and school improvement. *Harvard Educational Review, 72*(3), 293–329.

Paquin Morell, R. & Coburn, C. (2017). Access, activation and influence: How brokers mediate social capital among professional development providers. Paper prepared for the American Educational Research Association Annual Meeting. San Antonio, Texas.

Patashnik, E. M. & Zelizer, J. E. (2013). The struggle to remake politics: Liberal reform and the limits of policy feedback in the contemporary American state. *Perspectives on Politics, 11*(4), 1071–87.

Quint, J. C., Balu, R., Delaurentis, M., Rappaport, S., Smith, T. J., & Zhu, P. (2013). *The Success for All Model of School Reform: Early Findings from the Investing in Innovation (i3) Scale-Up*. New York: MDRC. Retrieved from: www.mdrc.org/publication/success-all-model-school-reform/file-full.

Redding, C., Cannata, M., & Taylor Haynes, K. (2017). With scale in mind: A continuous improvement model for implementation. *Peabody Journal of Education*.

Rice, J. K. & Malen, B. (2016). When theoretical models meet school realities: Educator responses to student growth measures in an incentive pay program. In Kappler Hewitt, K. & Amrein-Beardsley, A. (eds.) *Student Growth Measures in Policy and Practice* (pp. 29–47). New York: Palgrave Macmillan.

Roderick, M., Nagaoka, J., & Allensworth, E. (2005). Is the glass half full or mostly empty? Ending social promotion in Chicago. *Yearbook of the National Society for the Study of Education, 104*(2), 223–59.

Seeley-Brown, J. & Duguid, P. (2000). *The Social Life of Information*. Cambridge, MA: Harvard Business School.

Senge, P. (1994). *The Fifth Discipline: The Art and Practice of the Learning Organization*. New York: Doubleday.

Shulman, L. (1983). Autonomy and obligation: The remote control of teaching. In Shulman, L. & Sykes, G. (eds.) *Handbook of Teaching and Policy* (pp. 484–504). New York: Longman Publishing Group.

Slavin, R. E. (1996). *Every Child, Every School: Success For All*. Thousand Oaks, CA: Corwin Press.

Smylie, M. A. & Evans, A. E. (2006). Social capital and the problem of implementation. In Honig, M. I. (ed.) *New Directions in Education Policy Implementation: Confronting Complexity* (pp. 187–208). Albany, NY: SUNY Press.

Spillane, J. P. (1996). School districts matter: Local educational authorities and state instructional policy. *Educational Policy, 10*(1), 63–87.

Spillane, J. P. (1998). State policy and the non-monolithic nature of the local school district: Organizational and professional considerations. *American Educational Research Journal, 35*(1), 33–63.

Spillane, J. P. (1999). External reform initiatives and teachers' efforts to reconstruct their practice: The mediating role of teachers' zones of enactment. *Journal of Curriculum Studies, 31*(2), 143–75.

Spillane, J. P. & Callahan, K. A. (2000). Implementing state standards for science education: What district policy makers make of the hoopla. *Journal of Research in Science Teaching, 37*(5), 401–25.

Spillane, J. P. & Thompson, C. L. (1997). Reconstructing conceptions of local capacity: The local education agency's capacity for ambitious instructional reform. *Educational Evaluation and Policy Analysis, 19*(2), 185–203.

Spillane, J. P., Reiser, B. J., & Reimer, T. (2002). Policy implementation and cognition: Reframing and refocusing implementation research. *Review of Educational Research, 72*(3), 387–431.

Stein, M. K., & Coburn, C. E. (2008). Architectures for learning: A comparative analysis of two urban school districts. *American Journal of Education, 114*(4), 583–626.

Stovel, K. & Shaw, L. (2012). Brokerage. *Annual Review of Sociology, 38*(1), 139–58.

Talbert, J. E. & McLaughlin, M. W. (1994). Teacher professionalism in local school contexts. *American Journal of Education, 102*, 123–53.

Tarter, C. J. (1995). Middle school climate, faculty trust, and effectiveness: A path analysis. *Journal of Research and Development in Education, 29*(1), 41–9.

Tschannen-Moran, M. (2001). Collaboration and the need for trust. *Journal of Educational Administration, 39*(4), 308–31.

Useem, E., Offenberg, R., & Farley, E. (2007). *Closing the Teacher Quality Gap in Philadelphia: New Hope and Old Hurdles. The Third Study of Teacher Quality in Philadelphia, A Report from "Learning from Philadelphia's School Reform"*. Philadelphia, PA: Research for Action.

Weatherley, R. & Lipsky, M. (1977). Street-level bureaucrats and institutional innovation: Implementing special education reform. *Harvard Educational Review, 47*(2), 171–97.

Weick, K. E. (1976). Educational organizations as loosely coupled systems. *Administrative Science Quarterly, 21*(1), 1–19.

Weick, K. E. (1995). *Sensemaking in Organizations* (Vol. 3). Thousand Oaks, CA: Sage.

Wong, K. K. & Shen, F. X. (2001). Does school district takeover work? Assessing the effectiveness of city and state takeover as a school reform strategy. Paper presented at the 97th annual meeting of the American Political Science Association, San Francisco.

9

•••••

Sustainability and Scale

This chapter examines why change is so hard. One of the greatest dilemmas of educational research examines how to sustain promising practices. Even with indications of a successful innovation, maintaining that success over time can prove to be an enormous challenge in schools.

Sustainability focuses on whether the reform continues beyond the initial infusion of resources and support (Coburn, 2003; Datnow, Hubbard, & Mehan, 2002; Mitra, 2009; Taylor, 2005). Sustainability preserves fidelity to the original design and longevity of outcomes.

Once an initial infusion of resources and support disappears, most often changes tend to dissipate—and especially changes that affect the core of schooling, including what is taught, how it is taught, and who has a say in school decisions (Scott, 1995; Tyack & Cuban, 1995). Knowledge of how to sustain educational practice is thin (Datnow, 2005). Rather than providing a definitive set of answers, the available research instead more effectively poses a series of dilemmas regarding the preservation and generation of knowledge, supportive structures, and collaborative practices. This section discusses several potential supportive structures, including communication systems, multi-level support, knowledge generation, buffering structures, and intermediary organizations.

With the odds in favor of change failing, David Cohen and Jal Mehta (2017) consider the types of reforms that succeed: reforms that solve a longstanding problem of practice; reforms that reveal and define new problems; reforms that address strong pressure to make a change; reforms that provide innovative and accessible tools to implement a reform idea; reforms aligned with the values of the community, including practitioners, teachers, and parents. They also note that reforms that may fail on large-scale terms might thrive in smaller *niches* of change—subsystems that create a protected space for innovation while buffering and bridging this change from the broader political process. These niches could be at the district level or consist of a network of schools or districts.

Tyack and Cuban (1995) also examined reforms that were implemented smoothly. Ideas that are more peripheral to the concept of schooling are easier to change; structural add-ons that did not affect core principles tended to have greater influence. Also, reforms that were non-controversial, had influential constituencies, or strict mandates tended to last.

Research indicates that sustaining educational change requires persistence of vision and leadership. Sustained efforts tend to have a person facilitating the change effort who is able to dedicate at least 50 percent of their *time* to the change (Miles & Louis, 1990; Moffett, 2000) and a clear *system for communication* and sharing formative feedback on the initiative (Adelman & Taylor, 2003; Berends, Bodilly, & Kirby, 2002; Moffett 2000).

Often innovative ideas are at greatest risk when the visionary leader leaves. Educational change therefore requires *support from multiple levels*, including from the building and district levels and from the broader community (Berends, Bodilly, & Kirby, 2002; Coburn, 2003; Datnow et al., 2002; McLaughlin & Mitra, 2001). At each level of the system, reform initiatives require alliances for the change. These alliances can offer a critical mass of people who support the effort. They can also be powerful insiders who can leverage resources and priorities to help make the change happen (Anderson & Stiegelbauer, 1994; Datnow, 2005; Moffett, 2000). Policy entrepreneurs can also leverage change by building upon the work happening at other levels. For example, the creation of national assessment expectations in the No Child Left Behind legislation grew out of increasing state-level policy development on the topics of standards and assessments (Manna, 2006; McDonnell, 2009).

Growing research suggests that successful educational reforms are moving targets. Sustaining innovative change requires continuing the process of generating innovative, collaborative knowledge that can improve classroom practice, school culture, and organizational structures (Brown & Duguid, 2000; Cochran-Smith & Lytle, 1992; Nonaka & Nishiguchi, 2001; Talbert, Wood, & Lin, 2007). The dilemma exists, then, of how to continue to *encourage knowledge generation* beyond the initial investment of resources and energy (Coburn, 2003; McLaughlin & Mitra, 2001).

Absorptive capacity (Cohen & Levinthal, 1990) is a related concept from business literature. It focuses on the value of ongoing research and development for its own sake. Positioning an organization, or in this case a school, as a learning organization creates greater flexibility and responsiveness when innovation is needed. By already positioning oneself as a learning organization, responsiveness to imposed change tends to be more effective. A great predictor of an ability to learn in the future is prior knowledge and experience with the learning process. Recent research by Farrell and Coburn (forthcoming) examines conditions that enable district learning and reform. The ability for districts to have absorptive capacity requires consideration of "prior knowledge, communication pathways, strategic knowledge leadership, and resources to partner" (Farrell & Coburn, forthcoming, p. 1).

Sustainability requires structures and people that can support the ongoing development of ideas, to buffer criticism, and to build bridges with like-minded constituencies (Yonezawa & Stringfield, 2000). Building and district leaders are critical to the support of change and the buffering of reform from ideas and people who might reduce the effects of the changes (Honig & Hatch, 2004). Common planning time and the creation of professional learning communities are examples of structures that encourage change (McLaughlin & Talbert, 2001). Even in reforms with low resource needs, personnel need ongoing capacity building through professional development and other ways both to bring new ideas into a school and to transfer knowledge among members of the school community (Berends, Bodilly, & Kirby, 2002; Daly & Finnigan, 2011; Spillane, 2005). For example, the transfer of ideas with other schools doing similar work is important (Coburn, 2003; Cooper, Slavin, & Madden; 1997; Mitra, 2009; Muncey & McQuillan, 1996), as is the need for coaches, mentors, and critical friends—people who can provide an outside perspective on the tough work of change (Berends, Bodilly, & Kirby, 2002; Coburn & Russell, 2008; Honig, 2004).

Intermediary organizations, including non-profits, districts, and intermediary units can provide bridges between organizations that can help to sustain work. A noticeable common thread among sustainable initiatives (Lubienski, Scott, & DeBray, 2011) was a strong affiliation with an *intermediary organization* (IO) positioned outside of the school system—in Mitra (2009), for example, non-profits worked with schools on youth activism and community justice issues. Just as IOs can help with implementation, as discussed in Chapter 8, IOs also can help with sustaining change as well. Mitra (2009) found that the IOs mediated four needs—clarity of reform vision, leadership stability, ongoing funding, and knowledge sharing. These IOs, also called non-system actors, provide supporting roles such as coaching, professional development, provision of funds, and creation of reform visions. While they are a part of many reform initiatives, partnerships with IOs are usually considered to be short-term relationships during the implementation phase of an initiative. This research instead suggests that IOs might be better suited as long-term partners in many change efforts. This shift in conceptualizing the role of these organizations has implications for reform efforts in schools, including the need to engage in a more strategic analysis of potential opportunities for partnerships between schools and IOs. An awareness of the important roles that IOs can play in the long-term work toward change could help researchers, practitioners, and policy makers think more intentionally about how to plan for stabilizing such partnerships as an avenue toward sustaining reform initiatives.

Most change efforts eventually also require the transfer of financial responsibility from initial funding support. While initial funding often comes from an outside source, sustaining change usually necessitates ongoing assistance from within institutional walls (Coburn, 2003; McLaughlin & Mitra, 2001). To accomplish this shift, districts must increase funding and technical assistance to replace the support of outside funders. With most districts cash-strapped and pulled in multiple directions, perhaps it is not surprising that resource-hungry reforms tend to fail when resources run dry (Datnow et al., 2002).

●●●●●

Institutionalization

A persistence of a change effort does not equate sustainability with *institutionalization*. Rather than explaining how change occurs, institutional theory tends to focus on how the intransigent nature of schools prevents sustaining educational change (Burch, 2007; Fullan, 2001; Tyack & Cuban, 1995). At the heart of this theory is the idea that cultural beliefs and frames influence how we see the world. Through interactions, people and organizations over time can change these shared frames, which are then incorporated into new policies and institutions.

Tyack and Cuban's classic book *Tinkering Toward Utopia* (1995) provides one of the clearest descriptions of why changing schools is challenging. Change is harder to accomplish, they say, the closer it gets to the "grammar of schooling"—the core ideas that are considered fundamental to schooling, including reading, writing, and arithmetic, how classrooms are configured, and the roles of teacher and student. These concepts define what we collectively consider to be "school." Boyd (1978) also discussed ways in which visible elements of school, such as architecture, can be changed more easily than invisible elements of the technical core. Changing these fundamental ideas calls into question what a school is in our minds.

In organizational theory, the ability to make changes links to the proximity of the proposed change to the *technical core*; changes more at the *periphery* have a greater chance at lasting (Scott, 2002). The more a concept is central to a concept, the more it is related to *legitimacy*. Giving up that core principle can call into question the purpose and goals of that organization, structure, or idea. *Bridging* tactics strengthen interactions and relations between organizations and their environment. These bridging tactics include making an organization more like institutional expectations. Efforts in bridging strategies are trying to become more similar to the broader environmental pressures, such as conforming structures, procedures, and personnel to mimic legitimate organization (Meznar & Nigh, 1995; Scott, 2002; Suchman, 1995). Legitimacy can be established and preserved by codifying informal procedures (Zucker, 1988) and developing formal ties with external sources in the environment (Scott & Meyer, 1994). When facing instances of regulative uncertainty, for example, organizations facing greater normative pressure from their environments tend to develop more elaborate formal structures that connote visible symbols of their compliance to laws (Edelman, 1992). The greater the uncertainty in an organization, the more likely it will borrow structural forms that have been determined to be successful elsewhere (DiMaggio & Powell, 1983). Schools and districts seek to improve legitimacy and to avoid criticism by designing procedures and practices that are valued by successful districts or other accepted organizations (DiMaggio & Powell, 1983; Meyer & Rowan, 1978; Scott, 2002; Scott, Mendel, & Pollack, 1996; Zucker, 1988).

While much institutional research shows why change is hard, it is helpful to examine institutional scholarship that looks at spaces of agency in the face of isomorphism and the pressure to revert to the status quo. For example, Oliver

(1991) looked at ways individuals can strategically interact with institutional pressures that include levels of resistance and adaptation. She offers a typology of resistance levels, from "passive conformity" to the more intentional "proactive manipulation." She considers the institutional factors that influence the choice of these strategies.

One way that organizations and individuals can negotiate with institutional pressures is to protect an organization from external pressures using *buffering* strategies against environmental threats and to avoid crises, including coding mechanisms that create systematic uniformity regarding procedures and rules (Scott, 2002). Organizations may "decouple" their operations from their normative structure (Meyer & Rowan, 1977; Scott, 2002) by adopting policies without intending to implement them fully (Westphal & Zajac, 1994)—particularly in instances where insufficient regulation exists to monitor compliance or the penalties for non-compliance are considered less than the cost of compliance.

Box 9.1 Opting Out of No Child Left Behind

Organizations may even choose to detach from their environment (Honig & Hatch, 2004), such as Utah's deliberations regarding whether to refuse federal Title I money so that they did not have to comply with NCLB regulations. Utah is one of the most conservative states in the nation. It was therefore a political disaster for President George W. Bush, when Utah lawmakers considered resisting against Bush's first legislative priority. Utah opposed the increased federal control of schools, including Utah state representative Margaret Dayton. Federal officials convinced Utah that it could not afford the loss of over $106 million in education aid (Davis, 2005).

A choice of bridging or buffering strategies depends in part on how schools/districts/states construct their view of creating coherence between their policies and external environment pressures (Honig & Hatch, 2004). While an organization may establish new structures, adopt new procedures, and hire new personnel to demonstrate compliance, the content beneath these structures still may not fully comply with the intent of the law. Districts may intend to adopt similar responses during times of organizational crisis, but the district intentions to respond to external pressures are based on contexts including monetary, ideological, and human resources (DiMaggio & Powell, 1983; Dorado, 2002; Pfeffer & Salancik, 1978); the culture and identity of the organization (Carroll & Hannan, 1995; Oliver, 1991; Powell, 1991); the will and capacity of leaders and implementers (Honig, 2003; McLaughlin, 1987); conflicting, blending, or incomplete institutional demands and complex or incomplete institutional environments (Dorado, 2002; Edelman, 1992; Powell, 1991), including whether the district receives conflicting messages from state and federal authorities and the extent to which high-stakes accountability pressures contradict other policy messages (Darling-Hammond, 1990; Shulman, 1983); the extent of collaboration with other organizational and non-system actors (Mitra, 2006; Burch, 2007; Coburn, 2005; Honig, 2003); and the population that the organization serves (Oliver, 1991).

● ● ● ● ●

Pillars of Institutionalism

When considering how change occurs, Dick Scott's (1995) three pillars of insti-tutionalism is very helpful to understand the forces that drive it (see Table 9.1). At the left end of the spectrum are regulative changes, which align with the mandates that we discussed in the policy formation chapter (Chapter 7). Through force and consequences, behavior can change.

Regulative change requires ongoing external pressure, since if the regulation went away, it is assumed that the behavior would cease. If regulations persist for long periods of time, it is sometimes hoped that participants will internalize the change so that regulation is no longer necessary. Forced busing is an example of such a belief—that persistent enforced action could lead to changed hearts and minds.

Normative changes include cultural changes that are explicitly articulated. They could include the norms and values of a school, including the mission statement of the school the shared, and discussed processes for making deci-sions, and how meetings are run.

Cognitive changes occur beneath the surface. They are changes that have become so ingrained in the "way we do things here" that it is hard to talk about them as something separate or artiulate them to others (Coburn, 2003; Har-greaves & Fink, 2000; McLaughlin & Mitra, 2001; Pluye, Potvin, & Denis, 2004). Racial bias can include cognitive beliefs that are not fully considered as one enacts them. Driving to work and not remembering how one got there is another example of a cognitive process. The changes become a part of the iden-tity of a teacher, a school, or a district.

For organizations, nations, and groups seeking validity and legitimacy, *mimicry* of core principles (DiMaggio & Powell, 1983) of others who have greater power is common. One can even see this concept among teenagers who dress in certain brands, listen to certain music, and wear hairstyles to fit in. Countries do the same. Businesses do the same as well. The less they feel legitimate, the more they engage in mimicry. This tendency to trend to similar core ideas is a concept of *isomorphism* (meaning "same shape"). The concept explains why policies look similar across contexts. Much research has looked at these implications for educational change (see, e.g., Ogawa, 1992; Rowan, 1982, 1995, 2001; Rowan & Miskel, 1999; Tyack & Tobin, 1994). Indeed, schools define their

Table 9.1 Three Dimensions of Institutional Change

Regulative	Normative	Cognitive
Explicit exercises of power	Mobilization of bias	Shaping of consciousness
Force, rules, enforcement	Culture, shared norms and values, traditions	Myths, symbols—the unconscious

Source: Adapted from Scott (2002), Fowler, (2009, p. 30), and Gaventa (1980, p. 21).

purpose in part by how external pressures and cultural values define their purpose (Meyer & Rowan, 1977, 1978). Isomorphism helps to explain global trends in policy making, such as accountability pressures amplifying in schools around the globe.

• • • • •

Scale

Concepts of *scale* (Coburn, 2003) or *diffusion* (Rogers, 1995) look beyond whether something remains and considers whether it can spread to other contexts. Other fields call this concept *Type II translation*. Both of these terms explain the ease of which innovations spread more broadly to other locations and contexts.

Scale is a "nested" problem (Elmore, 1996), since it exists at all levels of the system, from classroom to school to district, state and federal. Due to loosely coupled systems (discussed in Chapter 8), new practices occur in isolation.

Traditional ideas of scale focused on different ways that spreading a reform can occur. Elmore describes the "naiveté" regarding how ideas might spread, given the constraints of educational systems. Metaphors of reproduction, contagion, and greenhouses have been used to explain potential growth. Elmore (1996) offered five theories that could serve as a basis for exploring processes of getting to scale. *Incremental growth* is a process of adding on new sites to a reform effort with attention focusing more on the new sites than the current efforts. *Cumulative growth* assumes that external support of a change will continue at the original sites while growth also moves on to other places. *Discontinuous growth* is a bit like a "Ponzi scheme" in the worst case of chain letters and related shady dealings promising money or goods to be sent forward from one person to five new people. In a more positive conception, it is the idea that each new convert to an idea is expected to spread the gospel to several others— similar to a business model for women's at-home businesses like Tupperware, Avon, and Creative Memories. *Unbalanced growth* extends the standard model of innovation to intentionally concentrate highly motivated individuals in one place to grow a new idea. *Cell division* is the final model presented by Elmore. Rather than concentrating talent, it involves increasing numbers of schools aligning with a particular theory. The reproduction focuses on concepts of quality teaching and learning.

In contrast to incremental growth, some scholars believe that policy is more often likely to happen in a diffusion process that aligns with the punctuated equilibrium concept shared in Chapter 7. Policy diffusion often progresses in an S-shaped curve, or a logistic growth curve (Figure 9.1). Adoption at first is slow when a new idea is being tried out. It speeds up as the idea takes hold during positive feedback as ideas diffuse. An idea then slows down again as saturation is reached due to negative feedback (Baumgartner & Jones, 2002).

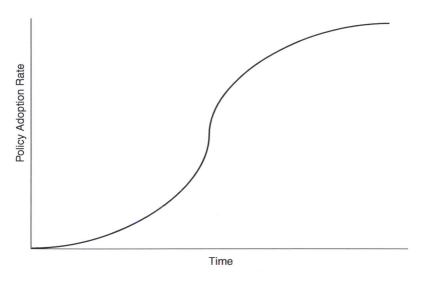

Figure 9.1 Policy Diffusion Curve. Baumgartner and Jones (2002).

●●●●●

A Comprehensive Model of Scale

Coburn (2003) offers a more sophisticated conceptualization of scale that emphasizes the preservation of current change as ideas are spread elsewhere. This concept of scale acknowledges that spreading an idea is not a matter of replication. Rather, the acknowledgement of mutual adaptation in implementation processes means that going to scale also assumes a level of changing a reform to fit local contexts if it is to spread. Tension thus builds with issues of fidelity—scaling up an idea offers many opportunities for violating the core principles of a reform effort and even to contradict the original intentions of a reform. Coburn presents four components of scale—breadth, sustainability, depth, and shift of reform ownership.

■ *Breadth* aligns with the more traditional notions of scale. It implies broadening/spreading a reform to new spaces—new classrooms, new districts. It also includes spread within a classroom to new curricula and ways of interacting in the classroom.

■ *Sustainability* is the persistence of change/reform work over time. In the face of competing priorities and demands, the change effort continues to have a place of priority on the agenda in the original schools even as the idea is spreading elsewhere.

■ *Depth* emphasizes a deepening of a reform. It might mean that a teacher uses a concept in more aspects of her practice, perhaps carrying the concept to a new course or subject. Research shows that consequential change involves teachers integrating new ideas with their own beliefs and previous experiences. The reform needs to fit into their way of teaching. In doing so, this practice becomes more taken for granted and taps deeper into norms and cognitive beliefs—it integrates into the belief system of how one operates.

■ *Shift in reform ownership* implies that external resources and energy are less needed to push for a reform because internal structures, budgets, training, and support are aligned with this reform goal. The school and district share greater ownership of the change and, at an organizational level, alignment occurs to encourage ongoing support of this new perspective/reform.

Evolution. Sustaining changes includes ongoing progress as a learning organization to adapt and adjust conceptual models in an ongoing manner. This component was not present in the original model, but has been proposed as a fifth dimension (Clarke & Dede, 2009; Dede, 2006; Rutledge, Brown, & Petrova, forthcoming). It is based on the conception that the revision of ideas is necessary to sustain innovation. Scale, then, is a process as much as a product.

●●●●●
Improvement Science

This concept of evolution as a component of scale is consistent upon the latest wave of scaling-up research that focuses on continuous improvement, or *design development* (Mintrop, 2016), as an element of scale. Continuous improvement consists of brief and smaller change cycles, conducted iteratively. The process includes identifying problems of practice, using data to assess outcomes, and adapting design frames to local contexts. Building out of conceptions of improvement science, total-quality management, design-based implementation research, and place-based research alliances, *rapid cycle testing* allows for the potential for improved implementation, sustainability, and scale (Cohen-Vogel, Cannata, Rutledge, & Socol, 2016)—also called "Plan Do Study Act" (PDSA; Cohen-Vogel et al., 2016; Langley, Nolan, Norman, & Provost, 2009).

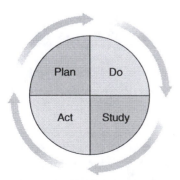

Figure 9.2 Rapid Improvement Cycles: The PDSA Model.

Development, implementation, and scale are no longer considered one-time linear processes but instead occur over and over again through inquiry-based processes of design, implementation, and scale. This cyclical nature of change amplifies the discussion in Chapter 5 that the policy process is not linear, but instead cyclical. Scale in this conception is a part of the design of the policy—the intention of spreading an idea is included in how the initial idea is developed and implemented (Redding, Cannata, & Taylor Haynes, 2017). Uniformity is not the goal, but instead an awareness of local contexts and a continual co-adaptation between design principles and contexts—a concept called scaling down by Erickson (2014) with a goal of shifting from "research-based practice to practice-based research" (p. 6).

Much of the recent development of understanding of scale has occurred through a five-year project, the National Center on Scaling Up Effective Schools (NCSU, 2017), which developed a new model for school systems to scale up practices of effective high schools. Through research–practice partnerships (discussed in Chapter 4), teachers and researchers participate together in these continuous processes, with each cycle building upon the learnings from the previous work.

The goal in this type of a system is to improve outcomes through continuous adjustment, rather than maintaining faithful to the original program design (Cannata, Cohen-Vogel, & Sorum, forthcoming). Adaptation of the design includes both "know how" and "know why"—the focus on not only a product but also the process by which innovation occurs (Cannata et al., forthcoming).

● ● ● ● ●

Comprehension Questions

■ What are the conditions that help to support sustainability? Scale? How are the concepts of scale and sustainability interrelated?

■ What is improvement science and how is it helping to conceptualize ways to deepen change in educational settings?

■ What does it mean for a reform to shift reform ownership?

■ What conditions help changes to be successful?

● ● ● ● ●

Discussion Questions

■ How does institutional theory help to explain why change is so hard? What have we learned from other chapters about how to seek change in this challenging environment?

■ What are buffering and bridging strategies? Can you think of any examples from your experiences? How do they influence a change process?

● ● ● ● ●

Activities

■ View the video of the original opening credits of the television show *Weeds*—it depicts a suburban neighborhood, the song *Little Boxes* playing in the background. Explain how this video depicts the ideas behind institutional theory—what unspoken norms are explicit in the scenes of this video?

■ Break into four groups based on Coburn's four components of scale: sustainability, depth, spread, and ownership. Consider the following:

  ☐ Definition

  ☐ What does success look like in this area?

  ☐ What hinders success in this area?

  ☐ How can the dimension be examined and researched?

● ● ● ● ●

Further Reading

Cannata, M., Cohen-Vogel, L., & Sorum, M. (forthcoming). Partnering for improvement: Improvement communities and their role in scale up. *Peabody Journal of Education*.

Coburn, C. E. (2003). Rethinking scale: Moving beyond numbers to deep and lasting change. *Educational Researcher, 32*(6), 3–12.

Erickson, F. (2014). Scaling down: A modest proposal for practice-based policy research in teaching. *Education Policy Analysis Archives, 22*(9).

Farrell, C. & Coburn, C. (2017). Absorptive capacity: A conceptual framework for understanding district central office learning. *Journal of Educational Change,* 18, 135–159.

Honig, M. I. & Hatch, T. C. (2004). Crafting coherence: How schools strategically manage multiple, external demands. *Educational Researcher, 33*(8), 16–30.

Mintrop, R. (2016). *Design-Based School Improvement: A Practical Guide for Education Leaders*. Cambridge, MA: Harvard Education Press.

Mitra, D. L. (2009). The role of intermediary organizations in sustaining student voice initiatives. *Teachers College Record, 111*(7), 1834–68.

Rutledge, S., Brown, S., & Petrova, K. (2017). Scaling personalization: Exploring the implementation of an academic and social emotional innovation in high schools. *Peabody Journal of Education*. Available online.

Tyack, D. & Cuban, L. (1995). *Tinkering Toward Utopia: Reflections on a Century of Public School Reform*. Cambridge, MA: Harvard University Press.

● ● ● ● ●

Reference List

Adelman, H. S. & Taylor, L. (2003). On sustainability of project innovations as systemic change. *Journal of Educational and Psychological Consultation, 14*(1), 1–25.

Anderson, S. E. & Stiegelbauer, S. (1994). Institutionalization and renewal in a restructured secondary school. *School Organisation, 14*(3), 279–93.

Baumgartner, F. R. & Jones, B. (eds.) (2002). *Policy Dynamics*. Chicago, IL: University of Chicago Press.

Berends, M., Bodilly, S. J., & Kirby, S. N. (2002). *Facing the Challenges of Whole-School Reform: New American Schools After a Decade*. Santa Monica, CA: The RAND Corporation.

Boyd, W. L. (1978). The changing politics of curriculum policy-making for American schools. *Review of Educational Research, 48*(4), 577–628.

Brown, J. S. & Duguid, P. (2000). Mysteries of the region: Knowledge dynamics in Silicon Valley. In Lee, C. M., Miller, W. F., Hancock, M. G., & Rowen, H. S. (eds.) *The Silicon Valley Edge: A Habitat for Innovation and Entrepreneurship* (pp. 16–39). Stanford, CA: Stanford University Press.

Burch, P. (2007). Educational policy and practice from the perspective of institutional theory: Crafting a wider lens. *Educational Researcher, 36*(2), 84–95.

Cannata, M., Cohen-Vogel, L., & Sorum, M. (2017). Partnering for improvement: Improvement communities and their role in scale up. *Peabody Journal of Education*. Available online.

Carroll, G. & Hannan, M. T. (1995). *Organizations in Industry: Strategy, Structure, and Selection*. New York: Oxford University Press.

Clarke, J. & Dede, C. (2009). Design for scalability: A case study of the River City curriculum. *Journal of Science Education Technology, 18*(4), 353–65.

Coburn, C. E. (2003). Rethinking scale: Moving beyond numbers to deep and lasting change. *Educational Researcher, 32*(6), 3–12.

Coburn, C. E. (2005). Shaping teacher sensemaking: School leaders and the enactment of reading policy. *Educational Policy, 19*(3), 476–509.

Coburn, C. E. & Russell, J. L. (2008). District policy and teachers' social networks. *Educational Evaluation and Policy Analysis, 30*(3), 203–35.

Cochran-Smith, M. & Lytle, S. L. (1992). Communities for teacher research: Fringe or forefront? *American Journal of Education, 100*(3), 298–324.

Cohen, D. & Mehta, J. (2017). Why reforms sometimes succeed: Understanding the conditions that produce reforms that last. *American Educational Research Journal, 54*(4), 644–90.

Cohen, W. M. & Levinthal, D. A. (1990). Absorptive capacity: A new perspective on learning and innovation. *Administrative Science Quarterly, 35*(1), 128–52.

Cohen-Vogel, L., Cannata, M., Rutledge, S., & Socol, A. R. (2016). A model of continuous improvement in high schools: A process for research, innovation design, implementation, and scale. *Teachers College Record, 118*(13), 1–26.

Cooper, R., Slavin, R. E., Madden, N. A., & Center for Research on the Education of Students Placed at Risk, Baltimore, MD. (1997). *Success for All: Exploring the Technical, Normative, Political, and Socio-Cultural Dimensions of Scaling Up*, Report no. 16. Baltimore, MD: Johns Hopkins University, Center for Social Organization of Schools.

Daly, A. J. & Finnigan, K. S. (2011). The ebb and flow of social network ties between district leaders under high-stakes accountability. *American Educational Research Journal, 48*(1), 39–79.

Darling-Hammond, L. (1990). Instructional policy into practice: The power of the bottom over the top. *Educational Evaluation and Policy Analysis, 12*(3), 339–47.

Datnow, A. (2005). The sustainability of comprehensive school reform models in changing district and state contexts. *Educational Administration Quarterly, 41*(1), 121–53.

Datnow, A., Hubbard, L., & Mehan, H. (2002). *Extending Educational Reform: From One School to Many*. New York: Routledge/Falmer.

Davis, M. (2005). Utah is unlikely fly in Bush's school ointment. *Education Week, 24.*

Dede, C. (2006). Scaling up: Evolving innovations beyond ideal settings to challenging contexts of practice. In Sawyer, R. K. (ed.) *Cambridge Handbook of the Learning Sciences* (pp. 551–66). Cambridge, UK: Cambridge University Press.

DiMaggio, P. J. & Powell, W. W. (1983). The iron cage revisited: Institutional isomorphism and collective rationality in organizational fields. *American Sociological Review, 48,* 63–82.

Dorado, S. (2002). Institutional environments, partaking and convening. *Organization Studies, 26*(3), 315–414.

Edelman, L. B. (1992). Legal ambiguity and symbolic structures: Organizational mediation of civil rights law. *American Journal of Sociology, 97,* 1531–76.

Elmore, R. (1996). Getting to scale with good educational practice. *Harvard Educational Review, 66*(1), 1–26.

Erickson, F. (2014). Scaling down: A modest proposal for practice-based policy research in teaching. *Education Policy Analysis Archives, 22*(9).

Farrell, C. & Coburn, C. (2017). Absorptive capacity: A conceptual framework for understanding district central office learning. *Journal of Educational Change,* 18, 135–159.

Fowler, F. C. (2009). *Policy Studies for Educational Leaders: An Introduction.* Harlow, Essex: Pearson.

Fullan, M. (2001). *Leading in a Culture of Change.* San Francisco, CA: Jossey-Bass.

Gaventa, J. (1980). *Power and Powerlessness: Quiescence and Rebellion in an Appalachian Valley.* Urbana, IL: University of Illinois Press.

Hargreaves, A. & Fink, D. (2000). The three dimensions of reform. *Educational Leadership, 57*(7), 30–3.

Honig, M. I. (2003). Building policy from practice: District central office administrators' roles and capacity for implementing collaborative education policy. *Educational Administration Quarterly, 39*(3), 292–338.

Honig, M. I. (2004). The new middle management: Intermediary organizations in education policy implementation. *Educational Evaluation and Policy Analysis, 26*(1), 65–87.

Honig, M. I. & Hatch, T. C. (2004). Crafting coherence: How schools strategically manage multiple, external demands. *Educational Researcher, 33*(8), 16–30.

Langley, G. L., Nolan, K. M., Norman, C. L., & Provost, L. P. (2009). *The Improvement Guide: A Practical Approach to Enhancing Organizational Performance* (2nd ed.). San Francisco, CA: Jossey-Bass.

Lubienski, C., Scott, J., & DeBray, E. (2011). The rise of intermediary organizations in knowledge production, advocacy, and educational policy. *Teachers College Record,* July 22.

Manna, P. (2006). *School's In: Federalism and the National Education Agenda.* Washington, DC: Georgetown University Press.

McDonnell, L. M. (2009). Repositioning politics in education's circle of knowledge. *Educational Researcher, 38*(6), 417–27.

McLaughlin, M. W. (1987). Learning from experience: Lessons from policy implementation. *Educational Evaluation and Policy Analysis, 9*(2), 171–8.

McLaughlin, M. W. & Mitra, D. (2001). Theory-based change and change-based theory: Going deeper, going broader. *Journal of Educational Change, 2*(4), 301–23.

McLaughlin, M. W. & Talbert, J. E. (2001). *Professional Communities and the Work of High School Teaching.* Chicago, IL: University of Chicago Press.

Meyer, J. W. & Rowan, B. (1977). Institutionalized organizations: Formal structure as myth and ceremony. *American Journal of Sociology, 83*(2), 340–63.

Meyer, J. W. & Rowan, B. (1978). The structure of educational organizations. In Meyer, J. W. (ed.) *Environments and Organizations* (pp. 78–109). San Francisco, CA: Jossey-Bass.

Meznar, M. & Nigh, D. (1995). Buffer or bridge? Environmental and organizational determinants of public affairs activities in American firms. *The Academy of Management Journal, 38*(4), 975–96.

Miles, M. B. & Louis, K. S. (1990). Mustering the will and skill for change. *Educational Leadership, 47*(8), 57–61.

Mintrop, R. (2016). *Design-Based School Improvement: A Practical Guide for Education Leaders.* Cambridge, MA: Harvard Education Press.

Mitra, D. L. (2006). Educational change on the inside and outside: The positioning of challengers. *International Journal of Leadership Education, 9*(4), 315–28.

Mitra, D. L. (2009). The role of intermediary organizations in sustaining student voice initiatives. *Teachers College Record, 111*(7), 1834–68.

Moffett, C. A. (2000). Sustaining change: The answers are blowing in the wind. *Educational Leadership, 57*(7), 35–8.

Muncey, D. E. & McQuillan, P. J. (1996). *Reform and Resistance in Schools and Classrooms: An Ethnographic View of the Coalition of Essential Schools.* New Haven, CT: Yale University Press.

National Center on Scaling Up Effective Schools, NCSU. (2017). Retrieved from: https://my.vanderbilt.edu/scalingupcenter/.

Nonaka, I. & Nishiguchi, T. (2001). *Knowledge Emergence: Social, Technical, and Evolutionary Dimensions of Knowledge Creation.* New York: Oxford University Press.

Ogawa, R. T. (1992). Institutional theory and examining leadership in schools. *International Journal of Educational Management, 6*(3), 14–21.

Oliver, C. (1991). Strategic responses to institutional processes. *Academy of Management Journal, 16*, 145–47.

Pfeffer, J. & Salancik, G. R. (1978). *The External Control of Organizations: A Resource Dependence Perspective.* New York: Harper & Row.

Pluye, P., Potvin, L., & Denis, J. L. (2004). Making public health programs last: Conceptualizing sustainability. *Evaluation and Program Planning, 27*(2), 121–33.

Powell, R. (1991). Absolute and relative gains in international relations theory. *The American Political Science Review, 85*(4), 1303–20.

Redding, C., Cannata, M., & Taylor Haynes, K. (2017). With scale in mind: A continuous improvement model for implementation. *Peabody Journal of Education.* Available online.

Rogers, E. M. (1995). *Diffusion of Innovations* (4th ed.). New York: Free Press.

Rowan, B. (1982). Organizational structure and the institutional environment: The case of public schools. *Administrative Science Quarterly, 27*, 259–79.

Rowan, B. (1995). Institutional analysis of educational organizations: Lines of theory and directions for research. In Ogawa R. T. (ed.) *Advances in Research and Theories of School Management and Educational Policy* (Vol. 3, pp. 1–20). Greenwich, CT: JAI.

Rowan, B. (2001). *The Ecology of School Improvement: Notes on the School Improvement Industry in the United States.* Philadelphia, PA: Consortium of Policy Research in Education.

Rowan, B. & Miskel, C. G. (1999). Institutional theory and the study of educational organizations. *Handbook of Research on Educational Administration, 2*, 359–383.

Rutledge, S., Brown, S., & Petrova, K. (2017). Scaling personalization: Exploring the implementation of an academic and social emotional innovation in high schools. *Peabody Journal of Education.* Available online.

Scott, W. R. (1995). *Institutions and Organizations.* Thousand Oaks, CA: Sage.

Scott, W. R. (2002). *Organizations. Rational, Natural, and Open Systems*, 5th ed. Upper Saddle River, NJ: Prentice Hall.

Scott, W. R. & Meyer, J. W. (eds.) (1994). *Institutional Environments and Organizations. Structural Complexity and Individualism.* Thousand Oaks, CA: Sage.

Scott, W. R., Mendel, P., & Pollack, S. (1996, March). Studying "everything else": Assessing the environments of an organizational field. Paper presented at Conference on Institutional Analysis, Tucson, AZ.

Shulman, L. (1983). Autonomy and obligation: The remote control of teaching. In Shulman, L. & Sykes, G. (eds.) *Handbook of Teaching and Policy* (pp. 484–504). New York: Longman Publishing Group.

Spillane, J. P. (2005). Distributed leadership. *The Educational Forum, 69*(2), 143–150.

Suchman, M. C. (1995). Managing legitimacy: Strategic and institutional approaches. *The Academy of Management Review, 20*(3), 571–610.

Talbert, J. E., Wood, A., & Lin, W. (2007). *Evaluation of BASRC Phase II: Evidence-Based System Reform: Outcomes, Challenges, Promising Practices.* Stanford University, CA: Center on Research on the Context of Teaching.

Taylor, J. E. (2005). Sustainability: Examining the survival of schools' comprehensive school reform efforts. Paper prepared for at the Annual Meeting of the American Educational Research Association, Montreal, Canada, April.

Tyack, D. & Cuban, L. (1995). *Tinkering Toward Utopia: A Century of Public School Reform.* Cambridge, MA: Harvard University Press.

Tyack, D. & Tobin, W. (1994). The "grammar" of schooling: Why has it been so hard to change? *American Educational Research Journal, 31*, 453–79.

Westphal, J. D. & Zajac, E. J. (1994). Substance and symbolism in CEOs' long-term incentive plans. *Administrative Science Quarterly, 39*(3), 367–90.

Yonezawa, S. & Stringfield, S. (2000). *Special Strategies for Educating Disadvantaged Students Follow-Up Study: Examining the Sustainability of Research Based School Reforms.* Baltimore, MD: Johns Hopkins University CRESPAR.

Zucker, L. G. (1988). *Institutional Patterns and Organizations: Culture and Environment.* Cambridge, MA: Ballinger Publishing Company.

III

●　●　●　●　●

Ideals of the U.S. Educational System

Since the first chapter of this book, we have defined policy as a struggle over ideals. This section examines how deeply held beliefs transform into creative solutions to address longstanding concerns. This section explores what ideals are central within the U.S. political structure and the beliefs of the major political parties.

10

•••••

Understanding U.S. Ideals

Political scientists have observed increasing polarization between political perspectives since the new millennium. With the advent of a broader range of media channels, people are choosing to listen increasingly to viewpoints most similar to their own, and the media often has sought to amplify discord because of the increase in ratings that it can bring (Mutz, 2015). The workplace is often one of the few places where people speak across political differences (Mutz & Mondak, 2006).

The Trump presidency symbolizes an intentional effort to increase dissonance between groups rather than seeking compromise and accommodation (Martin, 2017). Within such a political context, it is increasingly important to understand the range of ideals that have been at the heart of U.S. politics historically. Since the first chapter of this book, we have defined policy as a struggle over ideals. It involves how deeply held beliefs transform into creative solutions to address longstanding concerns. Drawing on previous work of core ideals in U.S. politics (Fowler, 2013; Fuhrman, Goertz, & Weinbaum, 2007; Wirt & Kirst, 1997), this chapter focuses on three core concepts—equity, market-based reforms, and societal control.

•••••

Equity

One set of longstanding ideals in U.S. policy focus on a set of concepts with similar goals—fraternity, equity, equality, and social justice. Included in this idea is the belief of helping all to achieve a minimal standard of living and opportunity, even if it might mean some personal sacrifice. This cluster of concepts also views the needs of the most struggling individual as important or more important than economic gain after a minimal level of growth is sustained.

States have sought greater evening-out of district expenditures through desegregation programs in the 1950s; programs for low-income students in the 1960s; attempts at finance equalization in the 1970s, desegregation, and minimum teacher and facility standards in the 1980s; and a push for standards and coherence in the 1990s to 2000s. States have created supported schools through the creation of school equipment. A principal rationale for state intervention is the belief that only the state can ensure equity and standardization of instruction and resources. Rationale is contested by local control advocates, who contend that flexibility is needed to adjust to diverse circumstances and local preferences (Wirt & Kirst, 1997). Efforts to desegregate schools since *Brown v. Board of Education of Topeka* (1954) have been ineffective. In fact, districts are more segregated along race and class lines than ever before (Orfield, Frankenberg, & Lee, 2003; Kahlenberg, 2001; Reardon, Grewal, Kalogrides, & Greenberg, 2012). Chapter 12 will explore equity in greater depth.

Equity consists of giving everyone the means to be successful, focusing on a minimum floor or standard. It focuses on fairness with recognition that we do not start out with equal opportunities and thus policies must adjust to compensate for deficits that individuals did not control. If all students are to reach the level of literacy, for example, some students come into kindergarten already fluently reading and others have never learned their letters. Relating to test scores, the metaphor of a track race has been used—for all students to reach the same level of proficiency in reading, for some it is a quick sprint, for others it is a marathon and some have already won the race before it has started. Equal results would mean varying levels of input depending on need.

Equality of opportunity is a lower standard. It consists of giving everyone the chance to compete for the same goals but does not consider the varying beginning points of any group. It is much less controversial because it opens up future systems without regard to what has already occurred. Allowing anyone to apply to a college is an example of equality of opportunity, but it does not guarantee equality of admission.

Fraternity is a related concept that consists of common bonds and allegiance between members of a society. These ties encourage putting the collective above individuals, such as Nordic nations and Japan. Policy demonstrating strong levels of fraternity tends to be higher in countries that are highly homogenous. For example, the famed Swedish model of social policy includes a broad safety net of childcare, schooling, health care, elderly care, and paid leave. These policies are paid for by a high taxation rate.

Social justice consists of efforts to look out for underprivileged groups when the majority does not do so. The exact belief of how much individual opportunities should be sacrificed for the broader good varies. Policies such as quotas, immigration, affirmative action, and marriage equality all fit within this realm.

●　●　●　●　●

Markets

Values that increase freedom and decentralize control as well as focus on economic efficiency highlight a market-driven approach. Chapter 11 explores a combination of efficiency and choice by focusing on market-driven philosophies that value the fiscal and economic health of a nation as the essential focus of policy. Behind these policies are values of efficiency, economic growth, and productivity.

Efficiency has been emphasized in reforms such as attempts to consolidate school districts to supposedly reduce expenses and has continued throughout the century. The number of local school districts dropped from 127,531 in 1932, to 89,000 in 1948, and to 13,491 in 2014 (National Center for Education Statistics, 2013–14; Tyack & Cuban, 1995). Standardization of teacher accreditation in the first half of the twentieth century and curricula in the final decades of the twentieth century into the present have also occurred in the name of efficiency. *Economic growth* values the strength of financial and employment indicators as a metric for the health of a nation. *Productivity* values the intensity of production based on the workforce and hours engaged in activity.

Market-driven philosophies also include the values of *liberty and freedom*. These concepts include the right or power to express free will, including the ability to do what one wants and what one has the power to do. Despite increased state power, the United States still holds a strong value toward local decision making. Education reforms often fail when they clash with existing practice or promote new ways to change the core technology of schools called the "grammar of schooling" (Tyack & Cuban, 1995). New forms of public schooling by way of charter schools, vouchers, and homeschooling also show unending interest in families and local communities controlling educational change.

Language within this set of values also includes *excellence, competition*, and *quality*. In all such instances, the ideas concentrate on the notion that competition with global forces necessitates a focus on developing the best and brightest to assure innovation, creativity, and growth, as well as national security. Often this focus on excellence might come at the cost of equity. Policy ideas might include financial support for educational development, such as science development in the post-Sputnik era.

● ● ● ● ●

Societal Control

Another ideal on societal control includes safety, order, and protection. Extremist views push against this focus on order. While contrasting in focus, this cluster of values focuses on who controls the state and how.

Policy focusing on *order/security/control* refers to conserving change and restricting behavior. It consists of a particular set or system of organizing and subduing social structures, institutions, relations, customs, values, and practices. Political and military order relates to physical protection from other nations. Often order and security are valued when an external threat is viewed as greater than the benefits of freedom, such as the dramatic reduction of privacy rights after the 9/11 terrorist attacks. Policy issues that are affected by this balance of freedom and control include gun control, privacy rights, and policies associated with the military and national security organizations. Order can also focus on moral order, such as socially conservative organizations seeking a greater political alignment with the church on social issues such as abortion, gay rights, contraception, and funds to private schools.

Extremism comes to exist when a minority who desire social change is forced to operate outside of the political realm to bring about that change. Often used with the terms fundamentalism and terrorism, it consists of a great mistrust of the political system and a disengagement from it. While fundamentalists tend to want to bring about change within a system, extremists tend to justify violence and the need to destroy the system (Nourbakhsh, 2016). Extremists want radical changes to occur—changes that often might need to include violence or dramatic separation from the broader society. Extremists also share an anti-globalization and an anti-government point of view, and often include notions of conspiracy and secrecy as justification for such radical actions. A minority perspective, extremism diverges from societal values and norms. *Right-wing extremism* includes very strong notions of personal liberty combined with valuing of tradition and the beliefs of previous generations. Superiority toward other groups is often expressed and therefore an opposition to egalitarianism. These beliefs tend to include a nationalistic focus that in extreme versions can be fascism. Examples include Nazi Germany, suicide bombers, and fringe groups seeking to use violence to cause chaos.

Left-wing extremism also has an isolationist tendency but views the market-driven economy as the cause of these problems. These individuals want to eliminate class distinctions and have an extreme bias toward collectivity, such as living in communal situations such as communes or kibbutzim. An extreme version of this perspective could be the original intentions and doctrines of socialism and communism.

●●●●●

U.S. Political Parties

While political parties evolve, over time we can view ways in which constellations of values have led to coalitions of individuals for periods of time. In the United States, Democrats and Republicans have dominated in a two-party system for 168 years. The Democrats emerged from the Democratic/Republican split in 1828 with the election of Andrew Jackson. The Republican Party was created from the Whig party in 1854. Prior to the Civil War, the North was primarily Republicans and the South was primarily Democrats.

With the election of Donald Trump and the support of Bernie Sanders in the 2016 election, populist outcry across the political spectrum signaled unrest in the current political structure. Populism tends to rise when people feel that the current political structures do not represent their voices and their beliefs (Horger, 2013; Sundquist, 1983; Inglehart & Norris, 2016).

The Republican Party has consisted of a coalition of four groups. The first group is *fiscal conservatives*, who have strong beliefs in the market system, with a focus on economic and budget concerns and the value of small government. This group has sometimes been referred to as "budget hawks." The Tea Party movement represented an extreme version of this perspective, focusing on dramatic reductions in spending in federal and state governments and opposing national health care, such as the Affordable Care Act passed in the Obama administration.

The second is *libertarians*, who have strong values of liberty, freedom, and small government. They tend to be liberal on social values, believing that people should have the right to make decisions about their own bodies and relationships. Libertarians and fiscal conservatives often coalesce on policy. Libertarians have run candidates in their own party, but often vote and run with Republicans because the U.S. system does not easily allow for the voting-in of third-party candidates. Thus, for example, Rand and Ron Paul from Kentucky are self-professed libertarians but align with the Republican Party rather than running under the Libertarian Party banner.

The next two groups in the Republican tent clash with the first two on many issues. The third group includes *military*—be it veterans, active military, and military families who depend on a strong presence of order, security, and control for their livelihood, and robust financial support of the military by the government. Military voting alignment with the Republican Party can be traced back to 1866 with the founding of the Grand Army of the Republic by Northern veterans of the Civil War interested in securing pensions for veterans and their widows. With a membership of nearly 500,000, their rhetoric supported the Republican Party and even went so far as to condemn Democrats as traitors who supported the succession of the Southern states (Inbody, 2008). More recently, Klingler and Chatagnier (2014) support the notion that veterans and active military are more conservative than their non-veteran counterparts and therefore much more likely to support Republican candidates. During the presidential campaign of 2016, polling of active duty military indicated a modest majority planned to vote for Republican candidate Donald Trump (54 percent) and a reluctance to support Hillary Clinton (25 percent) as the Democratic candidate, preferring Bernie Sanders by 13 percent (Shane & Altman, 2016). The unwillingness of the military to support Hillary Clinton was related to her close ties with the Obama administration, under which military spending began to drop after U.S. troops were removed from Iraq and Afghanistan and Congress allowed sequestration cuts to go into effect (Jacobson & Sherman, 2015).

The fourth group aligned with the Republican Party is also in contradiction with the first two. This group has been called the Religious Right in recent times and the Moral Majority before, and includes people with conservative social values of a strong moral order that could coalesce on religious principles, including socially conservative issues (abortion, gay rights, evolution, sex education) and the ability to attend religious schools with public dollars (vouchers).

The Christian Right supports socially conservative policies, including standards, evolution, and sex education. Christian Right organizations include the Christian Coalition, Pat Robertson and Eagle Forum (focusing on sex education), Focus on the Family (focused on family solidarity and child rearing), Concerned Women for America, and the Free Congress Foundation (focused on traditional female roles) (Spring, 2011). Since the 1990s, Christian organizations have focused on local education policies by taking control of school boards through targeted get-out-the-vote campaigns through large churches. *Stealth campaigning* was a process documented often in the 1990s when candidates did not reveal their conservative beliefs until after they were elected.

Box 10.1 Case Study: School Board Takeover

In an extreme example of local takeover, Hasidic Jews have taken over school boards in areas of New York through strong organizing of synagogue members. With a strong preference for private, religious schools, these school boards have moved to defund much of the public-school system in these districts and to sell land to synagogues (Glass, 2014).

"A Not-So-Simple Majority," *This American Life*, Episode 534, tells the story of Hasidic and Ultra-Orthodox Jewish community members getting elected to the school board in East Ramapo, New York school district to defund the public-school system. The narrative details efforts to gut the school budget to the point that students lacked sufficient courses to graduate.

Find on the web using the following search terms:

This American Life; Episode 534; September 12, 2014

On the Democratic side, the party has fewer factions but also less clarity of purpose. The central ideal in the party focuses on social justice. Most often self-identified as *progressives*—but previously called liberals and "New Politics liberals"—these individuals believe that the government needs to extend its reach to protect the underprivileged. Conservatives often refer to Democrats as "liberals"—a term that tends to have a derogative connotation since the George H. W. Bush presidency. Democratic policies focus heavily on the rights of individuals and the protection of the most vulnerable. Equity is a strong goal with a focus on race, class, and gender historically. Highly prizing the safety nets presented in northern European nations, policies of this group include a focus on childcare, health care, education, and workers' rights.

The election of Bill Clinton signaled a new wave of Democrats focused on attracting centrists. Called *Clinton Democrats* and aligned with beliefs of *neoliberals* in Europe, these individuals emphasize fiscal conservatism while still holding true to progressive ideals. In the biggest critique of Clinton Democrats, Bernie Sanders in the 2016 primary focused on ways in which Hillary Clinton was attached to big money and corporate wealth as a critique of the valuing of the market-driven system.

The *Green Party* continues to persist in the United States despite the difficulties of third-party efforts. Much like the Libertarians on the right, individuals in this party often vote for a majority party instead of for their own party due to the two-party, winner takes all system of voiting in the United States.

The party is based on a platform of four issues: peace (anti-war); ecology (reduce fossil fuels and encourage renewable resources); social justice (expand the safety net); and democracy (greater transparency of government, expand voting rights, increase public financing of elections). Most Green Party advocates vote with the Democratic Party due to the struggles of the third-party system, although the many defectors to Ralph Nader of the Green Party likely cost Al Gore the election in 2000.

While not very visible in the United States, Bernie Sanders, a professed *socialist*, had a strong run for the Democratic Party ticket in 2016. Socialists are opposed to market ideals and instead believe that policies must be in place to flatten the economic system, such as improve workers' rights and improve access to pay for college and homes. Socialists have a great deal in common with the Green Party but do not always have the same primary focus on the environment. The Social Democratic parties in European nations have had much greater success in national elections. This party advocates a peaceful evolution to a socialist system through broader safety nets of social policies and a graduate transition of society from capitalism to socialism using established political processes.

●●●●●

Comprehension Questions

■ Define the differences between fraternity, equity, equality and social justices.

■ Define the differences between efficiency, competition, and excellence.

■ What are the main coalitions within the Republican party?

●●●●●

Discussion Questions

■ In the current political climate of the United States, how are these factions and definitions of parties changing? Do the different factions within the parties make for strong allies or tenuous relationships?

■ Globally, how are alignments around ideals changing? Is globalism creating more shared values or greater factionalism, or both?

●●●●●

Activities

Have students break into groups to define the ideals discussed in this chapter and use external research to elaborate on them. Then have students choose the words/values/beliefs most important when selecting political candidates and three that are least important to them. Repeat the exercise for political parties—have students present the political party factions in greater depth and then have students identify with parties. Note—the identification of values and parties can be done anonymously through free online survey software or software associated with online coursework.

Create a spectrum of political parties and make a line across the room. Have students stand on the line in accordance with their beliefs.

● ● ● ● ●

Further Reading

Horger, M., (2013). Breaking up is hard to do: America's love affair with the two-party system. *Origins, 6*(10), July. Retrieved from: http://origins.osu.edu/article/breaking-hard-do-americas-love-affair-two-party-system.

Inglehart, R. & Norris, P. (2016). *Trump, Brexit, and the Rise of Populism: Economic Have-Nots and Cultural Backlash.* Research working papers, Harvard University John F. Kennedy School of Government. Retrieved from: https://research.hks.harvard.edu/publications/getFile.aspx?Id=1401.

● ● ● ● ●

Reference List

Fowler, F. C. (2013). *Policy Studies for Educational Leaders: An Introduction.* Upper Saddle River, NJ: Merrill.

Fuhrman, S. H., Goertz, M., & Weinbaum, E. (2007). Educational governance in the United States: Where are we? How did we get here? Why should we care? In Fuhrman, S. H., Cohen, D., & Mosher, F. (eds.) *The State of Education Policy Research* (pp. 41–61). Mahwah, NJ: Lawrence Erlbaum Associates.

Glass, I. (2014). 534: A not-so-simple majority. *This American Life.* Originally aired on 12 September. WBEZ and Chicago Public Media. Retrieved from: www.thisamericanlife.org/radio-archives/episode/534/a-not-so-simple-majority.

Horger, M. (2013). Breaking up is hard to do: America's love affair with the two-party system. *Origins, 6*(10), July. Retrieved from: http://origins.osu.edu/article/breaking-hard-do-americas-love-affair-two-party-system.

Inbody, C. D. S. (2008). Partisanship and the military: Voting patterns of the American military. In Reveron, D. S. & Hicks Stiehm, J. (eds.) *Inside Defense* (pp. 139–50). New York: Palgrave Macmillan US.

Inglehart, R. & Norris, P. (2016). *Trump, Brexit, and the Rise of Populism: Economic Have-Nots and Cultural Backlash.* Research working papers, Harvard University John F. Kennedy School of Government. Retrieved from: https://research.hks.harvard.edu/publications/getFile.aspx?Id=1401.

Jacobson, L. & Sherman, A. (2015). PolitiFact sheet: Military spending under Obama and Congress. *PolitiFact, Tampa Bay Times,* December 14. Retrieved from: www.politifact.com/truth-o-meter/article/2015/dec/14/politifact-sheet-our-guide-to-military-spending-/.

Kahlenberg, R. D. (2001). Learning from James Coleman. *Public Interest, 144,* 54–72.

Klingler, J. D. & Chatagnier, J. T. (2014). Are you doing your part? Veterans' political attitudes and Heinlein's conception of citizenship. *Armed Forces and Society, 40*(4), 673.

Martin, R. (2017). How the attacks on Trump reinforce his strategy. *Harvard Business Review*, January 12. Retrieved from: https://hbr.org/2017/01/how-the-attacks-on-trump-reinforce-his-strategy.

Mutz, D. (2015). *In-Your-Face Politics: The Consequences of Uncivil Media*. Princeton, NJ: Princeton University Press.

Mutz, D. C. & Mondak, J. J. (2006). The workplace as a context for cross-cutting political discourse. *Journal of Politics, 68*(1), 140–55.

National Center for Education Statistics. (2013–14). *Number of Public School Districts and Public and Private Elementary and Secondary Schools: Selected Years, 1869–70 Through 2013–14* [Table]. Retrieved from: http://nces.ed.gov/programs/digest/d14/tables/dt14_214.10.asp.

Nourbakhsh, Y. (2016). Extremism, its different types and influential factors that help shape it. In *Third ISA Forum of Sociology*, ISA conference, July 10–14.

Orfield, G., Frankenberg, E. D., & Lee, C. (2003). The resurgence of school segregation. *Educational Leadership, 60*(4), 16–20.

Reardon, S., Grewal, E., Kalogrides, D., & Greenberg, E. (2012). Brown fades: The end of court-ordered school desegregation and the resegregation of American public schools. *Journal of Policy Analysis and Management, 31*, 876–904.

Shane, L. & Altman, G. R. (2016). Military Times survey: Troops prefer Trump to Clinton by a huge margin. *Military Times*, May 9. Retrieved from: www.militarytimes.com/story/military/election/2016/05/09/military-times-survey-donald-trump-beats-hillary-clinton/84132402/.

Spring, J. (2011). *The Politics of American Education*. New York: Routledge.

Sundquist, J. L. (1983). *Dynamics of the Party System: Alignment and Realignment of Political Parties in the United States* (Rev. ed.). Washington, DC: Brookings Institution.

Tyack, D. & Cuban, L. (1995). *Tinkering Toward Utopia*. Cambridge, MA: Harvard Education Press.

Wirt, F. M., & Kirst, M. W. (1997). *The Political Dynamics of American Education*. Berkeley, CA: McCutchan Publishing Corporation.

11

●●●●●

Market-Driven Reform: The Foundation for the Accountability Movement[1]

Schools serve multiple, often conflicting purposes in the United States. While individual achievement is a key focus, the collective good is also a purpose. Inherently, public schools are political systems that balance values of academic achievement with equal opportunity and teaching of the democratic process.

This chapter looks at the market philosophies that undergirded the rise in in many reforms, including testing and charter school policy. The market system refers to a return to a preference for ideas associated with a laissez-faire system of economic liberalism, or a system in which economic transactions are freed from government interference. Related policies include deregulation, free trade, privatization, and fiscal austerity. Critics of the market approach tend to call it *neoliberalism*, citing evidence that market-driven policies create greater disparity and injustice between the wealthy and the poor and between wealthy nations and poorer nations (Apple, 2006).

This chapter will discuss the underpinnings of market theory and then discuss the policies that arise from a market-driven approach. Choice policies encourage movement of public funds to other schooling opportunities for students. More than one in ten students attend private schools and millions of families choose public schools through a choice program, often called a "voucher" (Lubienski & Lubienski, 2014, p. 44). The number of students participating in voucher programs has increased three-fold in the past ten years. In 2013–14, 5 percent of public school students—2.5 million students overall—attended charter schools (National Center for Education Statistics, 2015). Vouchers were a standard component of the Republican educational agenda in the 1990s and have received renewed attention from the Trump administration.

A choice policy with greater bipartisan support but still with controversy has been the rise in publicly funded "charter schools" since the 1990s. According to the National Center for Education Statistics, all but seven states have charter laws. Charter schools quadrupled during the first decade of the twenty-first century, from 340,000 to 1.6 million (Wohlstetter, Smith, & Farrell, 2013, p. 2). The number of students in charter schools has increased from 0.8 million to 2.5

million in the past ten years, ending in 2015. There are 5.1 percent of public school students enrolled in a charter school. The remainder of this chapter will examine the history of charter school development in the United States and consider the most current research documenting the impact of charter schools.

●●●●●

Market Theory

A market approach to education expects that bureaucracy creates problems. Increasing market mechanisms in the educational system would increase effectiveness, efficiency, and innovation (Lubienski, Scott, & DeBray, 2014). Effectiveness, according to this system of belief, would be increased by focusing on standardized measures of achievement and measuring students to ensure excellence. Organizations are considered the unit of change. As individuals make rational choices, organizations will be incentivized to make changes. Thus, the belief is not only that individuals could choose from a broader range of educational options, but this opportunity of choice will motivate the public institutions to change. This vision assumes that incentives are clear and will cause parents to make rational choices and organizations to adapt accordingly.

Market-driven reforms have been an increasing focus of educational policy in the United States in the past 30 years. Market-based educational reforms have become a part of the landscape of schooling in America (Wohlstetter et al., 2013). The most recent wave of market-driven reform rests in the principles designed by Milton Friedman in the 1950s (Friedman, 1995). Friedman believed in the power of the market to solve the ills of the education system. He based his work upon the principles of libertarianism, which focused on small government and the ability of people to have more agency in decisions about their lives (see Chapter 10). Friedman believed that the government should not provide services, such as public schooling or health care, because doing so creates a monopoly.

Friedman proposed a drastic version of a market-driven educational system. Beyond minimal financial support by the government, the control of education should be handed over to a purely private system in which families would purchase education from a range of providers. They would receive some financial assistance to do so from the state and could top off this assistance with any additional money to secure the educational program that they chose (Witte, 2009). Using economic language, Friedman believed that the externalities of the broader effects of education justify the funding but not the management of the system (Hochschild & Scovronick, 2003; Lubienski et al., 2014). Rather, private providers should offer a variety of school choices with a range of structures, formats, and visions. The role of government beyond provision of funds would be limited to protecting minimal standards, similar to health codes in other industries.

●●●●●

Rational Choice Theory

These principles emerged into the field of *rational choice theory*, an economic viewpoint that expects that people adjust their behaviors by weighing the costs and benefits of their choices. Applied to education, it assumes that failures in the educational system are a result of a lack of choice due to a public monopoly. As Ronald Reagan described, schools cannot solve the problem because they *are* the problem (Lubienski et al., 2014, p. 6). It also assumes that the types and range of schooling opportunities will be driven by the market—in this case, parents.

Rational choice theory assumes that families will readily change schools based on the quality of them, encouraging "good" schools to thrive and "bad" schools to close. It assumes that parents can have access to and will use information about the full range of schooling choices to select the best educational opportunity for their children. Yet research indicates that parents often lack access to information about schools and that the information is unequally distributed (Hochschild & Scovronick, 2003, p. 139). The most disadvantaged families have the least access to information (Goldhaber, 1999; Frankenberg, Siegel-Hawley, Wang, & Orfield, 2012).

Yet, research has shown that parents do not take full information into account. While parents report that they make choices based on the achievement data of schools, they actually are more likely to choose schools with similar demographics to their families instead (Buckley & Schneider, 2009; Hamilton & Guin, 2005; Hastings, Kane, & Staiger, 2005; Kleitz, Wieher, Tedin, & Matland, 2000).

The Republican Party continued to champion Friedman's ideas after the 1950s. Albert Hirschman (1970) argued that either schools should be made more democratic so that they are directly accountable to parents, or schools should be shifted to a market-based system to feel the effects of competition.

A broader enthusiasm of rational choice theory arose in the 1990s. The report by John Chubb and Terry Moe (1990), *Politics, Markets, and America's Schools*, served as a catalyst for this new wave of enthusiasm. Chubb and Moe discussed a broad version of choice, a plan in which private, religious, and secular schools would be included as well as the public system (Hochschild & Scovronick, 2003). They framed competition as the panacea for all of the perceived problems of the U.S. educational system that were discussed in *A Nation at Risk* seven years before (National Commission on Excellence in Education, 1983). Governmental control of public education hampered the natural market forces of choice, competition, and school autonomy from flourishing (Chubb & Moe, 1990, discussed in Lubienski et al., 2014 p. 6).

Business groups active in education championed this model, encouraging a more flexible system. For example, the report by the New Commission on the Skills of the American Work Force (National Center on Education and the Economy, 2006), *Tough Choices for Tough Times*, saw increasing globalism as a key indicator of the economic future. Under-skilled workers would suffer in this new economic framework. The report expected growth in creative work in research and design and a decline in routine labor. It encouraged greater career education and identification of career tracks at an earlier age in the United States, and the ongoing work of business groups also created a strong argument for the creation of the Common Core Standards (Committee for Economic Development, 2014), discussed in Chapter 2.

The rise of the influence of foundations and educational philanthropists in educational policy (discussed in Chapter 4) has especially focused on the increase of market-based reforms (Reckhow, 2013; Scott & Jabbar, 2014; Scott, 2009). These philanthropic donors have invested in intermediary organizations that provide implementation support to districts based on ideological perspectives more than evidence-based empirical research. The intermediaries, charter management organizations (CMOs), share selective evidence on the effectiveness of charter schools' efforts with district, state, and national allies (Castillo et al., 2015). The goal of these networks is to expand charter school creation and to broaden the political contexts that permit charter schools to exist.

●●●●●

Critique of a Market-Based System

Academic achievement in market models. While research in the 1980s and 1990s suggested the potential academic benefits of private schools over public ones (Bryk, Lee, & Holland, 1993; Coleman & Hoffer, 1987; Lubienski, Crane, & Lubienski, 2008, p. 690), recent research has caused serious question of these assumptions. In the largest study to examine the effects of market-based education to date, Lubienski and Lubienski (2006) found that public schools had *higher achievement levels* than demographically comparable private and charter schools. Thus, the primary assumption that market theory would increase achievement was not found in the largest scale study on the subject. Lubienski and Lubienski (2014) state:

> a growing body of evidence suggests that private, autonomous, choice-based schools are not necessarily more innovative or academically effective but instead often perform at lower levels even as they attract more able students. Public school students actually outperformed democratic peers in most types of private and independent schools.
>
> (p. 138)

Accounting for socioeconomic differences of the populations of students served, Lubienski and Lubienski found significant differences between public, private, and charter schools. The two notable exceptions were levels of teacher certification and reform-oriented instruction. These two variables were actually stronger in public schools, which the authors speculate might help to explain the larger academic gains in public schools. A deeper analysis looked for the causes of this weighty finding (Lubienski & Lubienski, 2014). The research found that market mechanisms such as deregulation and autonomy may in fact cause problems for schools rather than fix them. The Lubienski and Lubienski research states strongly that market-based reforms speculate on how markets should work in education, but there is little peer-reviewed, strong evidence to support the claims. Yet both these factors are neglected and even dismissed by marketists. They continue, "market initiatives continue to gain ground despite the fact that published, peer-reviewed studies consistently failed to find persuasive evidence that these programs are effective at achieving their promised goals" (p. 138).

Issues of equity are particularly a concern for market-based systems. Ironically, one of the first choice-based reforms was designed to increase equity. *Magnet schools* were created in the 1970s to reintegrate middle-class black and white families back into inner-city schools. Goals of magnet schools were to create high-quality, mission-specific programs focused on careers, the arts, and conceptual reforms such as open classrooms and back to basics. Over 3200 magnet schools still operate nationwide as of 2015 (National Center for Education Statistics, 2016). A few districts have broadened from magnets to controlled choice plans that have some parental choice but also district-focused racial balancing, including Montclair, NJ, Hartford, CT, and Cambridge, MA (Hochschild & Scovronick, 2003).

⊛ ⊛ ⊛ ⊛ ⊛

Vouchers

School voucher programs give families money to attend schools outside of the public system at reduced or no cost. Fitting with the tenets of the market system, vouchers are premised on the idea that the autonomy and independence of non-public schools along with the choice of discontented families will create opportunities and competitive incentives for the entire system.

The United States never adopted the voucher idea nationally, such as occurred in Chile and in Sweden (Wohlstetter et al., 2013). The first voucher experiment occurred in the early 1970s in Alum Rock Union Elementary School District—a district serving kindergarten through eighth grade. Funded in part by a federal grant from the Office of Economic Opportunity, the experiment only ran two of the expected five years due to lack of interest of district families. The experiment was subject to many restrictions that did not truly fit the ideal of a market reform, such as the California legislature refusing to let private schools be included in the choices of families (Hochschild & Scovronick, 2003).

One of the most famous voucher programs began in 1990 in Milwaukee—the Milwaukee Parental Choice Program, considered the nation's longest running voucher experiment. The experiment required private schools to randomly select students if they had too many applicants. Participants in the program tended to be black or Latino, poorer than the district average, from single families, and on governmental assistance. However, parent education and parent involvement tended to be higher than the average Milwaukee public school family (Witte, 1998). In 1998, religious schools were declared eligible by state law for the Milwaukee voucher program. The Wisconsin Court upheld this ruling and the U.S. Supreme Court let the state decision stand without ruling.

Subsequent voucher programs occurred in Washington, DC, Indiana, Louisiana, and Cleveland, Ohio. All of the programs targeted the vouchers toward disadvantaged students, including poor, special needs, and students otherwise not being served well by home schools (Wohlstetter et al., 2013). The vast majority in all voucher experiments chose religious schools, since these schools represent three-quarters of the existing private schools and are usually the only ones with tuition low enough to be covered by the vouchers (Witte, 2009). The Cleveland Scholarship and Tutoring program was the focus of the *Zelman v. Simmon-Harris* (2002) ruling by the U.S. Supreme Court, which ruled that state-funded voucher programs do not necessarily violate the Establishment Clause—the clause in the first amendment of the constitution that prohibits the establishment of religion by Congress.

Voucher programs have a history of uniting politically disparate groups—ultra conservatives uniting with leftist and often racially nationalist and locally active African Americans, such as in Minnesota, Massachusetts, and Cleveland. For example, the Milwaukee program was created by Polly Williams, an African American state legislator who was a former welfare recipient. Co-sponsors were Republican governor Tommy Thompson and ultra conservative activist Clint Bolick, co-founder of the Institute for Justice (Hochschild & Scovronick, 2003). Despite diverse coalitions, the rhetoric for the programs tended to be drawn from conservative politicians and policy advocates.

Contested research on vouchers. The research on vouchers is highly contested. Pro-voucher research argues that private schools are an effective tool for increasing academic outcomes for disadvantaged students (Forster, 2009; Greene, 2001; Howell, Wolf, Peterson, & Campbell, 2000; Watkins, 2006; Wolf, 2006). Small-scale research has cited significant learning gains for students attending private schools, including a report finding strong private school effects for Milwaukee students using vouchers. Similar studies were conducted in New York, Dayton, and the District of Columbia finding academic gains for African American students using vouchers (Friedman Foundation, 2009; Greene, 2001; Greene, Peterson, & Du, 1996; Greene, Peterson, & Du, 1998; Howell et al., 2000).

The pro-voucher research faces great scrutiny because it is rarely peer-reviewed—an academic process that provides a measure of rigor by having three other academics review the work anonymously and provide feedback on its rigor and merit. A closer look at the findings of high-quality studies of vouchers also indicates that voucher experiments rarely indicate significant achievement gains over time (Krueger & Zhu, 2004; Lubienski, 2016; Molnar, 1999; Witte, 1996). Considerable controversy exists regarding the results in Milwaukee especially; Witte (2009) reports that no researcher found any difference after four years in reading. The Cleveland and DC experiments did not generate significant achievement gains over time either. Researchers stress that it is important to take care to measure the effect of schools rather than differences in family background. Affluent and assertive families are likely to take advantage of choice programs (Lubienski & Lubienski, 2014).

A recent evaluation of the DC Scholarship Opportunity program (Dynarski, Rui, Webber, & Gutmann, 2017) raised strong concerns about the value of that voucher program. The program was established in 2004 as the only federally funded voucher program that permitted low-income students to attend private schools. The study looked at experiences after one year in the program for students who used the voucher in 2012, 2013, and 2014. The study found that, after one year, the program had a negative impact on mathematics achievement. It also had no impact on parental satisfaction and parental involvement. The only positive impact was parental perceptions of safety at school.

●●●●●

Charter Schools

Charter schools are publicly funded schools of choice, operating independently from school districts under an agreed-upon performance contract, or "charter." Charters may not charge tuition and must offer an unbiased admission process in exchange for regulatory freedom; the expectation is that they will be more innovative and responsive to family needs.

Fitting with a market model, the expectation also includes that the charters will encourage reform in the traditional school district. The goals of charter schools include classroom-focused, school-focused, and system-focused aims. At the classroom level, charters are expected to improve student achievement.

At the organizational level, charters are expected to encourage innovation in programming, governance, staffing, and finance, to improve opportunities for teacher leadership, and to increase school autonomy. At the system level, charters are expected to diversify the provision of education, to increase competition among schools, and to increase accountability (Wohlstetter et al., 2013).

A more recent phenomenon has been the creation of *cyber charter schools* in which students attend school from home or other remote locations. In 2014–15 there were 275,000 students in 25 states attending cyber charters. Sources of instruction include online instruction that can be software based, recorded instruction, or teacher-centered distance learning (Ahn, 2011; Huerta, González, & d'Entremont, 2006; Vergari, 2009). Online charters are an attractive option for unusual students—those who must work to help support families and students with an unusual talent or skill, such as a competitive athlete. They have proven helpful for students with unstable households (divorce, frequent moving) and for gifted students or students with disabilities who can work at their own unique pace. However, most online charter school students have been proven to lag behind traditional public school students on

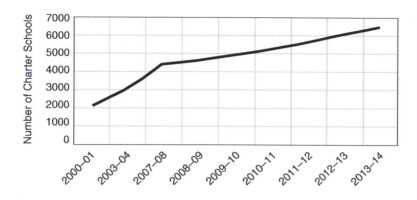

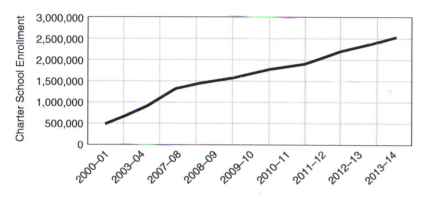

Figure 11.1 Charter School Trends (2001–14). U.S. Department of Education, National Center for Education Statistics, Common Core of Data (CCD), "Public Elementary/Secondary School Universe Survey," 1990–91 through 2013–14.

math and reading achievement, in some cases to the extent that it seemed as though they were not receiving schooling at all (Woodworth et al., 2015).

Cyber charters provide students with little live teaching contact time; most schooling is student driven, independent study. Keeping students engaged in this environment is a challenge. Parents are expected to play a much greater role in mediating student learning (Gill et al., 2015). Rural students are most likely to attend cyber charter schools (Mann, Kotok, Frankenberg, Fuller, & Schafft, 2016).

Recent research raises concerns about the quality of cyber charter schools, however. Cyber students show poor learning in math and reading across racial and poverty groups compared to charter and traditional schools (Woodworth et al., 2015). Legal scholars also question if cyber charters have enough safeguards to avoid fraud (DeJarnatt, 2015).

Funding of Charter Schools

Charter schools are funded by the public school system. The federal allocation for charter schools expanded greatly since the Obama administration and has expanded within the Trump administration. Charter funding was twice that of magnet schools and included supporting networks of charter schools, such as Aspire and Green Dot.

They are funded based on enrollment levels and a per-pupil formula. State laws vary regarding whether the district must pay full tuition for any local student choosing a charter or whether the state pays for a portion of the cost. Most states do not provide additional funds for building/facility expenses. Most states also do not fund charter schools at 100 percent of the funds allocated to traditional schools, including Alaska, Colorado, Minnesota, and New Jersey (Batdorff et al., 2014). As of 2017, seven states do not allow charters at all: Kentucky, Montana, Nebraska, North Dakota, South Dakota, Vermont, and West Virginia (Thomsen, 2016).

States decide who can authorize the creation of charter schools, but the intention was always to diversify who decides beyond districts. The premise behind charter school law was that districts with sole authority to authorize charters would rather block charter approval or make the approval process very difficult (Henig, 2013). State laws vary regarding authorizers, but they can include local districts, special-purpose charter school boards, non-profit organizations, state universities, mayor's office, or a combination of authorities. Authorizers have the job of choosing who gets a charter, monitoring compliance of current charters with applicable laws, and deciding when to revoke a charter (Vergari, 2009). Most charters are authorized for three years at a time and then need to be renewed, but the laws vary greatly. Arizona offers 15-year charters (Wohlstetter et al., 2013). As of 2015, over 1000 authorizing bodies existed nationwide—1032 authorizers in 44 states (National Association of Charter School Authorizers, 2015).

States also decide how charter schools are funded. In the state of Pennsylvania, original charter school legislation expected districts to fund 50 percent of the cost of sending a student to charter schools, and 50 percent by the state. Conservative governor Tom Corbett switched the funding structure to 100 percent district funded without district voice in determining who receives or keeps charters. The steep rise in district funds that must be sent to charter schools is causing great financial burden for districts. Rising health care costs and pensions are the other two reasons for fiscal concerns (Pennsylvania School Boards Association, 2015).

In a market system, the financial consequences of the loss of funding are supposed to incentivize districts and schools to improve. Emerging research is analyzing the extent to which these theories are true in practice. Hurya Jabbar (2015) examined networks of principals in New Orleans (a heavily charter school area). She found that the degree of competitive tension between schools depended on geography, the transfer/mobility of students, academic achievement, the personal qualities of the principal, and the charter school networks present.

History of Charters

The word "charter" was coined by American Federation of Teachers union president Al Shanker, building upon a paper written by educator colleague Ray Budde entitled "Education by Charter" (1989). Shanker's weekly columns in the *New York Times* championed the idea of teachers setting up autonomous schools, or schools within schools.

Leadership in Minnesota became intrigued by the charter idea. Minnesota leaders convened a conference of New York City's District Four, a district following Shanker's envisioned reform. The subsequent proposal was developed by Ted Kolderie and Joe Nathan in Minnesota, with support from a range of citizens and business groups, including the Citizen League, the Minnesota Business Partnership, a program leader from the progressive Urban Coalition, the president of the state PTA, and Republican governor Rudy Perpich. It emphasized a different vision than teacher leadership—one that focused more on the end of governments as the exclusive providers of education (Henig, 2013; Vergari, 2009).

The first charter in the United States was issued in Minnesota in 1991. State and district tuition dollars would follow students to schools of their choice, adding competition to school systems (Mazzoni, 1991). Minnesota had already been a leader of public choice policies prior to charters. The state developed cross-district open enrollment policies in 1988, despite opposition from the teachers' unions and school administrators. They also passed a Post-Secondary Education Options (PSEO) law that allowed high school students to earn dual credits (for high school and college) by taking courses at local colleges and universities (Henig, 2013; Vergari, 2009; Wohlstetter et al., 2013).

In 1992, California passed the next charter school law. Rather than facing teacher opposition, the California law was passed with union support because it was framed as a milder alternative to a voucher ballot initiative that narrowly failed the previous year. The voucher proposal was supported by the business community and heavily opposed by teacher unions (Wohlstetter et al., 2013).

Wohlstetter et al. (2013) have documented three waves of charter school development. The first wave of charter schools tended to be either existing public schools or new schools started by teachers, parents, and community organizations. Called "moms and pops," these schools tended to be standalone schools that focused on disadvantaged students, including special needs students and English language learners. Most of these schools were elementary schools. They tended to be smaller than district-run schools and nearly all of them localized decision making at the school site.

The second wave of charter schools began in the mid-1990s. By 1999, more than 1400 charter schools had been established in 32 states and the District of Columbia (Wohlstetter et al., 2013, p. 9). Federal laws were passed during this time, including the 1995 Public Charters Program, which encouraged states to apply for funds to bolster charter schools. The monies could be used for the creation, sustainability, and marketing of charter schools.

This second wave included the creation of charters sponsored by for-profit companies, called education management organizations (EMOs), or charter management organizations (CMOs), discussed also in Chapter 4. While they often were not allowed to directly acquire a charter, schools could affiliate with these organizations to receive a menu of services, including office support and curricula. Non-profits with a similar mission also joined in greater numbers. CMOs tended to uphold a particular educational philosophy. Foundations have greatly supported these ventures, including the Schools Venture Fund, Walton Family Foundation, and Charter School Growth Fund (Wohlstetter et al., 2013). An advocacy organization called the Center for Education Reform, headed by Jeanne Allen, a strong advocate for public choice, was formed in Washington, DC. The power of CMOs has been greatly increasing as they gain support through right-leaning foundations and ALEC (also discussed in Chapter 4).

A third wave of charter schools focused on refinements, beginning in 2005. The creation of a professional organization—the National Alliance for Public Charter Schools—signaled that charters were firmly established in the U.S. educational policy system. The focus of the third wave included creating standards of quality and exemplary practice (Wohlstetter et al., 2013). For example, Ted Kolderie, who helped create the original Minnesota charter school law, developed a Model Charter School law and sought to compare states to this ideal (Education/Evolving, 2004).

This third wave of reform also focused more on revising current laws. Henig (2013) documented the shift in charter school policy. The creation of laws tended to occur under Republican governors, who were 20 percent more likely to revise charter school laws (Wong & Langevin, 2007). Also, Republican governors played a key role in the creation of charter school laws but Democratic legislatures tended to take the role in revising the laws (Holyoke, Henig, Brown, & Lacireno-Paquet, 2009). Revision of charter school laws tended to increase flexibility and accountability (Shober, Manna, & Witte, 2006). States also began to revise the caps on charter schools during this era. Some states created absolute limits to the number of charters issued; others have increased numbers by reducing or removing caps on charter school numbers.

The Obama administration's Race to the Top legislation helped to encourage states to increase flexibility of charter school laws since unrestricted charters was one of the goals of the law, with billions of dollars of incentives encouraging states to do so. The U.S. Department of Education under the Obama administration also expanded the charter schools program and offered charter school funding through its i3, Investing in Innovation awards (Wohlstetter et al., 2013).

Research on charters. Evaluating the effectiveness of charter schools is important because the variance within charter schools is about as great as the variance of public schools. They vary greatly in size, student demographics, geographic location, and based on the parameters of state charter laws. Methodological issues also arise based on the data available, such as student versus school-level data, and aggregated or disaggregated data (Bulkley & Fisler, 2003).

The most comprehensive review of charter school research to date has been conducted by Wohlstetter et al. (2013) through an extensive literature review process that evaluated over 7000 publications, including giving a full text review of over 500 peer-reviewed journal articles between 2000 and 2011. Wohlstetter et al. (2013) looked carefully at evidence that charters were impacting education more broadly. They found:

1. Mixed findings about *the impact of performance* of students remaining at non-charter schools, concluding that a number of studies have found that the presence of charter schools has had a positive influence on student achievement more broadly (Booker, Gilpatrick, Gronberg, & Jansen, 2008; Bohte, 2004; Holmes, DeSimone, & Rupp, 2006; Stoddard & Kuhn, 2008; Ladner, 2007) and another set has found no evidence of broader student achievement (Bifulco & Ladd, 2005; Bulkley & Fisler, 2003; Lavertu & Witte, 2009; Zimmer et al., 2009).

2. A review of the research *did not find increased financial efficiency* in charter school operations. Instead, the problem of financial woes is one of the most common reasons for charter closures (Wohlstetter et al., 2013). Additionally, market competition does not lead to a reallocation of resources predicted by market theorists to become more effective. Instead it leads districts to focus more on marketing and on excluding costly students (Lubienski & Lubienski, 2014).

3. *Changes in the behavior of teachers, school, leaders, and district administrators* indicate an increase in efforts to market to students (Lubienski & Lubienski, 2014) as well as more polite behavior from administrators and staff (Wohlstetter et al., 2013).

4. Some studies indicate reduced *teacher quality* in charter schools—smaller numbers of credentialed teachers and less teaching experience in charter schools (Brown, Wohlstetter, & Liu, 2008), although this trend could be changing due to federal requirements of "highly qualified teachers" mandated during the NCLB era (NCLB, 2002). Recent studies indicate that charter school teachers are younger than comparative public school teachers. They tend to attend more selective undergraduate institutions but have lower GPAs (Baker & Dickerson, 2006; Cannata, 2008; Harris, 2007; Koppich, Holmes, & Plecki, 1998; Wohlstetter et al., 2013). Charter school teachers who leave the profession tend to have lower GPAs and pass rates. Other studies found that years of experience and years at the current school best predicted attrition (Miron & Applegate, 2007).

5. Wohlstetter et al. (2013) found overall *greater segregation* in charter schools than public schools but the effects on the non-charter schools were limited. They concluded that charter schools were not intentionally seeking to resegregate the system but not seeking to reduce segregation either. The research found that charter schools are not intentionally skimming high achieving students, although there is some evidence of skimming and

segregation occurring (Wohlstetter et al., 2013). Access to charters is affected by significant gaps geographically. Charter schools are often located in segregated neighborhoods (Frankenberg & Lee, 2003). Due to legislative silences on issues such as how students will be transported to charters and on geographic boundaries, new charters tend to be more segregated (Ausbrooks, 2002). Segregation patterns also differ based on regions of the country. The West and Southwest have charters enrolling more white students than the Northeast (Renzulli, 2006). Parent preference can also affect school segregation since parents tend to send their children to schools with other children of the same race (Ausbrooks, Barrett, & Daniel, 2005; Lacireno-Paquet & Brantley, 2008; Mickelson, Bottia, & Southworth, 2012; Weiher & Tedin, 2002).

●●●●●

Comprehension Questions

■ What are the key components of a market-driven system?
■ What is the definition of neoliberalism?
■ Why were magnet schools created?
■ Describe the controversy in voucher research.
■ What are the promises and pitfalls of charter schools overall?

●●●●●

Discussion Questions

■ How do various market-driven reforms align with values discussed in Chapter 10? With different political parties?
■ What is known about cyber charter schools? What is not known?
■ What incentives, intended and unintended, do market-driven reforms create for the public school system?
■ What assumptions and conditions must exist for market-driven reforms to be successful?

●●●●●

Activities

■ Explore the tool 50-State Comparison on Charter School Policies by Jennifer Thomson published on the Education Commission of the States website: www.ecs.org/charter-school-policies/.
■ How does the charter policy in your state compare to other states in the nation?

■ Design a National Issues Forum discussion on Preparing Today's Kids for Tomorrow's Jobs. Deliberate the three positions—a firm foundation (basic skills); academic competition (train for global economic needs); community first (train for local jobs): www.nifi.org/en/issue-guide/preparing-todays-kids-tomorrows-jobs.

■ Listen to or read the NPR report "Lessons From the Nation's Oldest Voucher Program," reported by Claudio Sanchez, *All Things Considered*, May 19, 2017: www.npr.org/sections/ed/2017/05/19/527429292/the-nations-oldest-voucher-program-beacon-of-hope-or-failed-experiment.

■ Listen to the NPR report "Lessons on Race and Vouchers From Milwaukee," reported by Claudio Sanchez, May 16, 2017: www.npr.org/sections/ed/2017/05/16/523612949/lessons-on-race-and-vouchers-from-milwaukee.

■ Listen to the NPR report "Kentucky's Unprecedented Success in School Funding Is on the Line," April 26, 2016: www.npr.org/sections/ed/2016/04/26/475305022/kentuckys-unprecedented-success-in-school-funding-is-on-the-line.

■ The central office at the school district has proposed to charter your neighborhood high school effective for the 2017–18 academic school year. The district is holding a meeting regarding the charter proposal and you will be attending the meeting. You will be a stakeholder placed into a discussion group:

1. Charter schools (such as):
   ☐ KIPP
   ☐ Uncommon
   ☐ Success Academy
   ☐ Harpswell Coastal Academy in Maine
   ☐ Green Dot of Los Angeles

2. Public schools (school districts)
   ☐ Current teacher
   ☐ Principal
   ☐ Superintendent
   ☐ Charter school administrator at the central office within the school district

3. Local union (we have chosen not to outline specific union organizations)

4. Parents
   ☐ Single parent with four kids who works two jobs
   ☐ Highly involved parent—two-parent household, partner is on city council
   ☐ PTA soccer parent
   ☐ Parent engaged in child's life, but absent from school life due to work demands

Discussion:

Split students into one of the four groups. Based on the conversation and the representatives in your group, do you think the charter school would be enacted?

First have within-group conversation and then have a cross-group discussion.

■ Read recent research on charter schools such as the resources suggested below to provide a brief summary for the class on how charter schools were used to rebuild New Orleans, and the controversies associated with this strategy.

Box 11.1 Case Study

One of the most documented stories of the charter system is the Harlem Children's Zone, founded by Geoffrey Canada. The Harlem Children's Zone website (hcz.org) has extensive material about the program. Several works have also been written about the program, including:

"Going Big," *This American Life* Radio, Episode 364, www.thisamericanlife. org/radio-archives/episode/364/going-big. About Harlem Children's Zone.
Tough, P. (2009). *Whatever it takes: Geoffrey Canada's quest to change Harlem and America.* Mariner books.
The documentary film *Waiting for Superman,* http://documentarylovers. com/film/waiting-for-superman/

And many critiques of the documentary, including:

"Waiting for Superman": Critics Say Much-Hyped Education Documentary Unfairly Targets Teachers Unions and Promotes Charter Schools

Find on the web using the following search terms:

Democracy Now; October 1, 2010; Waiting for Superman Critics

●●●●●

Note

1 Thank you to Sarah Moryken and John Allegro.

●●●●●

Further Reading

DeJarnatt, S. (2015). Keep following the money: Financial accountability and governance of cyber charter schools, Temple University Legal Studies Research Paper No. 2014–01 Retrieved from: https://papers.ssrn.com/sol3/papers.cfm?abstract_id=2370125.

Dynarski, M., Rui, N., Webber, A., & Gutmann, B. (2017). *Evaluation of the DC Opportunity Scholarship Program: Impacts After One Year* (NCEE 2017–4022). Washington, DC: National Center for Education Evaluation and Regional Assistance, Institute of Education Sciences, U.S. Department of Education.

Gill, B., Walsh, L., Wulsin, C. S., Matulewicz, H., Severn, V. Grau, E., Lee, A., & Kerwin, T. (2015). Inside online charter schools. *Mathematica*, Washington, DC. Retrieved from: www.mathematica-mpr.com//our-publications-and-findings/publications/inside-online-charter-schools.

Greene, J., Peterson, P., & Du J. (1998). School choice in Milwaukee: A randomized experiment. In Peterson, P. E. & Hassell, B. C. (eds.) *Learning from School Choice* (pp. 329–44). Washington, DC: Brookings Institution Press.

Jabbar, H. (2015). Competitive networks and school leaders' perceptions: The formation of an education marketplace in post-Katrina New Orleans. *American Educational Research Journal, 52*(6), 1093–131.

Lubienski, C. & Lubienski, S. T. (2014). *The Public School Advantage: Why Public Schools Outperform Private Schools*. Chicago, IL: University of Chicago.

Orfield, G. & Frankenberg, E. (2013). *Educational Delusions? Why Choice Can Deepen Inequality and How to Make It Fair*. Berkley, CA: University of California Press.

Wohlstetter, P., Smith, J., & Farrell, C. (2013). *Choices & Challengers: Charter School Performance In Perspective*. Cambridge, MA: Harvard Education Press.

● ● ● ● ●

Reference List

Ahn, J. (2011). Policy, technology, and practice in cyber charter schools: Framing the issues. *Teachers College Record, 113*(1), 1–26.

Apple, M. W. (2006). Understanding and interrupting neoliberalism and neoconservatism in education. *Pedagogies, 1*(1), 21–6.

Ausbrooks, C. (2002). Ensuring that underrepresented student groups have access to charter schools: What states are doing. *Planning & Changing, 33*(3–4), 185–96.

Ausbrooks, C. Y. B., Barrett, E. J., & Daniel, T. (2005). Texas charter school legislation and the evolution of open-enrollment charter schools. *Education Policy Analysis Archives, 13*(21).

Baker, B. & Dickerson, J. L. (2006). Charter schools, teacher labor market deregulation, and teacher quality: Evidence from the Schools and Staffing Survey. *Educational Policy, 20*(5), 752–78.

Batdorff, M., Maloney, L. May, J. Speakman, S., Wolf, P., & Cheng, A. (2014). *Charter School Funding: Inequity Expands*. Fayetteville: University of Arkansas.

Bifulco, R. & Ladd, H. D. (2005). Results from the Tar Heel state: Older students did better when in regular public schools. *Education Next, 5*(4), 60–6.

Bohte, J. (2004). Examining the impact of charter schools on performance in traditional public schools. *Policy Studies Journal, 32*(4), 501–20.

Booker, K., Gilpatrick, S., Gronberg, T., & Jansen, D. (2008). The effect of charter schools on traditional public school students in Texas: Are children who stay behind left behind? *Journal of Urban Economics, 64*(1), 123–45.

Brown, R., Wohlstetter, P., & Liu, S. (2008). Developing an indicator system for schools of choice: A balanced scorecard approach. *Journal of School Choice, 2*(4), 392–414.

Bryk, A. S., Lee, V. E., & Holland, P. B. (1993). I. Context. In Bryk, A. S., Lee, V. E., & Holland, P. B. (eds.) *Catholic Schools and the Common Good* (pp. 15–78). Cambridge, MA: Harvard University Press.

Buckley, J. & Schneider, M. (2009). *Charter Schools: Hope or Hype?* Princeton, NJ: Princeton University Press.

Budde, R. (1989). Education by charter. *Phi Delta Kappan, 70*(7), 518–20.

Bulkley, K & Fisler, J. (2003). A decade of charter schools: From theory to practice. *Educational Policy, 17*(3), 317–42.

Cannata, M. (2008). Teacher qualifications and work environments across school types. In Arsen, D., Belfield, C., Cannata, M., Chi, W. C., Cobb, C., Evergreen, S., Garn, G., Lubienski, C., Mead, J., Arlin Mickelson, R. A., Miron, G., Ni, Y., Southworth, S., Urschel, J., & Wilson, T. S. (eds.) *School Choice: Evidence and Recommendations.* Boulder, CO: Education Policy Research Unit and Education and the Public Interest Center. Retrieved from: http://nepc.colorado.edu/publication/school-choice-evidence-and-recommendations.

Castillo, E., Lalonde, P., Owens, S., DeBray, E., Scott, J., & Lubienski, C. (2015). E-advocacy among intermediary organizations: Brokering knowledge through blogs. Paper presented at the annual meeting of the American Educational Research Association, Chicago, IL, April.

Chubb, J. & Moe, T. (1990). *Politics, Markets, and America's Schools.* Washington, DC: Brookings Institution.

Coleman, J. S. & Hoffer, T. (1987). *Public and Private High Schools: The Impact of Communities.* New York: Basic Books.

Committee for Economic Development. (2014). *Business Leaders Support College- and Career-Readiness: Staying the Course on Common Core.* Washington, DC, September.

DeJarnatt, S. (2015). Keep following the money: Financial accountability and governance of cyber charter schools, Temple University Legal Studies Research Paper No. 2014–01 Retrieved from: https://papers.ssrn.com/sol3/papers.cfm?abstract_id=2370125.

Dynarski, M., Rui, N., Webber, A., & Gutmann, B. (2017). *Evaluation of the DC Opportunity Scholarship Program: Impacts After One Year* (NCEE 2017–4022). Washington, DC: National Center for Education Evaluation and Regional Assistance, Institute of Education Sciences, U.S. Department of Education.

Education/Evolving. (2004). *A Model RFP.* Saint Paul, MN: The Center for Policy Studies.

Forster, G. (2009). *A Win-Win Solution: The Empirical Evidence on How Vouchers Affect Public Schools.* Indianapolis, IN: Friedman Foundation for School Choice.

Frankenberg, E. & Lee, C. (2003). Charter schools and race: A lost opportunity for integrated education. *Education Policy Analysis Archives, 11*(32).

Frankenberg, E., Siegel-Hawley, G., Wang, J., & Orfield, G. (2012). *Choice Without Equity: Charter School Segregation and the Need for Civil Rights Standards.* Los Angeles, CA: Civil Rights Project

Friedman Foundation. (2009). *The ABCs of School Choice, 2007–2008 Edition.* Indianapolis, IN: Friedman Foundation for Educational Choice.

Friedman, M. (1995). *Public Schools: Make Them Private.* Washington, DC: Cato Institute.

Gill, B., Walsh, L., Wulsin, C. S., Matulewicz, H., Severn, V., Grau, E., Lee, A., & Kerwin, T. (2015). Inside online charter schools. *Mathematica.* Washington, DC. Retrieved from: www.mathematica-mpr.com//our-publications-and-findings/publications/inside-online-charter-schools.

Goldhaber, D. D. (1999). School choice: An examination of the empirical evidence on achievement, parental decision making, and equity. *Educational Researcher, 28*(9), 16–25.

Greene, J. P. (2001). The hidden research consensus for school choice. In Peterson, P. E. & Campbell, D. E. (eds.) *Charters, Vouchers, and Public Education* (pp. 83–101). Washington, DC: Brookings Institution.

Greene, J., Peterson, P., & Du, J. (1996). *The Effectiveness of School Choice in Milwaukee: A Secondary Analysis of Data from the Program's Evaluation.* Occasional paper 96–3, Cambridge, MA, Program on Education Public and Governance, Harvard University.

Greene, J., Peterson, P., & Du, J. (1998). School choice in Milwaukee: A randomized experiment. In Peterson, P. E. & Hassell, B. C. (eds.) *Learning from School Choice* (pp. 329–44). Washington, DC: Brookings Institution Press.

Hamilton, L. S, & Guin, K. (2005). Understanding how families choose schools. In Betts, J. R. & Loveless, T. (eds.) *Getting Choice Right: Ensuring Equity and Efficiency in Education Policy* (pp. 40–60). Washington, DC: Brookings Institution Press.

Harris, D. (2007). Should I stay or should I go? Comparing teacher mobility in Florida's charter and traditional public schools. *Peabody Journal of Education, 82*(2/3), 274–310.

Hastings, J. S., Kane, T. J., & Staiger, D. O. (2005). Parental preferences and school competition: Evidence from a public school choice program. NBER Working Paper #11805. Cambridge, MA: National Bureau of Economic Research, Inc.

Henig, J. (2013). *The End of Exceptionalism in American Education: The Changing Politics of School Reform.* Cambridge, MA: Harvard Education Press.

Hirschman, A. (1970). *Exit, Voice, and Loyalty. Response to Decline in Firms, Organizations and States.* Cambridge, MA: Harvard University Press.

Hochschild, J. & Scovronick, N. (2003). *The American Dream and the Public Schools.* New York: Oxford University Press.

Holmes, G. M., DeSimone, J., & Rupp, N. G. (2006). Friendly competition. *Education Next, 6*(1), 66–70.

Holyoke, T. T., Henig, J. R., Brown, H., & Lacireno-Paquet, N. (2009). Policy dynamics and the evolution of state charter school laws. *Policy Sciences, 42*(1), 33–55.

Howell, W., Wolf, P. J., Peterson, P. E., & Campbell, D. E. (2000). *Test-Score Effects of School Vouchers in Dayton, Ohio, New York City, and Washington, DC: Evidence from Randomized Field Trials.* Cambridge, MA: Harvard Program on Education Policy and Governance.

Huerta, L. A., González, M. F., & d'Entremont, C. (2006). Cyber and home school charter schools: Adopting policy to new forms of public schooling. *Peabody Journal of Education, 81*(1), 103–39.

Jabbar, H. (2015). Competitive networks and school leaders' perceptions: The formation of an education marketplace in post-Katrina New Orleans. *American Educational Research Journal, 52*(6), 1093–131.

Kleitz, B., Wieher, G., Tedin, K., & Matland, R. (2000). Choice, charter schools and household preferences. *Social Science Quarterly, 81*(3), 846–54.

Koppich, J., Holmes, P., & Plecki, M. (1998). *New Rules, New Roles? The Professional Work Lives of Charter School Teachers: A Preliminary Study.* Annapolis, MD: NEW Professional Library.

Krueger, A. & Zhu, P. (2004). Another look at the New York City School Voucher Experiment. *American Behavioral Scientist, 47*(5), 658–98.

Lacireno-Paquet, N. & Brantley, C. (2008). *Who Chooses Schools and Why: The Characteristics and Motivations of Families Who Actively Choose Schools.* Brief for Great Lakes Center for Education Research and Practice, East Lansing, MI.

Ladner, M. (2007). The impact of charter schools on catholic schools: A comparison of programs in Arizona and Michigan. *Catholic Education, 11*(1), 101–14.

Lavertu, S. & Witte, K. (2009). The impact of Milwaukee charter schools on student achievement. *Issues in Governance Studies, 23*. Washington, DC: The Brookings Institute.

Lubienski, C. (2016). Review of "A win-win solution" and "The participant effects of private school vouchers across the globe." National Education Policy Center, June.

Lubienski, C. & Lubienski, S. T. (2014). *The Public School Advantage: Why Public Schools Outperform Private Schools*. Chicago, IL: University of Chicago.

Lubienski, C., Crane, C., & Lubienski, S. (2008). What do we know about school effectiveness? Academic gains in public and private schools. *Phi Delta Kappan, 89*(9), 689–95.

Lubienski, C., Scott, J., & DeBray, E. (2014). The politics of research production, promotion, and utilization in educational policy. *Educational Policy, 28*(2), 131–44.

Lubienski, S. T. & Lubienski, C. (2006). School sector and academic achievement: A multilevel analysis of NAEP mathematics data. *American Education Research Journal, 43*(4), 651–98.

Mann, B., Kotok, S., Frankenberg, E., Fuller, E., & Schafft, K. (2016). Choice, cyber charter schools, and the educational marketplace for rural schools. *The Rural Educators, 37*(3).

Mazzoni, T. L. (1991). Analyzing state and school policy: An arena model. *Educational Evaluation and Policy Analysis, 13*(2), 115–38.

Mickelson, R. A., Bottia, M. C., & Southworth, S. (2012). School choice and segregation by race, class, and ability. In Mathis, W., Miron, G., & Welner, K. (eds.) S*chool Choice: The Evidence, Politics, and Policies for the 21st Century*. New York: Routledge.

Miron, G. & Applegate, B. (2007). *Teacher Attrition in Charter Schools*. Boulder, CO: Education Policy Research Unit and Education and the Public Interest Center.

Molnar, A. (1999). *Educational Vouchers: A Review of the Research*. Milwaukee, WI: Center for Education Research, Analysis, and Innovation, University of Wisconsin.

National Association of Charter School Authorizers. (2015). Charter school authorizers, September 3. Retrieved from: https://public.tableau.com/profile/nacsa#!/vizhome/NACSAAuthorizerContactInformation9315/Map.

National Center on Education and the Economy. (2006). *Tough Choices for Tough Times. The Report of the New Commission on the Skills of the American Work Force*. Washington, DC: NCEE.

National Center for Education Statistics. (2015). Percentage distribution of public charter schools, by enrollment size: School years 2003–04 and 2013–14. Retrieved from: http://nces.ed.gov/programs/coe/indicator_cgb.asp.

National Center for Education Statistics. (2016). Number of magnet schools year 2014–15. Retrieved from: https://nces.ed.gov/programs/digest/d16/tables/dt16_216.20.asp.

National Commission on Excellence in Education. (1983). *A Nation at Risk: The Imperative of Educational Reform*. Washington, DC: U.S. Government Printing Office.

NCLB. No Child Left Behind Act of 2001, Pub. L. No. 107–110, § 115, Stat. 1425 (2002).

Pennsylvania School Boards Association. (2015). *PSBA Special Report: The Critical Need for Charter School Reform*. www.psba.org.

Reckhow, S. (2013). *Follow the Money: How Foundation Dollars Change Public School Politics*. New York: Oxford University Press.

Renzulli, L. A. (2006). District segregation, race legislation, and black enrollment in charter schools. *Social Science Quarterly, 87*, 618–37.

Scott, J. (2009). The politics of venture philanthropy in charter school policy and advocacy. *Educational Policy, 23*(1), 106–36.

Scott, J. & Jabbar, H. (2014). The hub and the spokes: Foundations, intermediary organizations, incentivist reforms, and the politics of research evidence. *Educational Policy, 28*(2), 233–57.

Shober, A. F., Manna, P., & Witte, J. F. (2006). Flexibility meets accountability: State charter school laws and their influence on the formation of charter schools in the United States. *Policy Studies Journal, 34*(4), 563–87.

Stoddard, C. & Kuhn, P. (2008). Incentives and effort in the public sector: Have US education reforms increased teachers' work hours? *Economics and Education Review, 27*(1), 1–13.

Thomsen, J. (2016). *50-State Comparison: Charter School Policies.* Retrieved from: www.ecs.org/charter-school-policies/.

Vergari, S. (2009). Charter school policy issues and research questions. In Sykes, G., Schneider, B., & Plank, D. (eds.) *Handbook of Education Policy Research.* (pp. 478–90). New York: Routledge.

Watkins, S. (2006). Are public or private schools doing better? How the NCES study is being misinterpreted. *Heritage Foundation Backgrounder,* 1968, 1–4.

Weiher, G. R. & Tedin, K. L. (2002). Does choice lead to racially distinctive schools? Charter schools and household preferences. *Journal of Policy Analytics and Management, 21,* 79–92.

Witte, J. F. (1996). Reply to Green, Peterson and Du: "The effectiveness of school choice in Milwaukee. A secondary analysis of data from the program's evaluations." Madison, WI: Department of Political Science and the Robert La Follette Institute of Public Affairs, University of Wisconsin, Madison.

Witte, J. (1998). The Milwaukee Voucher Experiment. *Educational Evaluation and Policy Analysis, 20*(4), 229–51..

Witte, J. (2009). Vouchers. In Sykes, G., Schneider, B., & Plank, D. (eds.) *Handbook of Education Policy Research* (pp. 491–501). New York: Routledge.

Wohlstetter, P., Smith, J., & Farrell, C. (2013). *Choices & Challengers: Charter School Performance in Perspective.* Cambridge, MA: Harvard Education Press.

Wolf, P. J. (2006). School voucher programs: What the research says about parental school choice. *Brighton Young University Law Review,* 2008(1), 415–46.

Wong, K. K. & Langevin, W. E. (2007). Policy expansion of school choice in the American states. *Peabody Journal of Education, 82*(2), 440–72.

Woodworth, J. L., Raymond, M. E., Chirbas, K., Gonzalez, M., Negassi, Y., Snow, W., & Van Donge, C. (2015). *Online Charter School Study 2015.* Stanford, CA: Center for Research on Education Outcomes, Stanford University.

Zelman v. Simmons-Harris (00–1751) 536 U.S. 639 (2002) 234 F.3d 945, reversed.

Zimmer, R., Gill, R., Booker, K., Lavertu, S., Sass, T. R., & Witte, J. (2009). *Charter Schools in Eight States: Effects on Achievement, Attainment, Integration, and Competition.* MG-869. Pittsburgh: RAND.

12

●●●●●

Equity

Equity defines ways to increase access and fair treatment. It examines the ways in which educational policy can increase equity. For example, the passage of the Individuals with Disabilities Education Act (1975) created a set of rights of students with disabilities to demand an equitable education. Prior to this legislation, over one million children were denied enrollment in schooling due to disability (Future of Children, 1996). Today, one in ten children receives special education under IDEA.

A graphic conception originally created by Craig Froehle in 2012 (see Figure 12.1) compared people standing behind a fence watching a soccer match. People of different heights in the equality picture are all standing on the same size boxes trying to watch the game. Some can see and some cannot. In contrast, in the equity picture, how the boxes are distributed has changed to influence the access to viewing the game. Some need boxes of support, some do not. As this meme has traveled about social media, some have added words with the images, saying that equality is sameness; equity is fairness. Others have elaborated on this graphic to suggest that a liberation strategy would involve knocking the fence down entirely (Froehle, 2016).

●●●●●

Power

Ultimately issues of equity relate to issues of power and oppression. Theories of power observe the benefits ascribed by those who have power in keeping others

Figure 12.1 **Equality Versus Justice.**

from having more, whether explicitly or implicitly. Figure 12.1 implies this intentional power imbalance of giving the powerful more and making it even harder for the less empowered by digging a hole rather than allowing all to be treated the same.

Mayes et al. (2017) explore ranges of interpretation of power and education, including visual conceptions of power as a lighthouse, a label, a see-saw, a pie, a partnership, as well as theoretical traditions including critical, poststructural, and psychoanalytical. Fitting with Taylor and Robinson's discussion of "plural and context-specific relations of power" (2009, p. 173), the Mayes et al. work calls for conceptual resources that can analyze the movement of power, such as students and adults working together on student work. Each perspective on power provides its own lens that illuminates some strands of the concept.

Critical Pedagogy

Paulo Freire's work of critical pedagogy is one of the most famous critiques of a neoliberal educational system (Freire, 1970). Freire critiques the traditional education system as a banking model of students receiving information and facts from teachers. Freire instead advocated for a critical consciousness or conscious-raising model based on dialogue and inquiry between teachers and students called *praxis.*

This alternative approach builds out of the cultural knowledge or Funds of Knowledge (González, Moll, & Amanti, 2005) to raise critical consciousness to enable students to conceive of social justice and to make change part of the intention of scholarship. Scholars such as Michael Apple (2013) and Henry Giroux (1983) use the foundation of Freire's work to critique the ways in which the traditional school system reproduces race, class, and gender inequality (Torres & Van Heertum, 2009) and how school systems can oppress groups of people through social reproduction.

Critical policy analysis encourages questioning how policies adversely affect minoritized individuals, including asking questions such as: Why was this policy adopted? Who benefits and who faces consequences of this policy? How have these policies been justified? Whose interests are served by these policies? (Keway, cited in Taylor et al., 1997 cited in Stovall, 2009).

Critical Race Theory

Critical race theory (CRT) (Ladson-Billings, 1998; Solórzano & Yosso, 2001) explores the role of social reproduction of stereotypes and bias that undermine the ability of minoritized individuals to succeed. Issues studied include the School to Prison Pipeline, the overrepresentation of minoritized youth in special education and in discipline incidents. Critical race feminism notes ways in which women of color have felt excluded by the CRT movement (Wing, 1997).

The CRT movement began as critical legal studies designed to critique liberalism. CRT scholars assert that social class has become the dominant focus of equity work, and in education teachers feel more comfortable discussing class than race (Milner & Laughter, 2015). Color-blind tactics that ignore race (e.g., teachers stating "I don't see color") can create barriers to justice. Pathways to change involve narrative and dialogue about oppression, and specifically about race. For example, groundbreaking research has explored how intentional use of "race talk" when discussing school context and discipline issues in schools can lead to significant changes in school climate (Drame & Irby, 2015). The inability to explicitly discuss race has been shown to be a significant indicator of whether schools have the capacity to change (Payne, 2005). Through "transformative race talk," teachers speak transparently about race, use race-specific language, and address everyday school problems (Howard & del Rosario, 2000; Drame & Irby, 2015; Kegan & Lahey, 2001). By speaking about race directly instead of using color mute language, Irby and his colleagues found that teacher colleagues were more likely to talk about problems within the school when they used transformative race talk.

● ● ● ● ●

Equity and Accountability

While the standards and excellence movements have focused on all students achieving at the same level of proficiency, a focus on equity pays more attention to where students are beginning their educations and how far they have to go. Consider a running race in which one student only has to take a couple of steps to the finish line and another student has to run for miles. This metaphor is consistent with two children entering kindergarten with greatly different exposure to reading. One child is reading chapter books. Another child has yet to learn his letters. The first child has likely been exposed to language and literature materials for 2–3 years longer than the second child. The intensity of instruction and level of intervention necessary to have the second child reaching similar benchmarks to the first child will require a much greater amount of resources.

Opportunity to Learn as a Way to Frame Equity and Accountability

Scholars have referred to the concept of *Opportunity to Learn* (OTL) standards as a way to capture the differences in access to the fundamentals of learning. These disparities begin before birth with in utero access to nutrition, maternal stress, smoking and drug habits, and related risk factors. Once in public school settings in kindergarten, then include the quality of teachers, access to materials, the soundness of the physical facilities, access to out-of-school support and enrichment activities, nutrition, family stress, and more.

The concept of OTL was introduced in the 1960s as a means of helping to ensure validity of cross-national comparisons (Knoeppel, First, Della Sala, &

Ordu, 2014; McDonnell, 1995; Verstegen & Knoeppel, 1998). The concept was amplified in the policy arena in the mid-1990s when the concepts of the creation of educational standards for curricula and outcomes became prominent. When used as a statistical concept, the intention was not to assess students on knowledge that they had not been given a chance to learn. When it entered the policy arena, OTL took on normative implications regarding the purposes of education—the expectation that schools provided equal educational opportunity for all in the United States zeitgeist.

OTL was most visible in federal policy during the ESEA reauthorization during the Clinton administration. OTL language and standards were included in the original Goals 2000 proposal, defined as:

> the criteria for, and the basis of, assessing the sufficiency or quality of the resources, practices, and conditions necessary at each level of the education system (schools, local educational agencies, and States) to provide all students with an opportunity to learn the material in voluntary national content standards.
>
> (Pub L No 103227, 3 [7], cited in McDonnell, 1995, p. 312)

While OTL standards have not been adopted into law, the concept is still part of the conversations of progressive educators and policy makers. For example, the National Council of Teachers of English approved the importance of OTL standards in 1996, and reaffirmed this vision in 2012. Their vision of OTL included the importance of recognizing the multiple ways in which students learn and the need to enable teachers to teach all students.

One of the clearest guidelines for minimum standards of equity was provided in the *Williams vs. California* lawsuit in which the state of California was sued by nearly 100 San Francisco County students for failure to provide minimum standards of equity to its students. They defined equity as having three components—qualified teachers, adequate facilities, and sufficient supplies/equipment (Williams Settlement, 2004). High-quality coursework also has been included in subsequent conversations. Related conversations on disparities then refer to the "opportunity gap" as a needed focus for policy rather than just the "achievement gap" that is commonly used in policy discussions (Della Sala, Knoeppel, & Marion, 2017; Knoeppel, 2007).

● ● ● ● ●

Equity and the Courts

U.S. courts shape educational policy, and particularly related to equity. In highlighting the political nature of the courts, Wirt and Kirst quipped "court involvement in [educational policy] surprises only these who view the bench as a political eunuch" (1997, p. 262). Judges rule on case law by deliberating between competing values brought to them by the opposing sides. They must integrate this debate of values with the edicts of the constitution, which imposes constraints, as do professional canons and institutional traditions. The rulings by courts reflect an intersection of judicial values and court procedures, and these rulings create political consequences for the country (Wirt & Kirst, 1997).

Law defines the scope of educational practice by settling disputes, creating statutes and interpreting constitutional concepts (Mead, 2009, p. 286). Law bounds discretion by asking two questions: "May we?" and "Must we?" "May we" questions ask if a school or district has the scope of power to engage in activities that they want to do, such as testing students for drugs, limiting teacher contracts, or creating new structures of schooling such as charters. "Must we" questions are requirements that schools and districts may not want to do; in other words, "must" questions define the parameters of mandates discussed in the policy formation chapter (see Chapter 7). When leaders lack awareness of the boundaries of discretion, they unnecessarily may cause constraint or an overstepping of bounds. "Should we" is *not* a question of law but instead a policy question delegated to legislatures and executives (Mead, 2009).

Federal courts, state courts, and local school boards can all have the authority to define these boundaries. On education issues, the court tends to focus on two roles: *regulation* to control the behavior of other levels of government, and *legislation* to establish new rules. For example, federal courts have a manifest duty to resolve conflict occurring within the federal system and court rulings affect the scope of how the other branches of national government operate (Wirt & Kirst, 1997).

Despite ruling on many educational issues, judges tend to lack deep knowledge of educational processes. Judges rule based on expertise of the law rather than expertise of educational content or structure. One way judges gain more information about educational processes is through *amicus curiae* briefs. Latin for "friend of the court," amicus briefs are submitted by individuals or groups not directly involved with a court case, but are interested in influencing the outcome of the case. Amicus briefs are typically short documents that provide additional information to the court not available in other sources. They can include background information on the case, or an explanation of broader public opinion on the case (Kearney & Merrill, 2000; Simmons, 2009). Judges draw from content in amicus briefs to inform their final decisions.

Court rulings on school policy must be generalizable to extend beyond the bounds of education to be applicable to all of society (Henig, 2013) and are heavily based on precedent and, therefore, incremental change. Supreme Court Justices have lifetime appointments to encourage steady rulings based on the law rather than political will. State court selection varies from appointment to election, but most states' cultures encourage a nonpartisan focus to judge selection. These elections tend to have low voter turnout and a strong bias for incumbents (Henig, 2013; Superfine, 2010).

Race and the Courts

The most common way in which the United States historically has discussed equity is the role of race in the demographic composition of schools. The *Brown v. Board of Education of Topeka* (1954) ruling dramatically injected the government into the school system. In the eighteenth and nineteenth century, courts mainly focused on cases dealing with what are considered standard legal issues, including torts, contracts, and property (Tyack & Benavot, 1985; Superfine, 2010). The administrative progressive reforms of the 1920s, such as Taylorism, increased the courts' focus on bureaucratic and administrative functions related to increasing efficiency, centralization, and expansion of education. These decisions included hiring and firing, consolidation of schools and districts, and contracts with companies for goods and services (Tyack & Hansot, 1982).

Prior to the 1950s, the federal court system had very little involvement with education. Fewer than 300 court cases involving education occurred at the federal level (Cambron-McCabe, McCarthy, & Thomas, 2004, p. 22). The *Brown v. Board of Education of Topeka* (1954) ruling dramatically changed the role of the courts, creating a significant role for the court in addressing educational controversies. The ruling revised federal judicial purpose, traditions, politics, and dominant values (Henig, 2013). The political backlash of the Brown decision was very strong, with 80 percent of southerners opposing the ruling. By 1994, however, only 15 percent of southerners still opposed the ruling, showing the ways that court rulings can substantially change public opinion about education policy over time (Henig, 2013; Orfield, 1995).

The role of the courts in the first *Brown* decision introduced the idea of *substantive rights* in an education system. Substantive rights are upheld in large part with the support of the equal protection clause of the Fourteenth Amendment of the U.S. Constitution (Wirt & Kirst, 1997). Equal protection was extended to undocumented immigrants in 1982 in *Plyer v. Doe*. This concept of rights was extended over the next two decades by the courts to define many more constitutional boundaries (Mead, 2009), including: the right to free speech in *Tinker v. Des Moines Independent Community School District* (1969), fourth amendment protection from search and seizure in *New Jersey v. TLO* (1985), due process for students' requirements regarding suspensions in *Goss v. Lopez* (1975), and due process for teacher firing in *Board of Regents v. Roth* (1972), and free speech for teachers in *Pickering v. Board of Education* (1968).

A reversal in focus on desegregation rulings began in 1974 with *Millikein v. Bradley*. This ruling found that integration remedies that extended beyond the boundaries of one district needed to include evidence of intentional efforts to segregate. Subsequent to this ruling, cases in the 1990s showed a cultural preference within the courts for a deference to local control (Superfine, 2010), including *Board of Education v. Dowell* (1991), *Freeman v. Pitts* (1992), and *Missouri v. Jenkins* (1995), as well as a more recent ruling, *Parents Involved in Community Schools v. Seattle School District No. 1* (PICS, 2007).

Since then, scholars have noted a re-segregation of schools. White flight (affluent, white families moving away from mixed-race neighborhoods) and neighborhood residential transition have contributed to this shift. Even more important has been the court decisions of recent decades (Boger & Orfield, 2009). Once Nixon withdrew federal executive involvement in enforcing deseg-regation in 1969, the court became the primary policy maker regarding desegre-gation. A key issue has been the decline of school-assignment plans which made schools less segregated than neighborhoods (Reardon & Yun, 2003). The move toward increased re-segregation is related to the 1991 Supreme Court Decision *Board of Education of Oklahoma City v. Dowell*, in which federal courts were authorized to end desegregation plans in a marked reversal from previous rulings, with the premise that desegregation should be temporary. Federal dis-trict judges in the 1990s, particularly in the fourth circuit, took an activist role to enforce and expand re-segregation (Orfield & Lee, 2005).

Social Class and the Courts

In the 1970s, a wave of court cases at the state and federal level focused on rem-edying social class inequity through school finance reform. Lawsuits occurred in 45 states; plaintiffs prevailed in about half of the cases (Koski, 2007). The cases address disparities in per pupil spending between wealthy and poor dis-tricts. These court cases appeared in three waves (Superfine, 2010; Thro, 1989).

■ The first wave focused on challenges at the federal court level with a focus on the *equal protection clause* of the constitution. However, a Supreme Court ruling (*San Antonio Independent School District v. Rodriguez* in 1973) found that the equal protection clause was inadequate for school finance chal-lenges. Instead, the federal court ruled that state and local governments were better positioned to make school finance decisions.

■ With the decision-making power shifting to the states, the second wave in state courts focused on *providing funds equally* across all students. These cases drew on state constitutions that included an equal protection clause (Williams, 1985).

■ A third wave of reforms also occurred in state courts, with a focus on *adequacy* rather than equality. These cases drew on state constitution clauses focusing on providing a "thorough and efficient" education (First & Mirón, 1991).

Overall, most of the rulings on school finance reform have been vague guide-lines for states to follow. Only a few rulings have offered prescriptive guidelines for change. One of the most famous and discussed is the New Jersey state reforms guided by two *Abbott v. Burke* rulings (1990, 1998). The Abbott meas-ures were groundbreaking in their precise directedness to attempt to assure "parity" of resources between the poorest and wealthiest districts. The ruling was a directive for a comprehensive set of remediation, including the first state to mandate pre-school education. The court also designed an unprecedented "needs-based" supplemental support service system. The law also mandated unprecedented facility upgrade and new construction to address deteriorating schools in the poorest areas of New Jersey (Education Law Center, 2016). Schools receiving these services and funds have been referred to as "Abbott" schools in New Jersey.

●●●●●

Student Voice and the Right to Participate

In European nations, student voice has been reinforced by formal policies and national educational structures. Called "youth participation" in the United Nations Convention on the Rights of the Child (CRC), Articles 12 through 15 discuss youth participation as a series of rights, including access to information, expression of views, and freedom to form collective organization (United Nations, 1989). The CRC highlights the need to bolster the capacity of young people and adults to enable child participation and the need for strong standards and accountability to guide this process, and European policies have aligned with these goals.

Nationwide curricula, testing, and other educational policy structures increase the mandates for youth participation in most European nations (Lundy, 2007; Quinn & Owen, 2014.) UNESCO publishes regularly on youth participation in educational development and change (UNESCO, 2016). The New Zealand Ministry of Education states a vision for student voice on its website focused on involving students in assessment and change (Cook-Sather, 2014). The Ministry of Education in Ontario offers a deep and comprehensive program of youth voice, including a Ministry Student Advisory Council and related projects that prioritize student experience in provincial government (Courtney, 2016). The Swedish national curriculum includes formal standards for children to express views in matters that concern their learning and encourages to work "together with the pupils develop rules for working and participating" (Skolverket, 2011, p. 14).

In marked contrast to European nations, the United States lacks any formal policy to spur youth participation. While the democratic foundation of the United States includes the premise that participation is the fundamental right of citizenship (Ochoa-Becker, Morton, Autry, Johnstad, & Merrill, 2001), many U.S. policies inhibit the voices of young people. The United States is soon to become the only nation that has not ratified the CRC.[1] For example, it is illegal for young people under the age of 18 to serve on a voting decision-making board in the state of Pennsylvania. Other states have championed student voice, such as Vermont including students on the state board of education (Mitra, Serriere, & Kirshner, 2014).

Students can serve as important sources of information that otherwise are not available regarding implementation and experiences of educational change (Mitra, 2008; Rudduck, Day, & Wallace, 1997). When asking student opinions, students desired positive, strong relationships with their teachers as opposed to the isolation and lack of respect and appreciation that students reported they often felt (Yonezawa, McClure, & Jones, 2012). Students at Whitman High School in Northern California, for example, took teachers on tours of their neighborhood, including where they lived, worked, hung out on street corners, and where gangs staked out their territories (Mitra, 2003). Students felt that they truly did come to know their teachers better, and they believed that teachers came to better understand them as well. Teachers and students reported that they found the experience valuable, commenting that they developed a better understanding of student experience.

Student voice initiatives highlight the importance of teacher–student relationships and the overall culture of a school. Student voice can also influence teacher training, informing the practice of pre-service teachers (Cook-Sather, 2001) and university faculty (Cook-Sather, Bovill, & Felten, 2014). The goal in this process is encouraging teachers to rethink who is an authority of educational practice. When teachers and teachers-to-be learn how to listen to their students, teachers began to remove the stereotypes and labels that can be so easily attached to students.

Since effective implementation of reform benefits from participation by those most affected (McLaughlin, 1991), efforts to actively involve students can lead to improved student understanding of the educational changes in their schools (Mitra, 2004). Student information can be particularly useful for reshaping reform efforts when they are slowly or shallowly implemented (Yonezawa & Jones, 2007). U.S. research has examined ways that student critique can shift and deepen the work of the Common Core (Kornbluh, Ozer, Allen, & Kirshner, 2015).

Student voice builds upon efforts to increase student-centered learning (Toshalis & Nakkula, 2012). A cohort of states is taking the lead on changing graduation requirements so they are based on learning competencies rather than Carnegie Units (Council of Chief State School Officers, 2013; Sturgis, 2016). Many of these states are connecting this focus on competencies with personalization.

Vermont, for example, mandates that all students in grades 7–12 have Personalized Learning Plans to meet competencies. These plans could include blended learning, internships, dual enrollment, independent studies, and other broader interpretations of learning, with the focus on student goals and post-secondary plans driving how to encourage student engagement and investment in learning. To increase community and parent understanding of the legislation, Vermont's Agency of Education paired with Up for Learning, a statewide non-profit that focuses on helping schools deepen learning for young people through youth–adult partnerships. The organization developed two key initiatives to improve implementation of the law. First, a project called Communicating School Redesign (www.upforlearning.com/initiatives/communicating-school-redesign) consisted of student-led teams that designed communication campaigns to teach their local communities about the legislation. Second, the organization partnered with young people and a production company to develop a music video that taught the concepts of personalized learning through the song (www.upforlearn ing.com/our-time). The youth–adult partnership team then also created dialogue guides to scaffold community discussions of the video.

Given the potential challenges of designing and implementing student voice initiatives, understanding what conditions enable and sustain student voice initiatives is critical. The stark differences in traditional roles of young people and adults in schools require intentional efforts to create a new set of working conditions that include new norms, relationships, and organizational structures. Adults must learn how to lead by getting out of the way (Mitra, 2005) as a way to shift power from traditional systems, and they often need training to learn how to be a partner rather than a traditional teacher. Young people need to learn more about politics and policy of educational systems and to learn "adult speak" to be able to participate in decision-making processes. The following list outlines the types of conditions that can help to enable student voice, including partnership with an intermediary organization (Mitra, 2009):

- Securing sustainability by partnering with an intermediary organization.
- Sending signs that the youth–adult partnership is not "business as usual" through room arrangement, meeting design/protocols, and leadership roles.
- Emphasizing respect and trust among group members.
- Creating meaningful, but not equal roles.
- Creating visible victories.
- Providing dedicated time and space for collaboration.
- Building the capacity for youth and adults to fulfill their roles.

●●●●●

Policy Topics With an Equity Focus

With the predominant focus of educational reform since the 1980s focusing on excellence and assessment, the push for equity as a core value in educational systems is not always as prevalent in policy documents and governmental initiatives. While many equity policies have not been a focal point of educational policy in recent years, these policy ideas of how to make schools better continue to surface in policy conversations. Research continues to grow on the value of reforms such as early childhood education and community schools/wraparound services, including contributions to educational outcomes and cost effectiveness. In this section, we review some of the continuing policy conversations on how to improve equitable conversations.

Early Childhood Education

The United States is far behind other nations in providing early childhood learning opportunities. In a 2012 report, the Organization for Economic Cooperation and Development compared nations on early childhood education (2012). Only 69 percent of U.S. four-year-olds were enrolled in school, ranking the U.S. 28th out of the 38 nations studied; the top 15 countries in economic development all had enrollments over 90 percent, other than the U.S. Furthermore, most OECD nations (21 in the report) have young people beginning school at age three or younger.

Research has consistently shown the ways in which children provided with strong early childhood learning opportunities benefit in the long term. These benefits include:

1. *School readiness:* including vocabulary growth, math achievement, less likely to require special education or remedial classes (Clements & Sarama, 2011; Hernandez, 2012; Mann & Reynolds, 2006).

2. *Juvenile justice:* children less likely to have juvenile delinquency violations (Wilder Research, 2011) and for every dollar spent on preschool, 50 to 85 percent reduction in criminal costs.

3. *Social health:* less abuse of alcohol and drugs and greater psychological well-ness (Schweinhart & Fulcher-Dawson, 2009).

4. *Economic improvement:* reduced costs, increased revenues, and higher employment (Committee for Economic Development, 2006; Schweinhart & Fulcher-Dawson, 2009).

Previous efforts to expand early childhood education have focused on programs targeting poor children. A publicly funded program, *Head Start* promotes school readiness through programs that include preschool but also parent education, health care, nutrition, goal setting, screenings, and transition services. The program began in 1965 as a part of Lyndon Johnson's War on Poverty and has served more than 30 million children since then (Head Start, 2016).

Convergence effects have been found to occur in elementary years. That is, the marked impact of preschool investment tends to fade away by third grade (Hirokazu et al., 2013) with some speculation that this "fadeout" occurs due to struggling elementary schools that fail to capitalize on the early childhood gains; or the ability of schools to focus on the non-attenders of preschool may balance outcomes. Nevertheless, persistence of effects in the best-practice models of preschool programs, including longitudinal experimental designs such as Perry Preschool and Abecedarian (Campbell et al., 2012), indicates long-term benefits to society.

Universal preschool and current statistics suggest greater possibility for Early Childcare using a universal tactic. These programs would provide government-funded preschool to all students. Ten states offer universal pre-school in the United States (Curran, 2015). Georgia was the first in 1995, funded by a state-run lottery system. New York, Oklahoma, Florida, West Virginia, Vermont, Illinois, Massachusetts, Iowa, and Louisiana passed laws in the past two decades. Implementation has varied, even within these ten states, however. Only 14 percent of four-year-olds were enrolled in state-provided preschool in Massachusetts, compared to 79 percent in Florida (Barnett, Carolan, Fitzgerald, & Squires, 2012).

At times, this focus on public education has shifted from the current K–12 (kindergarten to 12th grade) system to encouraging a P–12, beginning at preschool. Research demonstrates growing evidence that early intervention is critical to successful student outcomes (Bushouse, 2009). Beyond academics, arguments for universal preschool include the growing cost of childcare for working families and the increasing number of moms in the workforce. Equity is also a key reason for the universal preschool policy push (Curran, 2015) because of the high cost of quality preschool education and the uneven availability of quality sites. Some areas of the country are beginning to legislate universal pre-kindergarten for four-year-olds, including in New York City.

Community Schools

Community schools consist of ways that schools partner with organizations such as city government, social service agencies, health organizations, and the judicial system in an attempt to harness their wide range of resources to improve opportunities for young people. In these partnerships, schools tend to be the hub around which services are coordinated. The school also tends to be open longer into the evening and year-round so that the building can be used to provide space for services, courses, training, and support for the neighborhood. Previous policy cycles called similar initiatives by the names of: *integrated services, collective impact, full-service schools, school-linked services, multi-sector collaborations,* and *wraparound services.*

A 2017 research brief by Jeannie Oakes, Anna Maier, and Julia Daniel stresses that the extensive research on community schools justifies the concept as an evidence-based strategy that should be a valid intervention under the *Every Student Succeeds Act (ESSA)* guidelines. The report defines community schools as having four components: "Integrated student supports; expanded learning time and opportunities; family and community engagement, and collaborative leadership and practices" (Oakes, Maier, & Daniel, 2017, p. 3).

It is the intention of multi-sector collaborations to break down agency "silos" that see only part of the problem. In most political systems, rather than being able to address children holistically, the services provided are privileged through the separation of health, education, and welfare departments. When a teacher learns that a student is struggling in her classroom, often the root causes of the struggles are under the auspices of many different policy units. A poor child may come to school with many needs, including being hungry, needing glasses to see the front of the room, and/or needing to transition through different schools due to homelessness or foster care placements. Parents may need support as well, such as training to find jobs, accessing substance treatment, or securing long-term housing. While the concept of neighborhood services occurring in one place dates back to the Progressive era, the policy concept took on new interest during the Clinton era in the mid-1990s. The creation of school-based health clinics became popular in urban and rural areas so that when students needed services, they were within reach. Schools also became used as 24-hour facilities for after-school programs, training programs for parents, and related community activities. These processes not only provided increased access to services, but also established the school building as a welcoming space. They encouraged families to interact with school personnel and to learn more about the range of services available in the community.

Collaborative models are based on the premise that reducing inequitable access to social systems can help to meet the needs of the youth who are struggling the most—greater support systems foster stronger youth development opportunities. Multi-sector, collaborative approaches are appealing to policy makers, funders, and practitioners because of their potential to (a) more comprehensively address the needs of young people that are interrelated across school, family, and community systems; (b) increase resources; and (c) ignite innovative ideas for addressing educational inequalities.

New relationships with shared goals and vision can be built due to perceived similarities and positive benefits (Monge & Contractor, 2003). Symbols of new relationships include common language (Knapp, 1995), a common agenda (Mitra & Frick, 2011), and shared urgency (Stone, Henig, Jones, & Pierannunzi, 2001). Struggling initiatives lacked clear goals or shared expectations (Annie E. Casey Foundation, 2013; McIntosh, Lyon, Carlson, Everette, & Loera, 2008).

Research looking at collaboration has found that efforts usually follow traditional political, social, and historical patterns of an area. Collaboration often builds upon a couple of particularly strong organizations that have historically built trust and show residents and officials that they meet the needs of community members. Creating the structure of a collaboration alone does not lead to change; respect, trust, communication, shared decision making, and reciprocity are critical to the success of multi-sector collaborations (Mellin et al., 2010; Mellin, Taylor, & Weist, 2013; Mellin & Weist, 2011).

Successful collaborations can shift traditional interaction patterns and create new relationships between the range of organizations in a community (Ansari & Weiss, 2006; Stone et al., 2001). Failed efforts often included conflicts between organizations over power and status (King & Ross, 2003), including issues of turf, trust, and bureaucracy (Kirst, 1993; Stone et al., 2001), as well as poorly defined roles and responsibilities (Flaherty et al., 1998). Funders such as the Schott Foundation's creation of the National Opportunity to Learn Network (2016) seek to bring together grassroots organizing efforts for policy efforts focusing on supplementing basic education in the form of early education, wraparound services, equitable discipline, and equitable school funding.

A recent multi-sector collaborative effort was Promise Neighborhoods, which began during the Obama administration. The program encouraged the creation and expansion of collaboration between non-profit organizations (including faith-based institutions) and institutions of higher education, with the goal of helping to prepare students for success in college and careers. The Promise Neighborhood initiative was modeled on the successes of the Harlem Children's Zone (HCZ), which demonstrated strong improvements in academic and socio-emotional outcomes of young people based on a premise of multi-sector collaboration. One of the models of collaboration, HCZ was founded by Geoffrey Canada for families living in Harlem, NY. The non-profit provides parenting workshops, preschool, charter schools, health programs, youth violence prevention efforts, social services, and college access support for thousands of families.

Comprehension Questions

■ What are the key court rulings in U.S. history that have influenced the role of schools in defining issues of equity?

■ What topics in education policy tend to be most focused on the issue of equity?

■ What is Opportunity to Learn and how has it been used as a political strategy?

■ Discuss the shifts in focus of early childhood education policy.

■ What are some of the ways that early childhood education improves outcomes for children?

■ Discuss the concept of community schools and related terms. What are the goals behind this set of policies?

Discussion Questions

■ Drawing on this chapter and the discussion from Chapter 10, what are the range of definitions of equity? Why is the topic contested?

■ How can critical race theory inform discussions of teaching practice?

■ Why do you think that the concept of Opportunity to Learn has not been codified into educational policy more often, including in the Elementary and Secondary Education Act?

■ Most countries in Europe have public school beginning in what we consider the preschool years—why has early childhood education remained a private system in the United States?

■ What are the responsibilities for a public school system? What ages should it extend to? What depth of services should the system provide? How do choices about the scope of schooling affect goals of equity-related aims?

■ What characteristics are shared among states that fund school districts more equitably? Fair distribution of school funding is not necessarily equal distribution of school funding. What are justifications for and against providing equal funding to school districts? What are contributing factors to shifts in school funding equity in a state over time?

● ● ● ● ●

Activities

■ Explore the online journal *International Journal of Student Voice* (https://ijsv.psu.edu/). Pick an article that provides a viewpoint that you have never thought about before. Discuss that article in a group.

■ Have students work in groups to understand the key court cases discussed in the chapter, including:

> *Brown v. Board of Education of Topeka (1954)*
> *Milliken v. Bradley (1974)*
> *San Antonio Independent School District v. Rodriguez (1973)*

☐ What was the key issue?

☐ What was the Supreme Court's ruling?

☐ How did the ruling affect educational equity?

■ Listen/read the NPR report "Preschool: Decades Worth of Studies, One Strong Message," reported by Claudio Sanchez, May 3, 2017.
Find on the web using the following search terms:

> *NPR; May 3, 2017; pre-k decades strong message; Sanchez*

■ Have students work in groups to assume roles and to discuss positions and viewpoints on a particular court case. Viewpoints could include legislators, governors, students, interest groups, and teachers.

■ Design a National Issues Forum discussion on three ways to address the achievement gap—demand accountability; close the spending gap; address root causes/poverty.
Find on the web using the following search terms:

> *NIFI; too many children left behind*

■ Examine the research by the School Funding Fairness project to examine disparities across states. School Funding Fairness—a series of graphs and charts illuminating disparities among states, published by Rutger's School of Education and the Education Law Center.
Find on the web using the following search terms:

> *School Funding Fairness*

■ View a documentary about equity in U.S. schools and hold a discussion about wthat they teach. Back to School: Five Docs to Watch About Education in America; *Frontline*, PBS Television.
Find on the web using the following search terms:

> *Frontline; PBS; Five School Docs*

■ "The Problem We All Live With," *This American Life* Radio, Episode 562 (about desegregation and a district integrating accidentally).
Find on the web using the following search terms:

> *This American Life Radio; Episode 562; July 31, 2015*

■ Explore the radio documentaries listed below to consider how desegregation policy occurs in the present day. "The Problem We All Live With—Part Two," *This American Life* Radio, Episode 563 (about a city trying intentionally to integrate all of its schools in Hartford, CT, and the Obama administration's verbal support of integration but lack of action).
Find on the web using the following search terms:

> *This American Life Radio; Episode 563; August 7, 2015*

●●●●●

Note

1 Somalia—the only other nation that has not ratified the CRC—indicated its plans to begin ratification in 2010.

●●●●●

Further Reading

Ansari, W. E. & Weiss, E. S. (2006). Quality of research on community partnerships: Developing the evidence base. *Health Education Research, 21,* 175–80.

Frankenberg, E. & Orfield, G. (eds.) (2012). *The Resegregation of Suburban Schools: A Hidden Crisis in American Education.* Cambridge, MA: Harvard Education Press.

McDonnell, L. M. (1995). Opportunity to learn as a research concept and a policy instrument. *Educational Evaluation and Policy Analysis, 17*(3), 305–22.

Mitra, D. L. (2009). Student voice and student roles in education policy and policy reform. In Plank, D. N., Sykes, G., & Schneider, B. (eds.) *AERA Handbook of Education Policy Research* (pp. 819–30). London: Routledge.

Oakes, J., Maier, A., & Daniel, J. (2017). *Community Schools: An Evidence-Based Strategy for Equitable School Improvement.* Palo Alto, CA: Learning Policy Institute.

Superfine, B. M. (2010). Court-drive reform and equal educational opportunity: Centralization, decentralization, and the shifting judicial role. *Review of Educational Research, 80*(1), 108–37.

●●●●●

Reference List

Abbott v. Burke, 575 A.2d 359 (N.J. 1990).
Abbott v. Burke, 710 A.2d 450 (N.J. 1998).

Annie E. Casey Foundation. (2013). *Community Change: Lessons Learned from Making Connections.* Retrieved from: www.aecf.org/resources/community-change-lessons-from-making-connections/.

Ansari, W. E. & Weiss, E. S. (2006). Quality of research on community partnerships: Developing the evidence base. *Health Education Research, 21,* 175–80.

Apple, M. W. (2013). *Education and Power.* New York: Routledge.

Barnett, W. S., Carolan, M. E., Fitzgerald, M. J., & Squires, M. J. H. (2012). *The State of Preschool 2012.* The National Institute of Early Education Research, Rutgers University.

Board of Education v. Dowell, 498 U.S. 237 (1991).

Board of Education of Oklahoma City v. Dowell 498 U.S. 237 (1991).

Board of Regents v. Roth, 408 US 564 (1972).

Boger, J. C. & Orfield, G. (eds.) (2009). *School Resegregation: Must the South Turn Back?* Chapel Hill, NC: University of North Carolina Press.

Brown v. Board of Education of Topeka, 347 U.S. 483 (1954).

Bushouse, B. K. (2009). *Universal Preschool: Policy Change, Stability, and the Pew Charitable Trusts.* New York: SUNY Press.

Cambron-McCabe, N. H., McCarthy, M. M., & Thomas, S. B. (2004). *Public School Law: Teachers' and Students' Rights.* Boston, MA: Allyn & Bacon.

Campbell, F. A., Pungello, E. P., Burchinal, M., Kainz, K., Pan, Y., Wasik, B. H., Barbarin, O. A., Sparling, J. J., & Ramey, C. T. (2012). Adult outcomes as a function of an early childhood educational program: An Abecedarian Project follow-up. *Developmental Psychology, 48,* 1033–43.

Clements, D. H. & Sarama, J. (2011). Early childhood mathematics intervention. *Science, 333*(6045), 968–70.

Committee for Economic Development. (2006). *The Economic Promise of Investing in High-Quality Preschool: Using Early Education to Improve Economic Growth and the Fiscal Sustainability of States and the Nation.* Washington, DC: Committee for Economic Development.

Cook-Sather, A. (2001). Between student and teacher: Learning to teach as translation. *Teaching Education, 12*(2), 177–90.

Cook-Sather, A. (2014). The trajectory of student voice in educational research. *New Zealand Journal of Educational Studies, 49*(2), 131–48.

Cook-Sather, A., Bovill, C., & Felten, P. (2014). *Engaging Students as Partners in Learning and Teaching: A Guide for Faculty.* Hoboken, NJ: John Wiley & Sons.

Council of Chief State School Officers. (2013). ILN overview video. *Personalized Learning Experiences.* Retrieved from: www.ccsso.org/Resources/Digital_Resources/ILN_Overview_Video.html.

Courtney, J. (2016). Ontario's student voice initiative: Looking back. *Connect,* 220, August. Retrieved from: http://research.acer.edu.au/cgi/viewcontent.cgi?article=1217&context=connect.

Curran, F. C. (2015). Expanding downward: Innovation, diffusion, and state policy adoptions of universal preschool. *Education Policy Analysis Archives, 23*(36).

Della Sala, M. R., Knoeppel, R. C., & Marion, R. (2017). Modeling the effects of educational resources on student achievement: Implications for resource allocation policies. *Education and Urban Society, 49*(2), 180–202.

Drame, E. R. & Irby, D. (2015). Positionality and racialization in a PAR project: Reflections and insight from a school reform collaboration. *The Qualitative Report, 20*(8), 1164–81. Retrieved from: http://nsuworks.nova.edu/tqr/vol20/iss8/2/.

Education Law Center. (2016). The history of *Abbott v. Burke*. Retrieved from: www. edlawcenter.org/cases/abbott-v-burke/abbott-history.html.

First, P. F. & Mirón, L. F. (1991). The social construction of adequacy. *Journal of Law and Education, 20*, 421–44.

Flaherty, L. T., Garrison, E. G., Waxman, R., Uris, P. F., Key, S. G., Glass-Siegel, M., & Weist, M. D. (1998). Optimizing the roles of school mental health professionals. *The Journal of School Health, 68*(10), 420–4.

Freeman v. Pitts, 503 U.S. 467 (1992).

Freire, Paulo. (1970). *Pedagogy of the oppressed*. New York: Continuum (1993), 125.

Froehle, C. (2016). The evolution of an accidental meme. *Medium*, April 14. Retrieved from: https://medium.com/@CRA1G/the-evolution-of-an-accidental-meme-ddc4e1 39e0e4.

Future of Children. (1996). Special education for students with disabilities: Executive summary. *The Future of Children, 6*(1), 1–8. Retrieved from: http://futureofchildren. org/publications/docs/06_01_ExecSummary.pdf.

Giroux, H. A. (1983). *Theory and Resistance in Education: A Pedagogy for the Opposition*. South Hadley, MA: Bergin & Garvey.

González, N., Moll, L. C., & Amanti, C. (eds.) (2005). *Funds of Knowledge: Theorizing Practices in Households, Communities, and Classrooms*. New York: Routledge.

Goss v. Lopez, 419 U.S. 565, 95 S. Ct. 729 (1975).

Head Start. (2016). Office of Administration for Children and Families, Early Childhood Learning and Knowledge Center. Retrieved from: https://eclkc.ohs.acf.hhs.gov/hslc/ hs/about.

Henig, J. (2013). *The End of Exceptionalism in American Education: The Changing Politics of School Reform*. Cambridge, MA: Harvard Education Press.

Hernandez, D. J. (2012). *Double Jeopardy: How Third-Grade Reading Skills and Poverty Influence High School Graduation*. Baltimore, MD: The Annie E. Casey Foundation.

Hirokazu, Y., Weiland, C., Brooks-Gunn, J., Burchinal, M., Espinosa, L., Gormley, W., Ludwig, K., Magnuson, A., Phillips, D., & Zaslow, M. (2013). *Investing in Our Future: The Evidence Base on Preschool Education*. Society for Research on Child Development, October. Retrieved from: http://fcd-us.org/resources/evidence-base-preschool.

Howard, T. C. & del Rosario, C. D. (2000). Talking race in teacher education: The need for racial dialogue in teacher education programs. *Action in Teacher Education, 21*(4), 127–37.

Individuals with Disabilities Education Act (1975). 34 CFR § 300.1.

Kearney, J. D. & Merrill, T. W. (2000). The influence of amicus curiae briefs on the Supreme Court. *University of Pennsylvania Law Review, 148*, 743–855.

Kegan, R. & Lahey, L. L. (2001). *How the Way We Talk Can Change the Way We Work: Seven Languages for Transformation*. Hoboken, NJ: John Wiley & Sons.

King, N. & Ross, A. (2003). Professional identities and inter-professional relations: Evaluations of collaborative community schemes. *Social Work in Health Care, 38*(2), 51–72.

Kirst, M. W. (1993). Financing school-linked services. *Education and Urban Society, 25*, 166–72.

Knapp, M. S. (1995). How shall we study comprehensive, collaborative services for children and families? *Educational Researcher, 24*(4), 5–16.

Knoeppel, R. C. (2007). Resource adequacy, equity, and the right to learn: Access to high-quality teachers in Kentucky. *Journal of Education Finance, 32*(4), 422–42.

Knoeppel, R. C., First, P. F., Della Sala, M. R., & Ordu, C. A. (2014). Finance equity, student achievement, and justice: A five state analysis of equality of opportunity. *Journal of Educational Administration, 52*(6), 812–32.

Kornbluh, M., Ozer, E. J., Allen, C. D., & Kirshner, B. (2015). Youth participatory action research as an approach to sociopolitical development and the new academic standards: Considerations for educators. *The Urban Review, 47*(5), 868–92.

Koski, W. S. (2007). Achieving "adequacy" in the classroom. *Boston Third World Law Journal, 27*, 13–43.

Ladson-Billings, G. (1998). Just what is critical race theory and what's it doing in a nice field like education? *International Journal of Qualitative Studies in Education, 11*(1), 7–24.

Lundy, L. (2007). "Voice" is not enough: Conceptualising Article 12 of the United Nations Convention on the Rights of the Child. *British Educational Research Journal, 33*(6), 927–42.

Mann, E. A. & Reynolds, A. J. (2006). Early intervention and juvenile delinquency prevention: Evidence from the Chicago Longitudinal Study. *Social Work Research, 30*(3), 153–67.

Mayes, E., Bakhshi, S., Wasner, V., Cook-Sather, A., Mohammad, M., Bishop, D. C., Groundwater-Smith, S., Prior, M., Nelson, E., McGregor, J., Carson, K., Webb, R., Flashman, L., McLaughlin, C., & Cowley, E. (2017). What can a conception of power do? Theories and images of power in student voice work. *International Journal of Student Voice*. Retrieved from: https://ijsv.psu.edu/?article=what-can-a-conception-of-power-do-theories-and-images-of-power-in-student-voice-work.

McDonnell, L. M. (1995). Opportunity to learn as a research concept and a policy instrument. *Educational Evaluation and Policy Analysis, 17*(3), 305–22.

McIntosh, J. M., Lyon, A. R., Carlson, G. A., Everette, C. D. B., & Loera, S. (2008). Measuring the mesosystem: A survey and critique of approaches to cross setting measurement for ecological research and models of collaborative care. *Families, Systems, & Health, 26*, 86–104.

McLaughlin, M. W. (1991). The RAND change agent study: Ten years later. In Odden, A. R. (ed.) *The Evolution of Education Policy Implementation* (pp. 143–56). Albany, New York: State University of New York Press.

Mead, J. (2009). The role of the law in educational policy formation, implementation and research. In Sykes, G., Schneider, B., & Plank, D. (eds.) *Handbook of Education Policy Research* (pp. 286–306). New York: Routledge.

Mellin, E. A. & Weist, M. D. (2011). Exploring school mental health collaboration in an urban community: A social capital perspective. *School Mental Health, 3*, 81–92.

Mellin, E. A., Bronstein, L. R., Anderson-Butcher, D., Amorose, A., Ball, A., & Green, J. H. (2010). Measuring interprofessional collaboration in expanded school mental health: Model refinement and scale development. *Journal of Interprofessional Care, 24*(5), 514–23.

Mellin, E. A., Taylor, L., & Weist, M. D. (2013). The Expanded School Mental Health Collaboration Instrument: Development and initial psychometrics. *School Mental Health, 6*(3), 151–62.

Milliken v. Bradley, 418 U.S. 717 (1974).

Milner, H. R. & Laughter, J. C. (2015). But good intentions are not enough: Preparing teachers to center race and poverty. *The Urban Review, 47*(2), 341–63.

Missouri v. Jenkins, 525 U.S. 70 (1995).

Mitra, D. L. (2003). Student voice in school reform: Reframing student-teacher relationships. *McGill Journal of Education, 38*(2), 289–304.

Mitra, D. L. (2004). The significance of students: Can increasing "student voice" in schools lead to gains in youth development. *Teachers College Record, 106*(4), 651–88.

Mitra, D. L. (2005). Adults advising youth: Leading while getting out of the way. *Educational Administration Quarterly, 41*(3), 520–53.

Mitra, D. L. (2008). *Student Voice in School Reform: Building Youth-Adult Partnerships that Strengthen Schools and Empower Youth.* Albany, NY: State University of New York Press.

Mitra, D. L. (2009). Student voice and student roles in education policy and policy reform. In Plank, D. N., Sykes, G., & Schneider, B. (eds.) *AERA Handbook of Education Policy Research* (pp. 819–30). London: Routledge.

Mitra, D. L. & Frick, W. C. (2011). Civic capacity in educational reform efforts: Finding agency in a time of globalization. *Educational Policy, 25*(5), 810–43.

Mitra, D., Serriere, S., & Kirshner, B. (2014). Youth participation in U.S. contexts: Student voice without a national mandate. *Children & Society, 28*(4), 292–304.

Monge, P. R. & Contractor, N. S. (2003). *Theories of Communication Networks.* New York: Oxford University Press.

National Opportunity to Learn Network. (2016). The Schott Foundation for Public Education, Web. 06, October.

New Jersey v. TLO, 469 U.S. 325, 105 S. Ct. 733 (1985).

Oakes, J., Maier, A., & Daniel, J. (2017). *Community Schools: An Evidence-Based Strategy for Equitable School Improvement.* Palo Alto, CA: Learning Policy Institute.

Ochoa-Becker, A. S., Morton, M. L., Autry, M. M., Johnstad, S., & Merrill, D. (2001). A search for decision making in three elementary classrooms: A pilot study. *Theory & Research in Social Education, 29*(2), 261–89.

Opportunity to Learn Standards, Statement of Principles. (2012). National Council of Teachers of English. Retrieved from: www.ncte.org/positions/statements/opptolearn standards.

Orfield, G. (1995). Public opinion and school desegregation. *Teachers College Record, 96*(4), 654–70.

Orfield, G., & Lee, C. (2005). *New Faces, Old Patterns? Segregation in the Multiracial South.* Civil Rights Project at Harvard University. Cambridge, MA: Harvard Education Publishing Group.

Organization for Economic Cooperation and Development. (2012). *Education at a Glance: OECD Indicators 2012—United States.* Retrieved from: www.oecd.org/edu/EAG%202012_e-book_EN_200912.pdf.

Parents Involved in Community Schools v. Seattle School District No. 1, 55 1 U.S. 70 1 (2007).

Payne, C. (2005). Still crazy after all these years: Race in the Chicago school system. *Consortium on Chicago School Research,* speech given by Professor Payne, University of Illinois at Chicago (UIC) College of Education, April 22.

Pickering v. Board of Education, 291 U.S. 563, 88 S. Ct. 1731 (1968).

Plyer v. Doe, 457 U.S. 202, 102 S.Ct. 382 (1982).

Quinn, S. & Owen, S. (2014). Freedom to grow: Children's perspectives of student voice. *Childhood Education, 90*(3), 192–201.

Reardon, S. & Yun, J. (2003). Integrating neighborhoods, segregating schools: The retreat from school desegregation in the South, 1990–2000. *North Carolina Law Review, 81,* May, 79–101.

Rudduck, J., Day, J., & Wallace, G. (1997). Students' perspectives on school improvement. In Hargreaves, A. (ed.) *Rethinking Educational Change With Heart and Mind (The 1997 ASCD Year Book)* (pp. 73–91). Alexandria, VA: Association for Supervision and Curriculum Development.

San Antonio Independent School District v. Rodriguez, 411 U.S. 1 (1973).

Schweinhart, L. & Fulcher-Dawson, R. (2009). Early childhood education. In Sykes, G., Schneider, B., & Plank, D. (eds.) *Handbook of Education Policy Research* (pp. 876–88). New York: Routledge.

Simmons, O. S. (2009). Picking friends from the crowd: Amicus participation as political symbolism. *Connecticut Law Review, 42*(1), 185–233.

Skolverket. (2011). *Curriculum for the Compulsory School, Preschool Class and the Leisure-Time Centre.* Stockholm: Ordförrådet AB.

Solórzano, D. G. & Yosso, T. J. (2001). From racial stereotyping and deficit discourses toward a critical race theory in teacher education. *Multicultural Education, 9*(1), 2–8.

Stone, C., Henig, J., Jones, B., & Pierannunzi, C. (2001). *Building Civic Capacity: The Politics of Reforming Urban Schools.* Lawrence, KS: University Press of Kansas.

Stovall, D. O. (2009). Race(ing), class(ing) and gender(ing) our work: Critical race theory, critical race feminism, epistemology, and new directions in educational policy research. In Sykes, G., Schneider, B., & Plank, D. (eds.) *Handbook of Education Policy Research* (pp. 258–66) New York: Routledge.

Sturgis, C. (2016). *Reaching the Tipping Point: Insights on Advancing Competency Education in New England,* International Association for K-12 Online Learning (iNACOL). Retrieved from: www.inacol.org/wp-content/uploads/2016/09/CompetencyWorks_ReachingTheTippingPoint_WhatIsCompetencyEducation.pdf.

Superfine, B. M. (2010). Court-drive reform and equal educational opportunity: Centralization, decentralization, and the shifting judicial role. *Review of Educational Research, 80*(1), 108–37.

Taylor, C. & Robinson, C. (2009). Student voice: Theorising power and participation. *Pedagogy, Culture & Society, 17*(2), 161–75.

Thro, W. (1989). To render them safe: The analysis of state constitutional provisions in school finance litigation. *Virginia Law Review, 75,* 1639–78.

Tinker v. Des Moines Independent Community School District, 393 U.S. 503 (1969).

Torres, C. A. & Van Heertum, R. (2009). Education and domination: Reforming policy and practice through critical theory. In Sykes, G., Schneider, B., & Plank, D. (eds.) *Handbook of Education Policy Research* (pp. 221–39). New York: Routledge.

Toshalis, E. & Nakkula, M. J. (2012). Motivation, engagement, and student voice. *The Education Digest, 78*(1), 29–35.

Tyack, D. & Benavot, A. (1985). Courts and public schools: Educational litigation in historical perspective. *Law and Society Review, 19*(3), 339–80.

Tyack, D. & Hansot, E. (1982). *Managers of Virtue: Public School Leadership in America, 1820–1980.* New York: Basic Books.

UNESCO. (2016). *World Youth Report: Youth Civic Engagement.* New York: United Nations.

United Nations. (1989). *Convention on the Rights of the Child.* Geneva: United Nations.

Verstegen, D. A. & Knoeppel, R. C. (1998). Equal education under the law: School finance reform and the courts. *Journal of Law & Politics, 14,* 555–89.

Wilder Research. (2011). *Cost-Savings Analysis of School Readiness in Illinois.* Prepared by Chase, R., Diaz, J., & Valorose, J. Saint Paul, MN: Wilder Research.

Williams, R. F. (1985). Equality guarantees in state constitutional law. *Texas Law Review,* 63, 1195–223.

Williams Settlement. (2004). What does it mean for california communities? UCLA's Institute for Democracy, Education, & Access. Retrieved from: http://justschools.gseis.ucla.edu/news/williams/.

Wing, A. K. (1997). A critical race feminist conceptualization of violence: South African and Palestinian women. *Albany Law Review, 60,* 943–76.

Wirt, F. & Kirst, M. (1997). *The Political Dynamics of American Education.* Berkeley, CA: McCutchan Publishing.

Yonezawa, S., & Jones, M. (2007). Using students' voices to inform and evaluate secondary school reform. In Thiessen, D. & Cook Sather, A. (eds.) *International Handbook of Student Experience in Elementary and Secondary School* (pp. 681–709). Dordrecht, Netherlands: Springer.

Yonezawa, S., McClure, L., & Jones, M. (2012). Personalization in schools. *The Education Digest, 78*(2), 41–7.

Index ●●●●●

Page numbers in *italics* denote tables, those in **bold** denote figures.

Taylor & Francis eBooks

Helping you to choose the right eBooks for your Library

Add Routledge titles to your library's digital collection today. Taylor and Francis ebooks contains over 50,000 titles in the Humanities, Social Sciences, Behavioural Sciences, Built Environment and Law.

Choose from a range of subject packages or create your own!

Benefits for you

» Free MARC records
» COUNTER-compliant usage statistics
» Flexible purchase and pricing options
» All titles DRM-free.

Benefits for your user

» Off-site, anytime access via Athens or referring URL
» Print or copy pages or chapters
» Full content search
» Bookmark, highlight and annotate text
» Access to thousands of pages of quality research at the click of a button.

REQUEST YOUR **FREE** INSTITUTIONAL TRIAL TODAY

Free Trials Available
We offer free trials to qualifying academic, corporate and government customers.

eCollections – Choose from over 30 subject eCollections, including:

Archaeology	Language Learning
Architecture	Law
Asian Studies	Literature
Business & Management	Media & Communication
Classical Studies	Middle East Studies
Construction	Music
Creative & Media Arts	Philosophy
Criminology & Criminal Justice	Planning
Economics	Politics
Education	Psychology & Mental Health
Energy	Religion
Engineering	Security
English Language & Linguistics	Social Work
Environment & Sustainability	Sociology
Geography	Sport
Health Studies	Theatre & Performance
History	Tourism, Hospitality & Events

For more information, pricing enquiries or to order a free trial, please contact your local sales team:
www.tandfebooks.com/page/sales

Routledge
Taylor & Francis Group

The home of
Routledge books

www.tandfebooks.com